Market Engineering

Henner Gimpel • Jan Krämer • Dirk Neumann •
Jella Pfeiffer • Stefan Seifert • Timm Teubner •
Daniel J. Veit • Anke Weidlich

Editors

Market Engineering

Insights from Two Decades of Research
on Markets and Information

 Springer

Editors

Henner Gimpel
University of Hohenheim
Stuttgart, Germany

Jan Krämer
University of Passau
Passau, Germany

Dirk Neumann
University of Freiburg
Freiburg im Breisgau, Germany

Jella Pfeiffer
University of Giessen
Giessen, Germany

Stefan Seifert
University of Bayreuth
Bayreuth, Germany

Timm Teubner
Technical University of Berlin
Berlin, Germany

Daniel J. Veit
University of Augsburg
Augsburg, Germany

Anke Weidlich
University of Freiburg
Freiburg im Breisgau, Germany

ISBN 978-3-030-66663-7   ISBN 978-3-030-66661-3   (eBook)
https://doi.org/10.1007/978-3-030-66661-3

Preface

This volume appears for a very special reason. Our academic father, Professor Dr. Christof Weinhardt, celebrates his 60th birthday this month.

We came together as eight of his former students to honor Christof and his achievements because we highly appreciate the particular impact he had on our academic careers. We invited all of Christof's students who remained in academia to contribute. Moreover, we asked exceptional people in Christof's life to write personal contributions. The result is a volume of 15 mostly scientific articles with 49 authors, which mirror many different aspects of the outcome of Christof's broad spectrum of academic personalities he gave stewardship to on his way.

How did it begin? Christof studied Wirtschaftsingenieurwesen (Industrial Engineering and Management) and subsequently defended his doctorate at the University of Karlsruhe (TH). He then defended his habilitation at the University of Giessen where, after a short sojourn at his first chaired position in Quantitative Business Administration at Bielefeld University, he received his full professorship in 1994. Six years later, he followed an offer to establish a new field of study back at his alma mater, where he took over the *Lehrstuhl für Informationsbetriebswirtschaftslehre* in November 2000.

Christof's achievements in research, service to his university, and service to the research community are impressive. His research and teaching focus on interdisciplinary topics related to market engineering, market design, information engineering, service science, and participation with applications in IT services, energy, finance, and telecommunications markets. In these areas, he published more than 150 peer-reviewed papers and books. Christof was a guest professor and visiting scholar in the USA, Canada, Australia, Singapore, Italy, and Austria. He always strived for interdisciplinary collaborations, collaborative research projects, and coordinated programs.

Christof is founder of the Karlsruhe Service Research Institute (KSRI), the Karlsruhe School of Services (KSOS), the Karlsruhe Decision & Design Lab (KD^{2}Lab), and the House of Participation (HoP) at the Karlsruhe Institute of Technology (KIT). He also served as Dean of the Department of Economics and Management and on the Strategy and Research Board of KIT. He headed the interdisciplinary DFG Research Training Group "Information and Market Engineering" and is a director of Forschungszentrum Informatik (FZI). Christof consulted the German Federal Parliament and was invited to join their Committee of Enquiry "Internet and the Digital Society" as an expert advisor. For our research community, Christof was Speaker of the Fachbereich Wirtschaftsinformatik of the Gesellschaft für Informatik, organizer of the 2007 international conference on Wirtschaftsinformatik, and member of the Review Board at DFG (Fachkollegiat), and he currently is the Editor-in-Chief of the journal *Business & Information Systems Engineering*.

Christof supported each and every one of us in developing our academic careers under his guidance. We all owe him many thanks. One particular thing about Christof is that he has an innate sense of people and their potential. This ability is not only centered around pure analytic capabilities. Christof takes a person into his environment in a very special way. Once offered, if one decides to take that path, it is a challenging journey with never a dull moment. On the one hand, Christof demands a lot from his students, including academic dedication and productivity and personal involvement in early-morning or late-night sessions developing new ideas, concepts, grant proposals, or entire research agendas. On the other hand, boarding Christof's ship has always been an opportunity to grow to one's full potential, as he has a lot to offer to all those who decide to take this chance.

Christof encourages his students to use a broad spectrum of methodologies, research approaches, and philosophies. From an epistemological perspective, one could say that he chose a pragmatist approach. One of his sayings, "Wissenschaft ist immer auch ein soziales System" (science is always a social system, too), underlines this beautifully. Christof established an academic ecosystem of the chair and multiple connected institutes, partially funded by public bodies and corporations, and he always managed to cover contemporary "hot" topics, thereby opening opportunities for many academically and industry-oriented students. His ability to constantly inspire skilled and passionate new students to become part of the team and to create an atmosphere in which critique and support were offered among the team members on a very advanced level helped us tremendously. With all this, Christof offered us an excellent platform for personal development, collegial teamwork, making friends, and developing the enthusiasm for pursuing our careers as professors. The further professional development of Christof's students who contributed to this volume shows that we succeeded. This development is certainly also largely due to Christof's dedication to making us all aware of what it means to enter a serious scientific engagement.

Tremendous success can also be seen in the fact that more than 94 students achieved their doctorate under Christof's guidance; many of them have bright careers in industry and, to date, 22 of Christof's students have become professors in Germany and abroad. Christof's personality inspired something in us all that made us achieve what we did.

What unites us in composing this volume—in its colorful and vivid diversity of academic traditions, epistemological stances, and personal perspectives—is the deep and wholehearted gratitude we owe to Professor Dr. Christof Weinhardt, our supervisor, mentor, and friend!

Stuttgart, Germany	Henner Gimpel
Passau, Germany	Jan Krämer
Freiburg, Germany	Dirk Neumann
Giessen, Germany	Jella Pfeiffer
Bayreuth, Germany	Stefan Seifert
Berlin, Germany	Timm Teubner
Augsburg, Germany	Daniel J. Veit
Freiburg, Germany	Anke Weidlich
April 2021	

Contents

Information and Market Engineering at KIT: Quo Vadis?

David Dann, Michael Thomas Knierim, Christian Peukert, Philipp Staudt, and Tim Straub

Abstract Information systems (IS) are nowadays at the core of many personal and institutional activities and influence daily life more than ever before. To understand, evaluate and envision the forms of how we interact with IS, interdisciplinary and multifaceted research efforts are required. At the Information and Market Engineering chair at the Karlsruhe Institute of Technology, this task is taken head-on via research that stretches from user experiences to system design. In this review, the present research foci at the department are outlined, together with a brief description of its origins and the global developments that underly the necessity of conducting these particular IS studies.

1 Introduction

With the turn of the millennium, information technology (IT) had become an omnipresent phenomenon in people's lives and minds. The fearfully anticipated Y2K problem vividly demonstrated how widely IT-based systems had spread and how dependent many aspects of our lives had become on it. However, in the following years, instead of slowing down, the speed of IT-based system diffusion rapidly increased, weaving these systems into the fabric of our lives more than ever. A striking example of this development is the ranking of global companies' market capitalization. Whereas in the beginning of the 2000s, companies like Exxon, General Electric, Total and Citibank were in the top five of publicly traded companies, they have step by step been overtaken by companies like Apple, Alphabet,

D. Dann (✉) · M. T. Knierim · C. Peukert · P. Staudt
Institute of Information Systems and Marketing (IISM), Karlsruhe Institute of Technology (KIT), Karlsruhe, Germany
e-mail: david.dann@kit.edu; michael.knierim@kit.edu; christian.peukert@kit.edu; philipp.staudt@kit.edu

T. Straub
Forschungszentrum Informatik (FZI), Karlsruhe, Germany
e-mail: straub@fzi.de

© The Author(s) 2021
H. Gimpel et al. (eds.), *Market Engineering*,
https://doi.org/10.1007/978-3-030-66661-3_1

1

Microsoft, Amazon and Facebook by the end of 2015.[1] Similarly, firmly established business sectors have been uprooted by the emerging digital competition, as can be seen in the sharing economy where services like Uber and Airbnb have become major competitors to traditional mobility and lodging offerings. Nowadays, almost all economic decisions in business and everyday life are supported by IT-based systems. These systems increasingly "cast in code" institutions and processes and influence the interactions and behaviour of decision-makers. Most recently, the importance of acknowledging the impact that these digitization processes have is embodied in the public and scholastic recognition of how social media platforms influence individual, social and institutional functioning. The wilful capitalization on biological reward mechanisms to increase IT use and the staggering increase of psychological ailments such as addictive tendencies, anxiety, stress and loneliness driven by the ever-attention-demanding social media applications and platforms (Kloker et al. 2020) represent issues on the individual and social level. On the institutional level, tendencies of increased political radicalization and public opinion manipulation (e.g. in elections) represent problematic and fundamental challenges imposed by today's ubiquity of IT-based systems. At the same time, IT-based systems still offer unprecedented potential to improve societies and human lives through democratic empowerment (e.g. through digital participation in governmental decision-making), ecological sustainability (e.g. through information and market access related to the ongoing energy transition) or data-driven economic and technological innovation (e.g. through the identification of insights in big data).

In this dynamic world, the interplay between economic decision-making and system design has become a core of IS research in general and research at the Information and Market Engineering (IM) chair at the Karlsruhe Institute of Technology (KIT) in particular. Over the years, research at the IM chair has covered a variety of topics that tackle the aforementioned individual, social and institutional challenges of IT-based systems. This chapter focuses on the most recent developments and research directions at the IM chair. In particular, this chapter aims to present a focused view on the present work in the sectors of energy markets, data analytics, user behaviour, digital experience and digital participation. This represents the work of research departments that are formed within the IM chair today. To provide an introduction on how these departments emerged, the following section provides a brief overview of the research topic developments in the form of IM dissertation-based text analysis. Afterwards, in the third section, an overview of the current department's work is given, including pressing global IT-based system developments and derived fields of research.

---

[1] Visual Capitalist Report, https://www.visualcapitalist.com/chart-largest-companies-market-cap-15-years/. Last accessed 30.10.2020.

2 A Brief Overview of Past IM Research

To gain an impression of the evolution of the research at the IM chair, abstracts and introductions of the dissertations that were completed since 2006 were analysed. The data includes all dissertations in that period that were available at the digital library of the KIT—55 dissertations in total. While this does not include all dissertations handed in at the chair, it suffices to give an overview of the prevalent research topics over the years. Using these dissertations, a wordcloud was created for the periods from 2006 to 2012 (Fig. 1), 2013 to 2016 (Fig. 2) and 2017 to 2020 (Fig. 3). The identified trends are based on a simple descriptive and subjective approach. That being said, every reader is invited to develop their own story around these results.

In the first wordcloud of 2006 to 2012 (there are only three dissertations from 2006 to 2008 that were included, which is why this is the longest period) in Fig. 1, the traditional topics of the IM chair are central. Markets, systems and auctions are essential to the dissertations in this period. Other words such as service, economic, electronic, network, price or performance further show that electronic markets

Fig. 1 Wordcloud of 23 dissertations at the IM chair in the period from 2006 to 2012

Fig. 2 Wordcloud of 18 dissertations at the IM chair in the period from 2013 to 2016

Fig. 3 Wordcloud of 14
dissertations at the IM chair
in the period from 2017 to
2020

represent the core and the legacy of the IM chair. Additionally, some topics that are central during this time and less relevant later are cloud and web-based services, retail markets or market liquidity.

Moving on to the period of 2013 to 2016 in Fig. 2, it can be seen that new domains are becoming important at the IM chair. While markets, auctions, systems and services are still central to research, healthcare, energy, grid, economics and regulation show that new directions are taken such as research on energy or telecommunication markets. Competition becomes a more important topic, but more user-centric research can also be observed in the emergence of terms like social, human, cognitive or arousal. This already announces the increasingly important experimental focus at the IM chair.

This trend continues in the period from 2017 to 2020 in Fig. 3. While markets and systems remain the centrepieces of research activities, other topics are less pronounced. Auctions, for example, are being replaced by mechanisms. Behaviour takes a more central role, and services are becoming less important. It can be seen that the user takes a central position shown by the words behaviour, users and decision. The energy domain retains its central role, while telecommunication and healthcare have disappeared. Data is more strongly pronounced, which might be driven by the stronger experimental focus and the evolution of data analytics as a research domain. The words welfare and acceptance imply a more economical approach to certain topics.

Building on this previous work, today, the scholastic work at the IM chair is carried forward in four research groups named (1) Smart Grids and Energy Markets, (2) Business Data Analytics, (3) Electronic Markets and User Behaviour and (4) Digital Experience and Participation. The work in these groups carries on the established focus of creating knowledge and value from analysing and developing information systems and markets. With an emphasis on beneficial behaviours and systems, research in these groups today tackles emerging challenges of the new decade that are detailed in the following section.

3 Present and Future of IM Research

3.1 Smart Grids and Energy Markets

One of the most important issues of our time is the reduction of greenhouse gas emissions to limit climate change. The electricity sector is one of the most carbon-intensive energy sectors, but it is also the easiest to decarbonize. Wind and solar energy can replace fossil-fuelled conventional generation. Furthermore, electricity can substitute fossil fuel in the transportation and heating sector (Golla et al. 2019). Therefore, decarbonizing the electricity sector is the most straightforward path to achieve global emission objectives. The European Union and its member states are committed to reducing carbon emissions, and Fridays for Future and affiliated organizations are gaining momentum worldwide. The research group Smart Grids and Energy Markets (SGEM) is committed to contributing to the decarbonization of all energy sectors through market mechanisms and information system solutions. The objective of the research group is stated as follows:

> We develop and evaluate economic mechanisms to coordinate supply and demand in digitalized energy systems. The overall objective is the development and the support of a sustainable energy system considering individual preferences and developments in our society.

The evolution of the SGEM group is described in a different chapter of this book. The group has accompanied the major evolution of energy markets in Europe and beyond. This includes research on market liberalization (van Dinther et al. 2006), market power (Veit et al. 2009), demand-side flexibility (Gärttner et al. 2018), electric vehicles (Schuller et al. 2015) and most recently decentralized electricity markets and market regionalization (Staudt et al. 2017). However, with the current trends of decarbonization, market engineering approaches are only gaining momentum in energy market research. Two major research directions are highlighted here that focus on energy consumer/user behaviour (Staudt et al. 2019) and on innovative energy market designs (Staudt and Oren 2020).

3.1.1 Support Systems for Energy Consumers

The objectives and preferences of users are always a central component when new coordinating mechanisms and market designs are developed. In this direction, the research group is working on several projects that allow the user to trade electricity locally and in the neighbourhood through IS and with the help of decision support systems (Golla et al. 2020). These support the user in the choice of the electricity rate (Vom Scheidt et al. 2019) and additional investment in infrastructures such as heat pumps or battery storage and help aggregators supply micromarkets at minimal costs with the use of available resources. The group is working at the interface of energy market research, green information systems and energy informatics, especially energy data analytics (vom Scheidt et al. 2020). Throughout these disciplines, the research is driven by an engineering approach in the design of markets, mechanisms and information systems which are then evaluated through simulations and field and laboratory experiments (Staudt et al. 2019). This way, the research group develops artefacts that support the energy transition as a whole. The results are currently applied in two major projects which is the development of citizen energy communities in three neighbourhoods in Landau and Ettlingen and through a battery storage research project in Baden-Württemberg. These projects already announce future trends in electricity market research.

3.1.2   Innovative Energy Market Designs

Citizen energy communities are promoted by the European Union as a way to have citizens participate in the energy transition (Golla et al. 2020). The according regulation will allow new solutions to trade and share locally produced electricity. This is an important research and business area that will support local suppliers and thus add to a further decentralization of the power sector. Furthermore, electric vehicles are finally entering the market in large quantities. This trend will be further intensified as charging infrastructure is added (Schmidt et al. 2020). Simultaneously, the prices for storage are decreasing, and production is becoming more environmentally friendly. This adds significant flexibility to the electricity system that needs to be coordinated. Finally, deep decarbonization is only possible through hydrogen electrolysis which will greatly change the electricity system as a whole. The development of market mechanisms and information systems according to this trend will take centre stage over the next decade. This further includes algorithms that support the coordination of the electricity system and grid to improve the integration of renewable generation and large loads added by hydrogen electrolysis. Data analytics and artificial intelligence will thus play a major role in future decarbonization of the electricity system.

3.2   Business Data Analytics

The topic of data analytics or science, especially in connection with big data, has increasingly become a focal point of public attention. Behind the great popularity of the topic is the fact that today more data than ever is available to support decision-making. In this context, data science explores the extraction of knowledge from mostly high-dimensional and heterogeneous data. The research group Business Data Analytics (BDA) aims to create value for businesses and society from the opportunities created by (big) data analytics and, in particular, methods within the broader terminology of artificial intelligence (AI).

In recent years, the BDA group has primarily worked on developing methods and models that allow for more precise, faster or valuable utilization of vast amounts of heterogeneous and unreliable data. In doing so, the research group has explicitly focused on subjects like the development and combination of analytical methods with forecasting models (Blanc and Setzer 2016), the development of novel analytical approaches in the context of geographic IS (Wiener et al. 2016) or the modelling and prediction of user behaviour based on heterogeneous field data (Schoch 2016).

At present, the group focuses its research on three major trends that have become critical for businesses looking to achieve competitive advantage through data science. The first trend is the search for qualitative improvements in recommendation systems (RS) that includes method hybridization and comprehensive analyses not only of the functionality of RS but also of their impact on socio-economic variables. The second trend is the development of interfaces and mechanisms to enable the exchange of data through markets or platforms, for example, through the process of incentive engineering. The third trend is the prediction of financial assets through innovative AI models and methods.

3.2.1 Recommendation Systems Innovation

RS have become commonplace in the digital landscape, perhaps best known from retail platforms like Amazon or Netflix, where customers receive daily recommendations for content that could be of interest to them. RS classify the usefulness that users attribute to individual items. To create these classifications, RS can be designed using different paradigms (e.g. collaborative filtering or content-based filtering). The combination of different RS paradigms to so-called hybrid RS can outperform individual approaches but requires an appropriate weighting of the individual RS. Available error data of individual RS allows finding an optimal weighting for each individual RS, which minimizes the accuracy of the hybrid RS. It can be shown that such hybrid RS outperform the results of the individual RS (Haubner and Setzer 2020).

In addition to methodological research on RS, the research group also conducts research to study RS from a socio-economic perspective. In particular, the existence of news RS embedded in major social networking platforms such as Facebook or Twitter has had an increasing influence on when and, above all, which news we consume. The resulting debates about emerging filter bubbles, in which individuals are continuously confronted with messages that confirm or reinforce their opinions, have gradually turned the role of RS into a socially highly relevant matter. Questions are raised as to whether RS can lead to increased polarization or even radicalization. Against this backdrop, research on responsible news RS examines whether and if so which configurations or paradigms of RS can lead to such filter bubbles. In doing so, guidelines for responsible news RS will be developed, which explicitly avoid these filter bubbles.

3.2.2   Data Markets and Platforms

Virtually all data analysis methods have one common demand: to achieve an adequate quality of modelling, the availability of large and accurate data sets is essential. In reality, however, this is often not guaranteed. There is either a lack of sufficient data to train meaningful models or the quality of the available data is insufficient. Therefore, the research group investigates the potential of combining high quality with swarm-based mass data in the form of open data crowdsensing services. Within this work, large training data sets are generated and published to reduce investment thresholds for future actors or start-ups and, thus, create the basis for innovative solutions. Furthermore, the use of these data sets and their future enrichment will be realized via a framework with a connected marketplace platform.

In business domains, the demand for data can be achieved by collaboration among companies within value networks. Within these networks, operators are often still acting too isolated and reserved concerning data availability, which, in turn, obstructs the creation of value. However, once all network partners follow a holistic perspective and act as one data-sharing entity, competitive advantages can be achieved (Badewitz et al. 2020). In the work on the management of collaborative value networks, it is investigated how companies and value networks can contribute to the overall performance of the network through data sharing. For this purpose, Industry 4.0 concepts are further developed into digitized collaboration tools, considering economic, security and data protection aspects. The availability of such cross-company data also opens up new data-driven business opportunities. In a complementary effort, together with industry partners, current research is investigating the potential of new business models derived from the Caruso data platform.[2] The platform harmonizes sensor data from vehicles of various international car manufacturers and provides access to in-vehicle data, which enables, for instance, new insurance concepts (pay-as-you-drive), services for workshop access or sharing concepts (e.g. car sharing).

3.2.3   Modelling Asset Development

The release of the digital peer-to-peer cash system Bitcoin in 2008 popularized the blockchain with its three key components: secure information transfer leveraging cryptographic protocols, a distributed database and a decentralized consensus mechanism. Since then, Bitcoin has become more and more popular. In 2019, Bitcoin already had a market capitalization of more than US$155 billion; this trend is steadily increasing. This success has already led several researchers to consider Bitcoin as a new asset class. However, the novelty of Bitcoin in the landscape of cash systems raises questions about which methods are suitable for analysing the Bitcoin market. Simultaneously, a literature review has shown that existing research

---

[2]https://www.caruso-dataplace.com/.

streams are currently not yet in a mature state. Existing approaches are difficult to compare and lack a scientific level of transparency and reproducibility (Jaquart et al. 2020a). Therefore, the BDA group is currently pursuing a research endeavour in which Bitcoin market's predictability is investigated using a variety of machine learning methods. For this purpose, both the methods and models identified in the former literature review article and so far unused state-of-the-art methods are being tested using various feature sets. So far, it can be shown that machine learning models can predict the market to a certain extent. Although within this study a first trading strategy cannot compensate for arising transaction costs, the proportion of explainable variance nevertheless encourages further research in this context (Jaquart et al. 2020b).

3.3 *Electronic Markets and User Behaviour*

Experiential and behavioural processes have become a central topic in human-computer interaction and IS in the last decade, especially in the context of digital system and platform use (Knierim et al. 2017b, Lux et al. 2018, Peukert et al. 2018b). This is due to an emerging consensus that aspects like emotion, motivation and trust critically interplay with decision-making quality and with individual and social functioning. For example, emotions have been determined as the cause of both irrational behaviour (Adam et al. 2011, Jung and Weinhardt 2018) and high-quality decision-making (Hariharan et al. 2016, Lux et al. 2018). Emotional salience and management have been considered a vitalizing and conflict-moderating aspect in digital participation platforms (Lux et al. 2015a, Peukert et al. 2018b) or a driver of small group performances and interaction satisfaction (Knierim et al. 2017a). Trust on the other hand has been identified as a central driver of readiness for economic transactions (Hawlitschek et al. 2016, Peukert et al. 2018b), and trust-facilitating systems have shown a clear competitive advantage for companies operating in the so-called sharing economy (Dann et al. 2020b; 2019). The research group Electronic Markets and User Behaviour (EMUB) dedicates its work to improving the understanding and design of digital systems that improve individual and social experiences in everyday life.

The basis for this (primarily experimental) research was established with the creation of the KD^2Lab. For more details on the lab's history and characteristics, see Hoffmann et al. (2021) in this book. In recent years, research emphasis of EMUB has, for example, been placed on the impact of choice architecture (nudges embedded in a system interface) on improved decision-making quality by reducing decision inertia in the context of computer-driven consumer investment decision (robo-advisory) (Jung and Weinhardt 2018) or on the value of including feedback on emotional states in real time to reduce irrational behaviour in financial decision-making (Astor et al. 2013, Lux et al. 2015b). A particular stream of research has focused on the effect of user interface design elements on the facilitation of trust in the sharing economy. Peer-to-peer sharing platforms differ from traditional e-commerce in the aspects that private individuals typically run both sides of the transaction (and not established corporations) and that part of the transaction can take place in "real" life (e.g. booking an apartment on Airbnb) (Dann et al. 2019). In this context, mutual trust has emerged as a fundamental transaction facilitator. Research in the EMUB group has identified that the manipulation of design aspects (e.g. profile pictures, star ratings, text reviews) decisively influences users' decisions to enter into a transaction on a peer-to-peer platform through both economic and social aspects (Dann et al. 2020b). Furthermore, studies identified that even the technological foundation of the platform itself impacts transaction intentions, for instance, because the blockchain's reputation as a "trust machine" is reflected in the perception of specific user groups (Dann et al. 2020a). Another stream of research has focused on leveraging multimodal data streams during IT system utilization to develop insights and models for improving user experiences in the context of knowledge work. In particular, neurophysiological data that can be collected continuously (through sensors worn on the body) has been utilized to build an understanding of how individual and social experiences can be unobtrusively detected in real time. Examples of this work are the research on using heart-rate analysis and feedback in small group interaction to improve intra- and inter-individual emotion management during teamwork (Knierim et al. 2017b;a) or the research on neurophysiological correlates of flow experiences (Knierim et al. 2019a; 2017c; 2019b). Especially the latter work tackles the challenge of how desirable experiential states (in terms of both individual and social performance, satisfaction and growth) can be observed and eventually facilitated.

At present, the research group focuses its research and education on two major trends in the context of digital system use that are becoming critical due to increased technological availability, ubiquity and sophistication. On the one hand, this refers to the increased demand for complex knowledge work due to advances in AI technology and how such complex work can be supported through IT-based system-enabled affect detection. On the other hand, this refers to the requirement of leveraging data-driven methods that are able to extract meaningful insights and predictions from diverse multimodal sensor data.

3.3.1 Affective Experience in Knowledge Work

Demands for unstructured knowledge work (KW) are growing, due to the rise of AI technologies that are replacing repetitive work in sales, administrative support or service tasks (Frey and Osborne 2017). As KW is by its nature complex and highly task- and situation-specific, it rarely comes with a single way of completing it. Additional developments, including flat hierarchies, self-directed work, job-crafting, open offices and digitally mediated collaboration, further extend this KW complexity (Bakker and van Woerkom 2017). Therefore, systems that aim to support KW are faced with the challenge of providing person-, task- and situation-independent approaches. A promising approach for this endeavour is the development of systems that support experiences, not specific tasks. To this extent, current projects are, for example, focusing on how flow experiences can be unobtrusively detected in individuals and small groups in the KW context (e.g. during the process of scientific writing) (Knierim et al. 2019a;b) using ECG and EEG measures and behavioural recordings (mouse and keyboard input). In another instance, research projects are investigating how comfortable wearable sensors can be used for recordings in more externally valid experimental scenarios and how these sensors can be used to track multiple physiological processes at once (e.g. extracting the ECG signal from an EEG recording). Furthermore, the integration of covert (i.e. physiological) and overt expressions of emotions (i.e. facial activity) into models that track affective experiences represents an effort that aims to enable more robust models that affect-adaptive systems can rely on.

3.3.2 Methods and Models for Adaptive Systems

Observing behavioural and neurophysiological data in real-world settings offers exciting possibilities like the support of physical health and mental well-being and the introduction of novel human-computer interaction modalities. The development of such applications is, however, strongly impeded by measurement complications in terms of internal validity, acquisition frequency and robustness and intra- and inter-individual variance. For example, while it is still often believed that physiological sensors provide objective measures of internal states (perhaps even unbeknownst to the individual), nowadays, it is a more common view that many derived features are multiply determined and that adaptive systems require large amounts of data (per person, per sample and per measurement domain) that allow differentiating meaning from noise in the observation. Therefore, research on methods and models for adaptive systems is currently moving towards more sophisticated and inductive analytic methods. This primarily includes the use of feature selection methods that allow identifying various shapes of variable relationships (e.g. using the maximal information coefficient to detect non-linear bivariate relationships; Reshef et al. 2011) and the use of transparent classification methods like explainable AI (XAI) (Gunning et al. 2019) that not only allow development of useful classifiers for adaptive systems but also provide insight into which features generated from sensor data meaningfully inform such classification outputs. Together these research efforts aim to enable the development of IT-based adaptive systems for the future of knowledge work that are able to support affective experiences in their natural context, in real time, so that positive individual and social experiences can be facilitated.

3.4 Digital Experience and Participation

Today's life is characterized by constant interaction with digital devices and systems, which affect almost all facets of our daily routines. The technological progress is—now for a considerable time—no longer only noticeable on a business level, but also in our private lives, digital devices have developed as permanent companions that continuously feed us with information of various kinds. Due to this ubiquity of digital devices, it is of utmost importance to investigate how users interact with these technologies, both on an individual and group level. One prerequisite, however, for people adopting these new technologies is that they demand a comprehensive digital experience. The term digital experience can be described as the resulting experience from the composition of multiple devices, digital artefacts or modes of interaction. Basically, it can be understood as the combination of separate user experiences to an overarching experience driven by digital technologies or services. Together, the activities of the research group Digital Experience and Participation (DXP) focus on the investigation of technology acceptance and digital experience, always with a strong emphasis on emerging digital technologies and interaction modalities.

In the past, the research group has primarily worked on understanding and designing the experience of digital technology users and subsequently supporting users to better capture, understand and process information and by doing so enable empowered decision-making. Specifically, this work has targeted the analysis of the decision-making process in different shopping scenarios, e.g. online, offline and virtual, and thereby also applied eye-tracking technology (Peukert et al. 2020, Pfeiffer et al. 2020). Furthermore, the research group has investigated how humans experience the interaction with others and with the underlying technology on participation and collaboration platforms. Here, it has been of importance to create a better understanding of how participants evaluate and consolidate proposals in participation processes through (feedback) mechanism design (Niemeyer et al. 2016, Wagenknecht et al. 2018), and how platforms and mechanisms need to be designed to incentivize actions that promote greater societal welfare (Straub et al. 2015). Moreover, the transfer of these participatory approaches to institutional and governmental processes paves the way for digital participation also for firms and public institutions. Firms, for instance, may take advantage of the crowd's wisdom in open innovation processes. However, when implementing, it is important to provide the right incentives, suitable rating scales, and to further reflect on the trade-off between anonymous and pseudonymous participation formats (Wagenknecht et al. 2017b;a).

At present, the research group focuses on two emerging trends that can be described as novel user experiences in immersive systems and as the pervasion of participatory and collaborative systems and its ensuing challenges. These developments are driven by emerging changes in the digital technology landscape, specifically the increased availability of immersive systems and the ubiquity of mobile-ready platforms. These changes have altered how people operate platforms or take part in markets, opening up entirely new ways to experience and participate. First, through the advent of immersive systems, the nature of how we interact with IS may switch to new forms generating an unprecedented digital experience. Advantages of these new interaction patterns, visualization techniques, sensory modalities and general potentials through an increased degree of immersion can, e.g., be used for behavioural change systems. Second, through participatory and collaborative IS, users of such systems are not only consumers but prosumers. While this might not be a new trend, to some extent this is true since the advent of the web 2.0; it is now used in a wide variety of societal, political and business-relevant contexts. Also, new trends such as digital citizen science open up challenges and blur boundaries between the offline and online world.

3.4.1 User Experience in Immersive Systems

Immersive systems have been around for quite some time, but only recently they have attracted much attention in IS research. Among others, the reasons for the raised attention are advances in and falling prices of the technology and the accompanying entry in the end-consumer market. The research activities of the chair mainly focused on VR shopping environments (Peukert et al. 2018a; 2020; 2019a;b, Pfeiffer et al. 2017). Various questions concerning the acceptance of VR shopping environments were addressed (Peukert et al. 2019a;b), but also how user assistance systems for virtual shopping environments can be designed (Peukert et al. 2018a; 2020, Pfeiffer et al. 2017). In particular, the concept of detecting different phases in consumers' decision-making process based on real-time analysis of eye-tracking data was introduced, aiming at designing context-aware user assistance systems (Peukert et al. 2020). Besides the application of immersive technology in a shopping context, first attempts have been made to observe how immersive experiences influence behaviour, in particular donation behaviour (Greif-Winzrieth et al. 2020). Moreover, a new stream of research combines immersive systems with e-participation platforms to better visualize information, e.g. how new construction projects will look like when finished, thereby empowering people to participate (Fegert et al. 2020).

3.4.2 Participatory and Collaborative Information Systems

Through lowered entry barriers, i.e. the technological availability and cost-efficiency of development tools, new services have paved the way for an unprecedented opportunity for collaboration and participation in everyday lives. Nowadays, people communicate via online messengers and apps, collaboratively build knowledge databases, work on crowdsourcing platforms, fund companies with capital gathered on crowdfunding platforms, develop new products in open innovation contests, make collaborative predictions on uncertain future events in prediction markets and Delphi markets and take part in political debates and decisions via online polls, discussion boards, e-participation platforms or participatory budgeting programmes (Fegert et al. 2019, Kloker et al. 2017, Niemeyer et al. 2016, Straub et al. 2014; 2015; 2016, Wagenknecht et al. 2017a). Now, a new wave of digital participation processes is being investigated and designed, which are primarily intended to enhance public participation in local government processes, e.g. urban planning or construction projects. For instance, within the research project Take Part, the implementation of the emerging technologies Augmented and Virtual Reality into e-participation is studied in several use cases around Karlsruhe investigating whether the application of immersive systems increases the overall participation in public projects (Fegert et al. 2019).

Lastly, the understanding of the integration of participatory approaches into platform design leads to a new field of application: Digital Citizen Science (Weinhardt et al. 2020). In contrast to classical citizen science approaches, the public might participate in research not only by providing or gathering data but that they might be empowered to actively contribute to science through formulating their own research questions, developing their own hypotheses and finally discussing those transparently and interactively with other citizens and researchers.

4 Concluding Thoughts

As IT-based systems are more fundamental and interconnected with everyday private and professional lives, with individual, social and institutional experiences and processes, the research that forms the basis for our understanding of how these systems develop and shape our lives is more pressing than ever before. While these systems are presently demonstrating difficult challenges, they are also amply demonstrating potentials to shape our present and future positively. IT-based systems offer unprecedented potential to improve societies and human lives through democratic empowerment (e.g. through digital participation in governmental decision-making), ecological sustainability (e.g. through information and market access related to the ongoing energy transition) or data-driven economic and technological innovation (e.g. through the identification of unknown insights in large and heterogeneous data). Hopefully, through this short review of how the scholastic work at the IM chair is tackling relevant issues and advancing promising developments, this chapter has presented the interested reader with a glimpse into the ongoing work in IM research groups and the overall developments in contemporary IS research.

References

Adam, M. T. P., Krämer, J., Jähnig, C., Seifert, S., & Weinhardt, C. (2011). Understanding auction fever: A framework for emotional bidding. *Electronic Markets, 21*(3), 197–207.

Astor, P. J., Adam, M. T. P., Jerčić, P., Schaaff, K., & Weinhardt, C. (2013). Integrating biosignals into information systems: A NeuroIS tool for improving emotion regulation. *Journal of Management Information Systems, 30*(3), 247–278.

Badewitz, W., Kloker, S., & Weinhardt, C. (2020). The Data Provision Game: Researching Revenue Sharing in Collaborative Data Networks. *22nd IEEE Conference on Business Informatics (CBI)*, 191–200.

Bakker, A. B. & van Woerkom, M. (2017). Flow at Work: a Self-Determination Perspective. *Occupational Health Science, 1*(1-2), 47–65.

Blanc, S. M. & Setzer, T. (2016). When to choose the simple average in forecast combination. *Journal of Business Research, 69*(10), 3951–3962.

Dann, D., Hawlitschek, F., Peukert, C., Martin, C., & Weinhardt, C. (2020a). Blockchain and Trust in the Platform Economy: The Case of Peer-to-Peer Sharing. *Wirtschaftsinformatik (WI)*, 1459–1473.

Dann, D., Teubner, T., Adam, M. T. P., & Weinhardt, C. (2020b). Where the host is part of the deal: Social and economic value in the platform economy. *Electronic Commerce Research and Applications, 40*, 100923.

Dann, D., Teubner, T., & Weinhardt, C. (2019). Poster child and guinea pig–insights from a structured literature review on Airbnb. *International Journal of Contemporary Hospitality Management, 31*(1), 427–473.

Fegert, J., Pfeiffer, J., Golubyeva, A., Pfeiffer-Leßmann, N., Hariharan, A., Renner, P., Pfeiffer, T., Hefke, M., Straub, T., & Weinhardt, C. (2019). Take Part Prototype: Creating New Ways of Participation Through Augmented and Virtual Reality. *29th Workshop an Information Technologies and Systems (WITS)*.

Fegert, J., Pfeiffer, J., Peukert, C., Golubyeva, A., & Weinhardt, C. (2020). Combining e-Participation with Augmented and Virtual Reality: Insights from a Design Science Research Project. *Proceedings of the International Conference on Information Systems (ICIS 2020)*, India.

Frey, C. B. & Osborne, M. A. (2017). The future of employment: How susceptible are jobs to computerisation? *Technological Forecasting and Social Change, 114*, 254–280.

Gärttner, J., Flath, C. M., & Weinhardt, C. (2018). Portfolio and contract design for demand response resources. *European Journal of Operational Research, 266*(1), 340–353.

Golla, A., Henni, S., & Staudt, P. (2020). Scaling the Concept of Citizen Energy Communities through a Platform-Based Decision Support System. *European Conference on Information Systems (ECIS)*, 1–7.

Golla, A., Staudt, P., & Weinhardt, C. (2019). Combining pvt generation and air conditioning: A cost analysis of surplus heat utilization. *International Conference on Smart Energy Systems and Technologies (SEST)*, 1–6.

Greif-Winzrieth, A., Knierim, M., Peukert, C., & Weinhardt, C. (2020). Feeling the Pain of Others in Need: Studying the Effect of VR on Donation Behavior Using EEG. *Proceedings of the 11th Retreat on NeuroIS*, 172–180.

Gunning, D., Stefik, M., Choi, J., Miller, T., Stumpf, S., & Yang, G.-Z. (2019). XAI—Explainable artificial intelligence. *Science Robotics, 4*(37).

Hariharan, A., Adam, M. T. P., Teubner, T., & Weinhardt, C. (2016). Think, feel, bid: The impact of environmental conditions on the role of bidders' cognitive and affective processes in auction bidding. *Electronic Markets, 26*(4), 339–355.

Haubner, N. & Setzer, T. (2020). Applying Optimal Weight Combination in Hybrid Recommender Systems. *Proceedings of the 53rd Hawaii International Conference on System Sciences (HICSS)*, 1552–1562.

Hawlitschek, F., Jansen, L.-E., Lux, E., Teubner, T., & Weinhardt, C. (2016). Colors and trust: the influence of user interface design on trust and reciprocity. *Proceedings of the 49th Hawaii International Conference on System Sciences (HICSS)*, 590–599.

Hoffmann, G., Greif-Winzrieth, A., Pfeiffer, J., Thomas, K., Peukert, C., & Adam, M. T. P. (2021). Karlsruhe Decision & Design Lab (KD^{2}Lab). In: Gimpel et al. (eds), *Market Engineering*, Springer, p. 19.

Jaquart, P., Dann, D., & Martin, C. (2020a). Machine Learning for Bitcoin Pricing — A Structured Literature Review. *Wirtschaftsinformatik (WI)*, 174–188.

Jaquart, P., Dann, D., & Weinhardt, C. (2020b). Using Machine Learning to Predict Short-Term Movements of the Bitcoin Market. *FinanceCom*, 21–40.

Jung, D. & Weinhardt, C. (2018). Robo-advisors and financial decision inertia: How choice architecture helps to reduce inertia in financial planning tools. *Proceedings of the 39th International Conference on Information Systems (ICIS)*.

Kloker, S., Riegel, M. L., & Weinhardt, C. (2020). Sensible or too Sensitive? Do Privacy Concerns Hinder the Acceptance of Digital Solutions to Treat Smartphone Addiction? *22nd IEEE Conference on Business Informatics (CBI)*, 10–19.

Kloker, S., Straub, T., & Weinhardt, C. (2017). Designing a crowd forecasting tool to combine prediction markets and real-time Delphi. *International Conference on Design Science Research in Information System and Technology (DESRIST)*, 468–473.

Knierim, M. T., Hariharan, A., Dorner, V., & Weinhardt, C. (2017b). Emotion Feedback in Small Group Collaboration: A Research Agenda for Group Emotion Management Support Systems. *Proceedings of the 17th International Conference on Group Decision and Negotiation (GDN)*, 1–12.

Knierim, M. T., Jung, D., Dorner, V., & Weinhardt, C. (2017a). Designing live biofeedback for groups to support emotion management in digital collaboration. *International Conference on Design Science Research in Information System and Technology (DESRIST)*, 479–484.

Knierim, M. T., Nadj, M., & Weinhardt, C. (2019a). Flow and optimal difficulty in the portable EEG: On the potentiality of using personalized frequency ranges for state detection. *Proceedings of the 3rd International Conference on Computer-Human Interaction Research and Applications (CHIRA)*, 183–190.

Knierim, M. T., Rissler, R., Dorner, V., Maedche, A., & Weinhardt, C. (2017c). The psychophysiology of flow: A systematic review of peripheral nervous system features. *Proceedings of the 9th Retreat on NeuroIS*, 109–120.

Knierim, M. T., Nadj, M., Li, M. X., & Weinhardt, C. (2019b). Flow in knowledge work groups - Autonomy as a driver or digitally mediated communication as a limiting factor? *Proceedings of the 40th International Conference on Information Systems (ICIS)*, 1–17.

Lux, E., Adam, M. T. P., Dorner, V., Helming, S., Knierim, M. T., & Weinhardt, C. (2018). Live Biofeedback as a User Interface Design Element: A Review of the Literature. *Communications of the Association for Information Systems*, *43*(1), 257–296.

Lux, E., Adam, M. T. P., Hawlitschek, F., & Pfeiffer, J. (2015b). Using Live Biofeedback for Decision Support: Investigating Influences of Emotion Regulation in Financial Decision Making. *Proceedings of the 7th Retreat on NeuroIS*, 1–12.

Lux, E., Hawlitschek, F., Teubner, T., Niemeyer, C., & Adam, M. T. (2015a). A Hot Topic-Group Affect Live Biofeedback for Participation Platforms. *Proceedings of the 7th retreat on neurois* (pp. 35–42).

Niemeyer, C., Wagenknecht, T., Teubner, T., & Weinhardt, C. (2016). Participatory Crowdfunding: An approach towards engaging employees and citizens in institutional budgeting decisions. *49th Hawaii International Conference on System Sciences (HICSS)*, 2800–2808.

Peukert, C., Adam, M. T. P., Hawlitschek, F., Helming, S., Lux, E., & Teubner, T. (2018b). Knowing me, knowing you: biosignals and trust in the surveillance economy. *Proceedings of the 39th International Conference on Information Systems (ICIS)*, 1–9.

Peukert, C., Brossok, F., Pfeiffer, J., Meißner, M., & Weinhardt, C. (2018a). Towards Designing Virtual Reality Shopping Environments. *Conference Booklet of the 13th International Conference on Design Science Research in Information Systems and Technology (DESRIST), Chennai, India*.

Peukert, C., Lechner, J., Pfeiffer, J., & Weinhardt, C. (2020). Intelligent Invocation: Towards Designing Context-Aware User Assistance Systems Based on Real-Time Eye Tracking Data Analysis. *Information systems and neuroscience* (pp. 73–82).

Peukert, C., Pfeiffer, J., Meißner, M., Pfeiffer, T., & Weinhardt, C. (2019a). Shopping in Virtual Reality Stores: The Influence of Immersion on System Adoption. *Journal of Management Information Systems*, *36*(3), 755–788.

Peukert, C., Pfeiffer, J., Meissner, M., Pfeiffer, T., & Weinhardt, C. (2019b). Acceptance of Imagined Versus Experienced Virtual Reality Shopping Environments: Insights from Two Experiments. *European Conference on Information Systems (ECIS)*, 1–16.

Pfeiffer, J., Pfeiffer, T., Greif-Winzrieth, A., Meißner, M., Renner, P., & Weinhardt, C. (2017). Adapting Human-Computer-Interaction of Attentive Smart Glasses to the Trade-Off Conflict in Purchase Decisions: An Experiment in a Virtual Supermarket. *International Conference on Augmented Cognition*, 219–235.

Pfeiffer, J., Pfeiffer, T., Meißner, M., & Weiss, E. (2020). Eye-Tracking-Based Classification of Information Search Behavior using Machine Learning: Evidence from Experiments in Physical Shops and Virtual Reality Shopping Environments. *Information Systems Research, 31*(3), 675–691.

Reshef, D. N., Reshef, Y. A., Finucane, H. K., Grossman, S. R., McVean, G., Turnbaugh, P. J., Lander, E. S., Mitzenmacher, M., & Sabeti, P. C. (2011). Detecting novel associations in large data sets. *Science, 334*(6062), 1518–1524.

Schmidt, M., Staudt, P., & Weinhardt, C. (2020). Evaluating the importance and impact of user behavior on public destination charging of electric vehicles. *Applied Energy, 258*, 114061.

Schoch, J. (2016). Modeling of battery life optimal charging strategies based on empirical mobility data. *it-Information Technology, 58*(1), 22–28.

Schuller, A., Flath, C. M., & Gottwalt, S. (2015). Quantifying load flexibility of electric vehicles for renewable energy integration. *Applied Energy, 151*, 335–344.

Staudt, P., Golla, A., Richter, B., Schmidt, M., vom Scheidt, F., & Weinhardt, C. (2019). Behavioral studies in energy economics: A review and research framework. *Local Energy, Global Markets, 42nd IAEE International Conference*, 1–17.

Staudt, P. & Oren, S. S. (2020). A Merchant Transmission Approach for Uniform-Price Electricity Markets. *Hawaii International Conference on System Sciences (HICSS)*, 1–10.

Staudt, P., Wegner, F., Garttner, J., & Weinhardt, C. (2017). Analysis of redispatch and transmission capacity pricing on a local electricity market setup. *14th International Conference on the European Energy Market (EEM)*, 1–6.

Straub, T., Gimpel, H., Teschner, F., & Weinhardt, C. (2014). Feedback and performance in crowd work: a real effort experiment. *Proceedings of the 22nd European Conference on Information Systems (ECIS)*.

Straub, T., Gimpel, H., Teschner, F., & Weinhardt, C. (2015). How (not) to incent crowd workers. *Business & Information Systems Engineering, 57*(3), 167–179.

Straub, T., Teubner, T., & Weinhardt, C. (2016). Risk Taking in Online Crowdsourcing Tournaments. *49th Hawaii International Conference on System Sciences (HICSS)*, 1851–1860.

van Dinther, C., Weidlich, A., & Block, C. (2006). Energiemaerkte der zukunft. *Universitaet Karlsruhe (TH)*.

Veit, D. J., Weidlich, A., & Krafft, J. A. (2009). An agent-based analysis of the German electricity market with transmission capacity constraints. *Energy Policy, 37*(10), 4132–4144.

Vom Scheidt, F., Staudt, P., & Weinhardt, C. (2019). Assessing the Economics of Residential Electricity Tariff Selection. *International Conference on Smart Energy Systems and Technologies (SEST)*, 1–6.

vom Scheidt, F., Medinová, H., Ludwig, N., Richter, B., Staudt, P., & Weinhardt, C. (2020). Data analytics in the electricity sector: A quantitative and qualitative literature review. *Energy and AI, 1*, 100009.

Wagenknecht, T., Crommelinck, J., Teubner, T., & Weinhardt, C. (2017b). When Life Gives You Lemons: How rating scales affect user activity and frustration in collaborative evaluation processes. *Wirtschaftsinformatik (WI)*.

Wagenknecht, T., Filpe, R., & Weinhardt, C. (2017a). Towards a design theory of computer-supported organizational participation. *Journal of Enterprise Information Management, 30*(1), 188–202.

Wagenknecht, T., Teubner, T., & Weinhardt, C. (2018). A Janus-faced matter–The role of user anonymity for communication persuasiveness in online discussions. *Information & Management, 55*(8), 1024–1037.

Weinhardt, C., Kloker, S., Hinz, O., & van der Aalst, W. M. P. (2020). Citizen science in information systems research. *Business and Information Systems Engineering, 62*, 273–277.

Wiener, P., Stein, M., Seebacher, D., Bruns, J., Frank, M., Simko, V., Zander, S., & Nimis, J. (2016). Biggis: a continuous refinement approach to master heterogeneity and uncertainty in spatio-temporal big data. *Proceedings of the 24th ACM SIGSPATIAL International Conference on Advances in Geographic Information Systems*, 1–4.

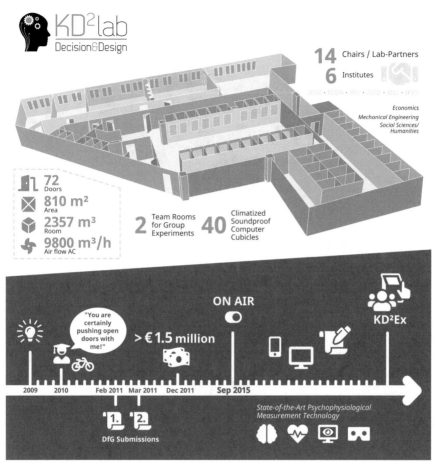

KD²lab
Decision&Design

14 Chairs / Lab-Partners

6 Institutes

IISM · ECON · IIP · AIFB · IISG · IPEK

Economics
Mechanical Engineering
Social Sciences/
Humanities

72 Doors

810 m² Area

2357 m³ Room

9800 m³/h Air flow AC

2 Team Rooms for Group Experiments

40 Climatized Soundproof Computer Cubicles

ON AIR

KD²Ex

"You are certainly pushing open doors with me!"

> € 1.5 million

2009   2010   Feb 2011   Mar 2011   Dec 2011   **Sep 2015**

1. **2.**
DfG Submissions

State-of-the-Art Psychophysiological Measurement Technology

Experiments

170
2015 - 2020

*State: Sep. 2020

65 Experimenters

1271 Bookings

2207 Sessions

20 Graduations

26.807 Participations

239 max. per day

Authors: Greta Hoffmann, Anke Greif-Winzrieth, Jella Pfeiffer, Michael Knierim, Christian Peukert, Marc Adam

Market Success: The Quest for the Objectives and Success Factors of Markets

Henner Gimpel, Lisa Hanny, Marion Ott, Jonathan Wagner, Martin Weibelzahl, Martin Bichler, and Steffi Ober

Abstract Markets are an essential tool to coordinate complex systems. Engineering markets requires the consideration of numerous objectives and factors that will eventually determine the market's success. These objectives and factors are frequently not well defined or elaborated. Hence, this chapter aims to support market design through a perspective on what determines market success. To this end, we review the literature, consider examples of market success and failure, and reflect on our ongoing work regarding future electricity market design. We provide a framework for market objectives and success factors with a focus on electricity markets. The framework could spur the identification of objectives and success factors of markets in other domains, and inform the engineering of future electricity markets.

H. Gimpel (✉)
Faculty of Business, Economics and Social Sciences, University of Hohenheim, Stuttgart, Germany

Faculty of Mathematics, Natural Sciences, and Materials Engineering, University of Augsburg, Augsburg, Germany

FIM Research Center and Project Group Business and Information Systems Engineering of Fraunhofer FIT, Augsburg/Bayreuth, Germany
e-mail: henner.gimpel@fim-rc.de

L. Hanny · J. Wagner · M. Weibelzahl
FIM Research Center and Project Group Business and Information Systems Engineering of Fraunhofer FIT, Augsburg/Bayreuth, Germany
e-mail: lisa.hanny@fim-rc.de; jonathan.wagner@fim-rc.de; martin.weibelzahl@fim-rc.de

M. Ott
ZEW – Leibniz Centre for European Economic Research, Mannheim, Germany
e-mail: Marion.Ott@zew.de

M. Bichler
Department of Computer Science, Technical University of Munich, Munich, Germany
e-mail: bichler@in.tum.de

S. Ober
NABU Bundesverband, Berlin, Germany
e-mail: steffi.ober@nabu.de

© The Author(s) 2021
H. Gimpel et al. (eds.), *Market Engineering*,
https://doi.org/10.1007/978-3-030-66661-3_2

1 Introduction

> Science is concerned with what is possible while engineering is concerned with choosing, from among the many possible ways, one that meets a number of often poorly stated economic and practical objectives.—Richard Hamming (1969)[1]

Rising global temperatures and natural catastrophes call for active policy interventions in terms of CO_2 reductions and sustainable use of natural resources. The energy sector plays a vital role in addressing climate change because many CO_2 emissions are energy related (IPCC 2014). Stressing the need to tackle this issue globally, the United Nations has included the provision of sustainable, reliable, and affordable energy in their 2030 agenda for sustainable development (SDG7) (Fuso Nerini et al. 2018). On a national basis, Germany is adopting similar plans, including increasing the share of renewable energies, phasing out coal power plants, and reducing greenhouse gas emissions by 2030 by 55% compared to 1990 (Deutscher Bundestag 2019). Under the European Commission's Green Deal, Germany further strives for climate neutrality by 2050.

In facilitating the transition toward clean energy, energy markets—and, more specifically, electricity markets—serve a critical enabling function. This function can be explained by the potential of markets to promote allocation and information efficiencies. Moreover, markets may also steer individual behavior to efficient market outcomes via price signals. In some cases, however, prices may not accurately reflect reality, which results in market failures due to, for example, negative externalities or abuse of market power (Andrew 2008). These concerns also apply to electricity markets since these are inherently characterized by high entry barriers, imperfect information, social and environmental costs, transmission and storage constraints, as well as inelastic demand, which may all lead to incorrect price signals (Cramton 2017; Wilson 2002). The increasing share of renewable energy production further underlines the need for well-functioning markets, as the resulting generation decentralization and price volatilities require enhanced market coordination and information flows (Lösch and Schneider 2016).

Setting up well-functioning electricity markets is not a trivial task, as it usually involves a complex set of (conflicting) market objectives. Moreover, a given market's overall success can be evaluated only by assessing market structure and outcomes against the backdrop of various economic, social, legal, technological, and physical factors. Further, "market success factors" may contribute to successfully achieving the objectives. Disentangling these market success factors allows for describing, explaining, monitoring, and predicting the success of different market designs and contributing to choosing a satisfying or even the best design.

Therefore, this chapter's aim is as follows:

---

[1]Richard W. Hamming was an American mathematician who received the Turing Award in 1968. The quote is from his Turing Award lecture (Hamming 1969, p. 5).

Identify and structure the multitude of market objectives and their corresponding success factors to support scholarly and practical approaches to designing and engineering electricity markets.

By understanding the critical determinants of market success, this chapter is a step toward a future-proof and sustainable electricity market design that complies with the overarching goal of delivering reliable electricity at the least cost to consumers (Cramton 2017). While we focus on electricity markets, we believe that most of the objectives and success factors can also be applied to other markets.

This chapter provides a comprehensive framework to achieve its aim, which allows for discussion of market objectives and market success factors beyond the traditional mechanism design of economic theory. Moreover, our framework contributes to existing work by mapping market objectives and market success factors. The framework is derived from an interdisciplinary literature review in the fields of—among others—economics, social sciences, information systems, operations research, computer science, and law. Moreover, the framework comprises insights from exemplary electricity markets and interdisciplinary market design workshops within the German Kopernikus project SynErgie (Sauer et al. 2019).

The remainder of this chapter is structured as follows: Section 2 lays out theoretical concepts. Section 3 presents the core artifact of this work, the market success framework. Section 4 discusses our framework's practical usage, limitations, and perspectives for future research. Section 5 concludes.

2 Theoretical Background

2.1 Market Design and Market Engineering

Markets are designed and engineered. "A market is a set of humanly devised rules that structure the interaction and exchange of information by self-interested participants in order to carry out exchange transactions at a relatively low cost. As such, markets are constrained by a sociocultural and legal framework" (Gimpel et al. 2008). Markets are information processing systems and services that support equating supply and demand, finding prices, and deciding on allocations and transactions. Markets are also entrepreneurial activities, and they may compete with other markets unless the regulatory framework ensures a monopoly position. Markets are the outcome of both evolutionary, emergent phenomena and purposeful design. Market design thus requires attention to all of a market's complications and details (Roth 2002). Therefore, "market design calls for an engineering approach" (Roth 2002, p. 1341). Others go even further and require a detail-focused "plumbing mindset." "The economist-plumber stands on the shoulder of scientists and engineers, but does not have the safety net of a bounded set of assumptions" (Duflo 2017, p. 3).

Market design and market engineering are closely related concepts. One can understand market design as an object (the design artifact) or as an activity (the process of designing). As an activity, market design is the art of designing institutions so that the behavioral incentives for individual market participants are in line with the market architect's overarching objectives (Ockenfels 2018). Market engineering is "the use of legal frameworks, economic mechanisms, management science models as well as information and communication technologies for the purpose of: (1) designing and constructing places where goods and services can be bought and sold; and (2) providing services associated with buying and selling" (Gimpel et al. 2008, p. 3). Market engineering is a process that produces (among other things) a market design artifact. As such, market engineering is close to the activity of market design. Both concepts also originate from an interdisciplinary background (Roth 2002; Wilson 2002). Market design was initially rooted in micro-economics but was soon extended to a broad range of other research areas such as computer science and operations research (Baliga and Vohra 2003; Roth 2008). Market engineering was coined by Christof Weinhardt and his team in the early 2000s (Weinhardt et al. 2003, 2006; Neumann 2004; Holtmann 2004; Weinhardt and Gimpel 2007; Gimpel et al. 2008). Christof and his team had a background in economics and information systems and leveraged the respective literature. They added multiple perspectives from their interdisciplinary work and collaboration with researchers from various disciplines, along with economics and information systems including management, finance, operations research, computer science, and law, to name but a few. The engineering perspective stresses the holistic view of markets, the notion that details matter, the need for an interdisciplinary approach, and the use of multiple methodologies (Gimpel et al. 2008; Roth 2002; Weinhardt et al. 2003). In sum, market engineering offers a broader and more holistic perspective on designing and engineering markets. In contrast, market design is used for a longer time, more widely, and (within its scope) more deeply.

2.2   Market Structure and Success

The object being analyzed and designed in market engineering is a market. A market involves multiple elements, as shown in Fig. 1. This perspective originates from Smith's (2003) micro-economic system framework, extensions offered by Weinhardt et al. (2003) and Gimpel et al. (2008), and further extensions suggested here. The market is embedded in the *socioeconomic, legal, technological, and physical environment*. A specifically relevant part of that environment might be a *regulatory authority* surveilling the market structure, participants' behavior, and outcomes to enforce or adjust the regulation.

The *market structure* resides within the environment. It contains the definition of the *transaction objects* which might be offered, sought, or traded via the market (e.g., block contracts for consecutive hours of energy supply one day ahead). Further, *participation rules* define who is allowed to enter the market or

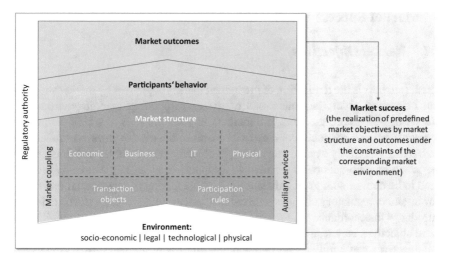

Fig. 1 Framework for market engineering (extension of Weinhardt et al. [2003] and Gimpel et al. [2008])

not (e.g., prequalification requirements for entering a balancing power market). The market structure has four further sub-structures: the *economic structure*, the *business structure*, the *IT structure*, and the additional *physical infrastructure.* The economic structure (also referred to as market microstructure) includes the bidding language, transparency rules, allocation rules, and price determination. The business structure focuses on the market as an entrepreneurial endeavor. It provides for the market institution's financing, the cost structure, revenue streams, personnel recruitment, development, dispatch, etc. The IT structure includes all the IT software and hardware belonging to an electronic market. The additional physical infrastructure includes any other physical assets (beyond IT hardware) that belong to the market (e.g., buildings for displaying goods being offered, for fiduciary storage, for facilitating the in-person exchange of traders, or for settlement). The relative importance of these structures might vary across markets. The market structure is flanked by *market coupling* (e.g., the markets for electric power being linked to markets for fossil fuels) and by *auxiliary services* that are not at the core of the market process but support participants (e.g., weather or price forecasting services).

On top of all this, there is the *market participants' behavior*. This behavior will typically result from the environment; the actors' options, values, and preferences; and the market structure. Behavior and structure jointly determine *market outcomes* (e.g., allocation or prices). A key challenge in market engineering is designing the market structure so that—given the environment—the behavior of the participants outside the control of the market designer and engineer results in the desired outcome and market success.

3   Market Success Framework

3.1   Market Objectives

Market success is the realization of predefined market objectives by market structure and outcomes under the constraints of the corresponding market environment. *Market objectives* are the aims of a market; they are the ends to which the market is engineered and operated. For electricity markets, the market objectives reflect the underlying electricity system and society's objectives as a whole, and thus exceed the scope of pure economic efficiency (Kominers et al. 2017). Market objectives need to be chosen with great care since the whole market is designed around them. For instance, regulatory changes or fiscal instruments (e.g., taxes or public debt) are introduced in accordance with market objectives. The lack of a concise definition of these objectives may result in unintended and unforeseen market outcomes.

Objectives can conflict with one another, and trade-offs need to be considered when deciding on the overall objectives. For instance, electricity markets typically face a trade-off between short-run and long-run efficiency (Biggar and Hesamzadeh 2014). Even if efficient electricity production with existing plants is achieved in the short term, concerns may arise in the long term over which investments in new plants and technologies and retirement of existing plants are necessary for efficiency. However, whether one or multiple market objectives are attainable in practice hinges on various conditions that we refer to as success factors. *Market success factors* are elements of a market's structure, auxiliary services, coupling, environment, or participants' behavior that directly influence the attainment of market objectives, thereby marking the difference between market success and market failure.

Figure 2 provides an overview of the market success framework. It lists the objectives and success factors, which are further detailed in the chapter.

Table 1 provides a list of common market objectives. The list comprises traditional economic criteria (e.g., short-run and long-run efficiency) and complements these with other essential perspectives relating to, for example, social well-being (support of the broader economy and society), sustainability (environmental/human health protection), or fairness (distributive justice). The list addresses electricity markets explicitly and captures the essential commodity aspect of electricity (security of supply). While we believe that each of the objectives listed may be a legitimate objective for an electricity market, we do not claim that the list is exhaustive. The list of objectives expands and complements traditional economic design desiderata such as allocative efficiency, individual rationality, budget balance, incentive compatibility, and core stability (Mas-Colell et al. 1995). In particular, the latter might often be challenging to achieve in a strict sense in complex real-world electricity markets. In contrast, the list of objectives in this chapter focuses on long-term-oriented objectives from a broad social perspective.

Fig. 2 Overview of the market success framework

3.1.1 Short-Run Efficiency

In economic terms, the objective of short-run efficiency is achieving allocative (or Pareto) efficiency (Dierker 1986). In the context of electricity, a market is allocatively efficient when the market price approaches the cost of supplying an additional unit of electricity (Green 2000; Munoz et al. 2018). Thereby, price signals are essential for steering supply and demand toward allocatively efficient outcomes. For prices to perform this function—and thus to serve as a reliable indicator of current market conditions—they need to reflect all relevant information available in a given market. For instance, prices need to reflect the costs of different power plants or local grid constraints. Marginal costs, on the other hand, comprise important supply-side information and may include, for example, the costs of fuel needed to arrive at an additional unit of energy (Munoz et al. 2018). Allocative efficiency may be achieved by maximizing gains from trade, which can be defined as the

Table 1 Electricity market objectives

Market objectives	Key aspects
Short-run efficiency	• Timeframe: Short run • Maximization of welfare or gains from trade • Minimization of costs • Requires inclusion of all affected parties and costs
Long-run efficiency	• Timeframe: Long run • Maximization of welfare • Requires incentivizing efficient investments in assets and network, as well as for decommissioning • Efficient allocation of risk
Support of the broader economy and society	• International competitiveness • Low financial burden on consumers • Innovativeness of the energy sector • High employment in the energy sector
Security of supply	• Reliability: Security of supply and energy system security • Robustness: Ability of the energy system to cope with disruptions and operate under unusual circumstances such as outages or IT security leaks • Resilience: Ability of the energy system to maintain services under stress and in turbulent environments
Distributive justice	• Different distributive rules such as egalitarian, merit, or utilitarian • Distribution by region, origin, income, age, etc. • Justice such as procedural or cosmopolitan justice
Environmental protection	• Protection of natural resources in quantity and quality, as well as of natural ecosystems • Sustainable use of natural resources • Climate neutrality • CO_2 reduction
Human health and flourishing protection	• Promote health, for example, by avoiding noise emissions, radiation, or toxic substances along the whole energy lifecycle • Promote well-being, happiness, life satisfaction, virtue, and close personal relationships

"improvement in consumer incomes and producer revenues that arise from the increased exchange of goods and services" (Sauma and Oren 2007, p. 1397).

To reach efficient market outcomes, electricity markets need to aggregate all information and reliably consider all available assets and network constraints. This rule implies that market mechanisms successfully avoid costly ex-post adjustments in the form of redispatch. Thus, redispatch refers to rearranging the schedule of (conventional) power plants such that all transmission constraints are respected, and demand is met (van den Bergh et al. 2015). Since efficient markets already consider the actual value or cost of electricity, externalities such as fossil fuel combustion are fully captured by market mechanisms and thus internalized (Andrew 2008). If externalities are internalized, short-run efficiency can align nicely with market objectives in the sustainability domain, such as environmental protection.

3.1.2 Long-Run Efficiency

The objective of long-run efficiency is "ensuring the market provides the proper incentives for efficient long-run investment" (Cramton 2017, p. 591). For electricity markets, the term "proper" refers to at least three aspects of long-run investment. First, investments need to be made in the "right" technologies. For example, for the German Energiewende, investments should be made in renewables instead of fossil power plants. Second, investments should be made in optimal asset capacities and network capacities. Third, investments need to be made in the right locations of the system (Cramton 2017). Another critical aspect of the objective of long-run efficiency relates to market power. No market participant or coalition should be able to manipulate the market outcomes to their advantage. Instead, it is essential that free competition is possible and that barriers to market entry and exit are low. Free competition also includes support for new market players or small-scale entrants such as prosumers.

Moreover, long-run efficiency also addresses the "missing money problem," which captures the idea that electricity prices do not fully reflect the value of investment needed to meet customers' expectations for reliable electric services (Hogan 2017). Hence, conventional power plants, which mostly perform as base load or back-up generators, may not recover their fixed costs due to low returns. Low returns may stem from a drop in prices, which is usually explained by high feed-in from renewable energy sources and low(er) demand linked to increasing energy efficiency (Hogan 2017). Lastly, long-run efficiency also comprises the co-existence of markets with different timescales (e.g., futures, day-ahead, or intraday) that allow for hedging against risks.

3.1.3 Support of the Broader Economy and Society

As discussed in Sect. 2.1, every market operates in a broader environment. Similarly, the electricity market operates within the context of the broader economy and, ultimately, society. There are multiple links and possible feedback channels between the broader economy (and society) and the electricity market (Brown and Spiegel 2019). Interaction effects may occur, for example, via market prices, employment rates, innovations, or the abuse of market power. For instance, as a significant production cost component, electricity prices may influence the (international) competitiveness of the manufacturing industry (Kwon et al. 2016; Moreno et al. 2014). In this case, electricity prices influence the competitive environment of non-electricity markets and bear consequences for the whole society via employment rates and tax income. Similar effects arise concerning market power, where monopoly electricity providers may also extend their powerful position to other markets (or society), for example, by controlling electricity prices (or outputs). On the retail level, electricity prices further have an essential impact on consumer rent and individual households' economic and social well-being (Brennan 2007). Lastly, it is essential to note that prices guide market participants on both the wholesale and retail level. This guidance implies that price components need to be understood by all relevant players so that economic decisions can be based on "true" market signals (Vucetie et al. 2001). Hence, this objective seeks to reduce the complexity of electricity prices, which is frequently introduced by additional levies and taxes, so that informed decision-making is possible. Informed decisions not only influence social participation but also positively affect short-run efficiency. Increased transparency may generally contribute to efficient allocation and pricing (Francis et al. 2009).

3.1.4 Security of Supply

From a short-term perspective, supply security refers to the readiness of existing capacities to meet the current load. Markets require proper incentives for the provision of reserves (Creti and Fabra 2007). From a long-run perspective, supply security involves performance attributes that stimulate investment in generation, transmission, distribution, metering, and control capacities to ensure stable system operation (Creti and Fabra 2007). More generally, the objective of security of supply refers to the market design supporting the reliable operation of the whole electricity system. Reliability in the electricity sector may be defined using two components: adequacy and security. First, "adequacy refers to the ability of the system to supply customer requirements under normal operating conditions" (McCarthy et al. 2007, p. 2153). Second, security includes the system's dynamic response to unexpected disturbances and relates to its ability to tolerate them (McCarthy et al. 2007). In sum, reliability can broadly be described as the system's ability to supply the electricity desired by consumers when and where it is demanded. Subcategories of reliability are resilience and robustness. Thus, resilience is traditionally used in an interdisciplinary context and provides a measure of stability related to objects' ability to promptly recover from an exogenous shock and promptly return to the equilibrium state (Mola et al. 2018). Within the power industry, resilience is defined as the system's ability to maintain or recover quickly to a stable state, allowing it to continue operations in the presence of significant mishaps or continuous stress (Ibanez et al. 2016). Common elements of resilient electricity systems are, for example, continuous feedback and monitoring of critical systems and consistent planning of communications and IT services to minimize human error (Carvalho et al. 2006). A system is robust if it is resilient for given events under all defined states (Ibanez et al. 2016).

To achieve reliability in practice, electricity markets need to allow for adjustments in the very short term in the case of instabilities. The existence of well-functioning balancing markets as well as redispatch activities can contribute to such adjustments. To mitigate the need for these costly short-term measures, electricity markets must account for available flexibilities already early on. Flexibilities can be provided through electricity generation or demand, storage technologies, transmission line expansions, or sector coupling (Heffron et al. 2020). In order to trade flexibility, separate flexibility markets may be needed that complement wholesale electricity markets (Hirth and Schlecht 2019). Objectives relating to economic efficiency need to create appropriate incentives for flexibility investments. Hence, the security of supply and long-run efficiency are closely interlinked objectives (Jamasb and Pollitt 2008).

3.1.5 Distributive Justice

The outcome of every market will produce both benefits and costs. Distributive justice as a market objective refers to how these benefits and costs are distributed among the market participants. The answer to the question of what justice means in such a context is highly critical. Nevertheless, market design and engineering need to consider the distributive effects resulting from how the market is organized (Traber 2017). There are different rules according to which the benefits and costs can be distributed. For instance, an egalitarian rule assigns everyone identical benefits and costs; a merit-based rule assigns benefits and costs in proportion to the contribution that market participants have made to the market outcome; a utilitarian rule assigns benefits and costs such that the greatest overall utility is achieved (with the notion of utility itself being subject to debate). Further, an inequitable distribution can also show itself according to, for example, region, origin, income, or age.

For electricity markets, distributive concerns often evolve around zonal or nodal pricing schemes (Ding and Fuller 2005). Smaller bidding zones usually involve price heterogeneity between different regions and favor one region over another (Egerer et al. 2016). Regional disparities may then have a considerable impact on the economy (or society) as a whole and the corresponding market objective. However, the growing decentralization of electricity systems and high shares of renewable energy sources may demand regionally differentiated prices in terms of economic efficiency (Neuhoff 2011). Uniform pricing may run counter to the objective of short-run efficiency. Further issues arise concerning how countries finance their energy transitions, such as the German Energiewende, as the related costs and benefits are typically distributed over different generations (Healy and Barry 2017). More precisely, the (economic) costs are mainly borne by today's generation to not further destroy the next generations' natural environment. Cross-generational settings often lead to underestimating long-run costs and thus underinvestment (Winkler 2009). Distributive justice, under certain circumstances, falls short of long-run efficiency objectives. Distributive justice may further be concerned with issues around energy poverty. Energy poverty relates to (un)equal access to modern energy services and the underlying pre-conditions for electricity usage (González-Eguino 2015; Sovacool 2012). For instance, poorer households may have to face higher electricity bills due to less energy-efficient buildings and devices (Reames 2016). In this case, distributive justice is again closely linked to objectives relating to economic and social development.

3.1.6 Environmental Protection

In essence, the market objective of environmental protection relates to the protection of natural resources in quantity and quality and the protection of ecosystems (including wildlife). This objective does not exclude the use of natural resources per se but calls for doing so sustainably, that is, in such a way that resources can be renewed. In the context of electricity, environmental protection translates into climate neutrality of electricity generation and avoidance of negative externalities for the environment (Capros et al. 2019). This shift is captured by the German Energiewende, for instance, which strives to increasingly replace conventional power plants with renewables to generate "clean" energy. Note that environmental protection is closely linked to short-run and long-run economic efficiency since externalities need to be reflected in prices (short run), and "green" investments need to be stipulated (long run). Furthermore, environmental protection may influence the broader economy and society.

3.1.7 Human Health and Flourishing Protection

Generating, transmitting, and consuming electricity comes with by-products such as noise emissions, radiation, or toxic substances. These by-products may negatively affect human health and flourishing (Treyer et al. 2014). For instance, the combustion of fossil fuels such as coal produces particulate matter, which—when it occurs in high concentrations—settles in the human lung and causes lasting damage. Therefore, the objective of human health and flourishing protection calls for electricity markets in which such adverse impacts are minimized. The installation of air filtration systems in coal power plants and, more generally, a shift toward renewable electricity production are measures supporting this objective (Akella et al. 2009). Beyond health, a possible objective could be that a market does not interfere with or even promote factors related to human flourishing such as well-being, happiness, life satisfaction, virtue, and close personal relationships. Analogous to the previous objective—environmental protection—human health and flourishing are also closely related to short-run and long-run efficiency and the broader economy and society. Additionally, human health also strongly depends on the previous objective of environmental protection.

In summary, we identify seven different market objectives that are distinguishable but also interrelated. The market objectives may be conducive to or inhibit one another, requiring trade-offs. However, whether one or several of the above objectives are achieved depends on success factors. In the following, we outline different success factors that directly impact market objectives and thereby foster or inhibit a market design's overall success.

3.2 Market Success Factors

3.2.1 Objective Orientation

While it may sound trivial that market design should be aligned with the market's objectives, it is somewhat challenging to determine what this means in practice. First, objective orientation implies that the market designer and engineer have determined the market's objectives. Second, objective orientation implies that the market design is catered to the market objectives. Third, effectivity means that a given market design is well suited to achieve the chosen market objectives (Cramton 2017). Market design provides instruments that effectively guide the individual behavior of the market participants.

Linking this success factor to the previously outlined market objectives, it becomes clear that all objectives are somehow affected by the degree of "objective orientation." Hence, all the above objectives may more likely be reached if market design directly addresses them.

3.2.2 Participation

Whether market design finally contributes to achieving the chosen objectives crucially hinges on market participation. Only if market players transact in a given market, the market can achieve its objectives. Hence, (potential) market participants should not be excluded from the marketplace, and market entry barriers should be low (Pavić et al. 2017). In addition, markets have to create the appropriate short- and long-term incentives to use them and not rely on agreements and transactions outside the market. In other words, no market participant should be able to do better by transacting outside the marketplace (Roth 2012). Fluctuating prices may incentivize market players to participate in local markets for flexibility in the short term. In contrast, in the long term, market players may be encouraged to invest in sufficient capacity to profit from price peaks (Graßl and Reinhart 2014).

Concerning market objectives, market participation may be closely linked to both short-run and long-run efficiency. In particular, markets may operate efficiently only if sufficient information and all stakeholders are considered. Goods are allocated to the participant with the highest valuation, or contracts to the participant with the lowest costs.

3.2.3 Incentives for Market-Conducive Behavior

Market designers and engineers need to create incentives that induce behavior conducive to the efficient functioning of the respective market. Market participants need to be incentivized to support market objectives and act following market rules and institutions. More precisely, no market participant or coalition should be able to manipulate market mechanisms, to engage in tacit collusion, or to bid or game strategically (Kominers et al. 2017; Kumar and Wen 2001). Market designers and engineers therefore need to create a market in which it is safe for market participants to reveal information and in which the market outcome is stable such that no market player or coalition can gain an advantage by deviating from it. If achieving the market objective depends on the participants' disclosure of information, it must be in the market participant's best interest to do so (e.g., due to dominant strategy or Bayesian incentive compatibility) (Roth 2007, 2012; Wolak 2019).

Considering the link between this success factor and the market objectives, incentivizing market-conducive behavior may support short-run and long-run efficiency and contribute to a market's support of the broader economy and society. For instance, the disclosure of private information and the resolution of conflicting interests fosters efficient market allocations as well as "true" price signals; the lack of opportunities to exploit market power and form strategic coalitions positively contributes to the objective of long-run efficiency; installing market incentives that foster technological innovations and adoptions may cause positive spill-overs to the broader economy and society because research and development activities need to be conducted and innovations can be used for applications outside the electricity domain.

3.2.4 Integration and Interconnection

Markets are typically interconnected with "neighboring" markets. For example, there is not just one energy market, but rather many neighboring submarkets on which different energy resources and services are traded, for example, the gas market, oil market, and electricity market. Moreover, markets are typically integrated into the broader market environment. For instance, the markets for different energy resources and services are influenced by numerous other markets whose transaction object is not energy but, for example, consumer goods, tourism, or labor (Heffron et al. 2020). Further, the electricity market itself comprises several submarkets, for example sequential markets for the same final good such as forward markets and real-time markets for energy. Therefore, market designers and engineers must be aware of possible feedbacks between neighboring and larger markets. In particular, they must ensure that neighboring markets are aligned with one another. Each market is efficiently integrated into the broader market environment to reduce or completely prevent friction between the various (sub)markets.

By linking this success factor with the market objectives, integrating markets into the broader market environment may significantly contribute to the market's support of the broader economy and society; interconnecting a market with its adjacent markets can notably contribute to short- and long-run efficiency.

3.2.5 Coordinated Timing

Within a given market, coordinated timing refers to the absence of time lags and sufficient time for market participants to reflect and make a decision. Market participants have sufficient time to (re)consider and evaluate different alternatives and make informed decisions (Roth 2007). Moreover, market designers and engineers need to consider possible interactions with different (sub)markets to ensure that no market participant is excluded from market interactions due to incompatible timing and the speed with which changes can be implemented in the existing market design.

Concerning the market objectives, coordinated timing predominantly influences the objectives of short-run and long-run efficiency. For instance, sufficient decision time allows market participants to consider and aggregate all available pieces of information in the short run. In the long run, coordinated timing enables participation in different (sub)markets and does not structurally exclude participants from market interactions.

3.2.6 Realizability in IT Systems

Electricity markets are complex markets whose functioning today largely depends on IT systems. For example, the market outcomes on power exchanges are calculated using algorithms, bids of suppliers and buyers are transmitted digitally, and network operators rely on computers to manage their network. Accordingly, market success depends heavily on the speed of the computations, the quality of their outcomes, and the security of the IT systems. Further, changes in the market design must ultimately be represented by the IT system and implemented in the existing structure.

Concerning the market objectives, this success factor mainly contributes to short- and long-run efficiency and supply security. Among the market objectives, these three objectives are most strongly affected when IT systems do not function properly.

3.2.7 Legitimacy

The concept of legitimacy is frequently discussed from an interdisciplinary perspective including, for example, important studies in political science (Lipset 1959), philosophy (Habermas 1975), psychology (Tyler 2006), and sociology (Johnson et al. 2006). More recently, legitimacy also extends to further domains, including, for example, electricity systems (Fuchs 2019; Renner and Giampietro 2020). In the electricity context, legitimacy is understood from an organizational (or managerial) perspective, referring to the "generalized perception that the actions of an entity are desirable, proper, and appropriate" (Suchman 1995, p. 574). The rights and identity of a regulator are publicly agreed on. Questions of legitimacy nowadays mainly relate to market design issues involving, for example, legitimacy of market operators, market participants, and institutional changes (Fuchs 2019). Thus, creating a broad social consensus on decision rights and relevant institutions constitutes a major success factor for market design. Consensus can usually be achieved if market incentives and institutions are aligned with socially accepted market objectives.

As indicated by the Fukushima incident, legitimacy can positively impact the objectives of environmental protection and human health. Environmental and human health protection are prerequisites for legitimate market design and thus already imply objective compatibility. Moreover, legitimacy is closely linked to distributive justice. If markets involve an unequal distribution of resources and outcomes are perceived as "unfair," market success is inhibited due to legitimacy concerns.

3.2.8 Legality

Another important driver of market success is legality, meaning that market design aligns with current law and jurisprudence. Legality requires decision-makers, in our case market designers and engineers, to resolve disputes by applying legal rules that have been declared beforehand, and not to alter the legal situation retrospectively at their discretion (Robinson 2005). One exemplary legal aspect that needs to be considered in market design is the protection of business secrets. Making the protection of confidential information enforceable by law allows market participants to truthfully reveal their valuation (or cost) to the market operator when engaging in market interactions, which is also an essential prerequisite for overall market success.

Considering market objectives, legality is connected to all of the above objectives in one way or another. First and foremost, legality impacts short-run efficiency via trust formation and the protection of business secrets. Moreover, flexible law amendments may positively contribute to short-run efficiency via swift adaptations to changes in the market environment, for example, an increasing share of renewable energies. However, note that a flexible legal framework may increase uncertainty of future expectations and negatively impact long-run efficiency, possibly leading to a conflict between short-run and long-run objectives. Further, the legal framework in electricity markets may impact the broader economy and society, as it significantly influences electricity prices and thus the financial burden of electricity on the household and industry level.

3.2.9 Technological Factors

Markets rely on various technologies, both analog and digital. Market designers and engineers must ensure that markets are designed to be technology-neutral for markets to select the "right" technologies (in the sense of being efficient, effective, cost-effective, etc.). Technology neutrality of markets is the only way to make sure that the technologies prevail in open competition. However, some objectives may require the privileged treatment of specific technologies, such as renewable energy generation in electricity markets, to achieve environmental objectives (Gawel et al. 2017). Moreover, market designers and engineers should anticipate technological developments in the short term, midterm, and long term and consider such possible developments when implementing new market rules.

Linking this success factor to the market objectives may contribute to short- and long-run efficiency, the security of supply, environmental protection, and human health and flourishing protection, for example, if more power plants are built that emit fewer pollutants into the environment.

3.2.10   Transparency

Another essential success factor for markets is transparency (Cramton 2017). Transparency implies that the market's rules, particularly how the participants' behavior translates into market outcomes, are unambiguously specified and communicated to the market participants. Common knowledge of the rules allows market participants to anticipate other participants' behavior and consequences and act accordingly. Transparency about the market outcome, if not in conflict with information confidentiality, may increase trust in the market. Moreover, market rules need to be connected to a transparent period of validity, enabling foresighted decision-making and long-term planning. This also implies that market participants can make reliable predictions for the future with intertemporal planning being a possibility. Focusing on market rules, it becomes clear that they need to be designed clearly and unambiguously.

Linking transparency to market objectives, this success factor impacts both short-run and long-run efficiency. Market participants can easily understand existing market rules, including price formation, and correctly anticipate others' behavior in a transparent environment. This knowledge and understanding allows market participants to base their decisions on all available information correctly and is necessary for short-run efficient market outcomes. Transparency further fosters security of supply, as important market information may be exchanged more easily between system-relevant stakeholders (e.g., electricity providers or grid operators), and congestion problems can be anticipated with higher accuracy through market indicators.

3.2.11   Simplicity

Simplicity can be regarded as a necessary extension of transparency (Cramton 2017). Provided that market participants' valuations (or costs) are made transparent, it is further crucial that these preferences can be expressed simply and effectively. Hence, market participants face minimum transaction costs when placing their bids. Since markets operate simply and predictably, distorting interventions by the regulator are minimized. The absence of ex-post adjustments allows market participants to gain experience with a given market design, and learning effects are possible. Another aspect of simplicity is the ease with which market designs are practically implemented. A given market design easily fits into the existing social, legal, technological, and economic environment and can be implemented via existing infrastructure.

Simplicity affects the objectives of short-run and long-run efficiency, as it contributes to reducing implementation hurdles and false expectations. More precisely, the unambiguous and straightforward disclosure of preferences and comprehensible market rules supports short-run efficient outcomes. The reduced need for ex-post adjustments and market interventions further enhances efficient market operation in the long run, creating a stable investment environment. Simplicity also positively impacts the objective of security of supply since unintended miscoordinations are limited due to a consistent understanding of market rules.

4 Intended Usage and Limitations of the Market Success Framework

The proposed framework of market objectives and success factors provides a holistic overview of functional market design requirements and serves as practical guidance for researchers, policymakers, and practitioners. It may be used along the whole lifecycle of markets from their initial conception up to the operation and eventual shutdown (Weinhardt et al. 2003; Neumann 2004; Gimpel et al. 2008). Thereby, our framework may assist all relevant stakeholders and decision-makers throughout the process of designing, evaluating, and monitoring markets. In this context, relevant user groups are regulators, market designers and engineers, and researchers from various fields, including economics, operations research, information systems, computer science, and law. Specifically, we see at least four possible ways to use the market success framework:

1. The framework, most notably the objectives, may serve as a starting point for eliciting needs and requirements for a market. Further, it may serve as a reference frame for structuring various perspectives, needs, and requirements. While the framework presented in this chapter might be a starting point, we assume that the framework is adapted to fit the specific market to be designed.
2. The market success framework may be used in the design phase. The objectives will serve as guiding principles for market designers and engineers, and the success factors offer more specific guidance on which aspects to consider. Again, we assume that the framework serves as a starting point from which the list of success factors and their interrelations with the objectives need to be tailored for a specific market.
3. Once one or multiple potential market designs are developed, they should be evaluated and refined to the point where a single satisfying design is selected. In this evaluation, the objectives—adapted to the specific market—are the

dimensions to be considered for judging the likely market success. On a more operational level, the success factors—adapted to the specific market—provide a list of factors to consider for evaluating the market.

4. Once the market is in operation, it should be monitored and re-evaluated based on its structure and outcomes in the field. Similar to the evaluation during the design phase, for an evaluation in the operation phase, the market success framework provides both the objectives and the success factors to consider. It is likely that the market operators, regulators, and competition authorities will, over time, reconsider objectives and success factors and gradually evolve them.

The market success framework may be used from two different perspectives. First, it may be used descriptively as an analytical framework to support market design. Second, it may be used to normatively judge the quality of market designs and derive recommendations on how markets ought to be designed. No matter which perspective is ultimately adopted, the market success framework seeks to structure existing market engineering processes and provides a common ground for future work.

Quite naturally, our work has limitations. The proposed list of market objectives and success factors is not exhaustive and is explicitly tailored to electricity markets. Hence, market designers, engineers, and researchers may extend our framework to other fields of application and add more objectives and success factors to the list. Moreover, our framework does not include suggestions concerning the operationalization and measurement of the proposed success factors. Therefore, future work may aim to establish objective criteria to state the degree of success factor achievement reliably. In addition, our framework does not provide information on the relative importance of the objectives and success factors. Possible extensions in this field may include a selection and weighting process to distinguish between primary (obligatory) and secondary (optional) market success factors.

5 Conclusion

Societal and technological changes call for active and detailed engineering of markets to cope with and manage increased market complexity. The emergence of new market participants, technological innovations, and the plurality of social values and constructs open up a complex field in which market designers and engineers need to make decisions regarding possibly conflicting market objectives and specific measures they want to implement. Hence, this work provides a structured overview of different market objectives and the corresponding factors that contribute to achieving these objectives and ultimately determine market success. This work's focus mainly lies in electricity markets. The ongoing energy transition poses various new challenges to market designers, engineers, and regulators, which will most likely increase in the coming years. More precisely, the energy transition brings about fundamental changes in the market environment and therefore calls for market design adaptations. Against this background, the energy transition will only realize its full potential if changes in the market environment are effectively addressed by market design. Even though this work is mainly centered around electricity markets, our framework may also be extended to other application fields. Further research may tailor this framework to a range of other markets in which market design interventions are required due to market failures, malfunctioning, or changes in the overall market environment. Hence, our framework provides an essential basis for understanding market performance (or quality) and, ultimately, market success.

Acknowledgments The authors gratefully acknowledge the financial support of the Kopernikus project SynErgie by the Federal Ministry of Education and Research (BMBF) and the project supervision by the project management organization Projektträger Jülich (PtJ). The authors thank all participants in SynErgie Cluster IV for the fruitful discussions.

References

Akella AK, Saini RP, Sharma MP (2009) Social, economical and environmental impacts of renewable energy systems. Renewable Energy 34:390–396. https://doi.org/10.1016/j.renene.2008.05.002

Andrew B (2008) Market failure, government failure and externalities in climate change mitigation: The case for a carbon tax. Public Admin. Dev. 28:393–401. https://doi.org/10.1002/pad.517

Baliga S, Vohra R (2003) Market Research and Market Design. Advances in Theoretical Economics 3. https://doi.org/10.2202/1534-5963.1059

Biggar DR, Hesamzadeh MR (eds) (2014) The Economics of Electricity Markets. John Wiley & Sons Ltd, Chichester, United Kingdom

Brennan TJ (2007) Consumer preference not to choose: Methodological and policy implications. Energy Policy 35:1616–1627. https://doi.org/10.1016/j.enpol.2006.04.023

Brown B, Spiegel SJ (2019) Coal, Climate Justice, and the Cultural Politics of Energy Transition. Global Environmental Politics 19:149–168. https://doi.org/10.1162/glep_a_00501

Capros P, Zazias G, Evangelopoulou S, Kannavou M, Fotiou T, Siskos P, Vita A de, Sakellaris K (2019) Energy-system modelling of the EU strategy towards climate-neutrality. Energy Policy 134:110960. https://doi.org/10.1016/j.enpol.2019.110960

Carvalho PVRd, Santos ILd, Gomes JO, Silva Borges, Marcos R., Huber GJ (2006) The Role of Nuclear Power Plant Operators' Communications in Providing Resilience and Stability in System Operation. Proceedings of 2nd Symposium on Resilience Engineering

Cramton P (2017) Electricity market design. Oxford Review of Economic Policy 33:589–612. https://doi.org/10.1093/oxrep/grx041

Creti A, Fabra N (2007) Supply security and short-run capacity markets for electricity. Energy Economics 29:259–276. https://doi.org/10.1016/j.eneco.2006.04.007

Deutscher Bundestag (2019) Gesetz zur Einführung eines Bundes-Klimaschutzgesetzes und zur Änderung weiterer Vorschriften vom 12. Dezember 2019, §3 (1). Bundesgesetzblatt:2513–2521

Dierker E (1986) When does marginal cost pricing lead to Pareto efficiency? J. Econ. 46:41–66. https://doi.org/10.1007/BF03051785

Ding F, Fuller JD (2005) Nodal, Uniform, or Zonal Pricing: Distribution of Economic Surplus. IEEE Trans. Power Syst. 20:875–882. https://doi.org/10.1109/TPWRS.2005.846042

Duflo E (2017) The Economist as Plumber. American Economic Review 107:1–26. https://doi.org/10.1257/aer.p20171153

Egerer J, Weibezahn J, Hermann H (2016) Two price zones for the German electricity market — Market implications and distributional effects. Energy Economics 59:365–381. https://doi.org/10.1016/j.eneco.2016.08.002

Francis JR, Huang S, Khurana IK, Pereira R (2009) Does Corporate Transparency Contribute to Efficient Resource Allocation? Journal of Accounting Research 47:943–989. https://doi.org/10.1111/j.1475-679X.2009.00340.x

Fuchs G (2019) Legitimacy and field development: Electricity transition(s) in Germany. Global Transitions 1:141–147. https://doi.org/10.1016/j.glt.2019.10.001

Fuso Nerini F, Tomei J, To LS, Bisaga I, Parikh P, Black M, Borrion A, Spataru C, Castán Broto V, Anandarajah G, Milligan B, Mulugetta Y (2018) Mapping synergies and trade-offs between energy and the Sustainable Development Goals. Nat Energy 3:10–15. https://doi.org/10.1038/s41560-017-0036-5

Gawel E, Lehmann P, Purkus A, Söderholm P, Witte K (2017) Rationales for technology-specific RES support and their relevance for German policy. Energy Policy 102:16–26. https://doi.org/10.1016/j.enpol.2016.12.007

Gimpel H, Jennings NR, Kersten GE, Ockenfels A, Weinhardt C (2008) Market Engineering: A Research Agenda. In: Gimpel H, Jennings NR, Kersten GE, Ockenfels A, Weinhardt C (eds) Negotiation, Auctions, and Market Engineering, vol 2. Springer Berlin Heidelberg, Berlin, Heidelberg, p. 1

González-Eguino M (2015) Energy poverty: An overview. Renewable and Sustainable Energy Reviews 47:377–385. https://doi.org/10.1016/j.rser.2015.03.013

Graßl M, Reinhart G (2014) Evaluating Measures for Adapting the Energy Demand of a Production System to Volatile Energy Prices. Procedia CIRP 15:129–134. https://doi.org/10.1016/j.procir.2014.06.081

Green R (2000) Competition in generation: the economic foundations. Proc. IEEE 88:128–139. https://doi.org/10.1109/5.823994

Habermas J (1975) Legitimation crisis. Beacon Press, Boston, Mass

Hamming RW (1969) One Man's View of Computer Science. J. ACM 16:3–12. https://doi.org/10.1145/321495.321497

Healy N, Barry J (2017) Politicizing energy justice and energy system transitions: Fossil fuel divestment and a "just transition". Energy Policy 108:451–459. https://doi.org/10.1016/j.enpol.2017.06.014

Heffron R, Körner M-F, Wagner J, Weibelzahl M, Fridgen G (2020) Industrial demand-side flexibility: A key element of a just energy transition and industrial development. Applied Energy 269:115026. https://doi.org/10.1016/j.apenergy.2020.115026

Hirth L, Schlecht I (2019) Market-Based Redispatch in Zonal Electricity Markets: Inc-Dec Gaming as a Consequence of Inconsistent Power Market Design (not Market Power). ZBW - Leibniz Information Centre for Economics, Kiel, Hamburg. http://hdl.handle.net/10419/222925

Hogan M (2017) Follow the missing money: Ensuring reliability at least cost to consumers in the transition to a low-carbon power system. The Electricity Journal 30:55–61. https://doi.org/10.1016/j.tej.2016.12.006

Holtmann C (2004) Organisation von Märkten. Market Engineering für den elektronischen Wertpapierhandel. Doctoral Dissertation, Universität Karlsruhe

Ibanez E, Lavrenz S, Gkritza K, Giraldo DAM, Krishnan V, McCalley JD, Somani AK (2016) Resilience and robustness in long-term planning of the national energy and transportation system. IJCIS 12:82. https://doi.org/10.1504/IJCIS.2016.075869

IPCC (2014) Climate Change 2014: Synthesis Report. Contribution of Working Groups I, II and III to the Fifth Assessment Report of the Intergovernmental Panel on Climate Change [Core Writing Team, R.K. Pachauri and L.A. Meyer (eds.)]. IPCC, Geneva, Switzerland. https://www.ipcc.ch/site/assets/uploads/2018/02/SYR_AR5_FINAL_full.pdf

Jamasb T, Pollitt M (2008) Security of supply and regulation of energy networks. Energy Policy 36:4584–4589. https://doi.org/10.1016/j.enpol.2008.09.007

Johnson C, Dowd TJ, Ridgeway CL (2006) Legitimacy as a Social Process. Annu. Rev. Sociol. 32:53–78. https://doi.org/10.1146/annurev.soc.32.061604.123101

Kominers SD, Teytelboym A, Crawford VP (2017) An invitation to market design. Oxford Review of Economic Policy 33:541–571. https://doi.org/10.1093/oxrep/grx063

Kumar DA, Wen F (2001) Market power in electricity supply. IEEE Trans. On Energy Conversion 16:352–360. https://doi.org/10.1109/60.969475

Kwon S, Cho S-H, Roberts RK, Kim HJ, Park K, Edward Yu T (2016) Effects of electricity-price policy on electricity demand and manufacturing output. Energy 102:324–334. https://doi.org/10.1016/j.energy.2016.02.027

Lipset SM (1959) Some Social Requisites of Democracy: Economic Development and Political Legitimacy. Am Polit Sci Rev 53:69–105. https://doi.org/10.2307/1951731

Lösch A, Schneider C (2016) Transforming power/knowledge apparatuses: the smart grid in the German energy transition. Innovation: The European Journal of Social Science Research 29:262–284. https://doi.org/10.1080/13511610.2016.1154783

Mas-Colell A, Whinston MD, Green JR (1995) Microeconomic theory. Oxford Univ. Press, New York, NY

McCarthy RW, Ogden JM, Sperling D (2007) Assessing reliability in energy supply systems. Energy Policy 35:2151–2162. https://doi.org/10.1016/j.enpol.2006.06.016

Mola M, Feofilovs M, Romagnoli F (2018) Energy resilience: research trends at urban, municipal and country levels. Energy Procedia 147:104–113. https://doi.org/10.1016/j.egypro.2018.07.039

Moreno B, García-Álvarez MT, Ramos C, Fernández-Vázquez E (2014) A General Maximum Entropy Econometric approach to model industrial electricity prices in Spain: A challenge for the competitiveness. Applied Energy 135:815–824. https://doi.org/10.1016/j.apenergy.2014.04.060

Munoz FD, Wogrin S, Oren SS, Hobbs BF (2018) Economic Inefficiencies of Cost-based Electricity Market Designs. EJ 39. https://doi.org/10.5547/01956574.39.3.fmun

Neuhoff K (2011) Opening the Electricity Market to Renewable Energy: Making Better Use of the Grid. DIW Economic Bulletin 1:16–23

Neumann DG (2004) Market engineering: A structured design process for electronic markets. Doctoral Dissertation, Universität Karlsruhe

Ockenfels A (2018) Marktdesign. https://wirtschaftslexikon.gabler.de/definition/marktdesign-51491/version-274653. Accessed 29 October 2020

Pavić I, Beus M, Pandžić H, Capuder T, Štritof I (2017) Electricity markets overview - Market participation possibilities for renewable and distributed energy resources. 2017 14th International Conference on the European Energy Market (EEM)

Reames TG (2016) Targeting energy justice: Exploring spatial, racial/ethnic and socio-economic disparities in urban residential heating energy efficiency. Energy Policy 97:549–558. https://doi.org/10.1016/j.enpol.2016.07.048

Renner A, Giampietro M (2020) Socio-technical discourses of European electricity decarbonization: Contesting narrative credibility and legitimacy with quantitative story-telling. Energy Research & Social Science 59:101279. https://doi.org/10.1016/j.erss.2019.101279

Robinson PH (2005) Fair Notice and Fair Adjudication: Two Kinds of Legality. University of Pennsylvania Law Review:335–398

Roth AE (2002) The Economist as Engineer: Game Theory, Experimentation, and Computation as Tools for Design Economics. Econometrica 70:1341–1378. https://doi.org/10.1111/1468-0262.00335

Roth AE (2007) The Art of Designing Markets. Harvard Business Review 85:118–126

Roth AE (2008) What Have We Learned from Market Design? The Economic Journal 118:285–310. https://doi.org/10.1111/j.1468-0297.2007.02121.x

Roth AE (2012) The Theory and Practice of Market Design. Nobel Prize in Economics documents

Sauer A, Abele E, Buhl HU (eds) (2019) Energieflexibilität in der deutschen Industrie: Ergebnisse aus dem Kopernikus-Projekt - Synchronisierte und energieadaptive Produktionstechnik zur flexiblen Ausrichtung von Industrieprozessen auf eine fluktuierende Energieversorgung - SynErgie. Fraunhofer Verlag, Stuttgart

Sauma EE, Oren SS (2007) Economic Criteria for Planning Transmission Investment in Restructured Electricity Markets. IEEE Trans. Power Syst. 22:1394–1405. https://doi.org/10.1109/TPWRS.2007.907149

Smith VL (2003) Markets, institutions and experiments. In: Nadel L (ed) Encyclopedia of Cognitive Science. Nature Publishing Group

Sovacool BK (2012) The political economy of energy poverty: A review of key challenges. Energy for Sustainable Development 16:272–282. https://doi.org/10.1016/j.esd.2012.05.006

Suchman MC (1995) Managing Legitimacy: Strategic and Institutional Approaches. The Academy of Management Review 20:571. https://doi.org/10.2307/258788

Traber T (2017) Capacity Remuneration Mechanisms for Reliability in the Integrated European Electricity Market: Effects on Welfare and Distribution through 2023. Utilities Policy 46:1–14. https://doi.org/10.1016/j.jup.2016.10.005

Treyer K, Bauer C, Simons A (2014) Human health impacts in the life cycle of future European electricity generation. Energy Policy 74:S31-S44. https://doi.org/10.1016/j.enpol.2014.03.034

Tyler TR (2006) Psychological perspectives on legitimacy and legitimation. Annu Rev Psychol 57:375–400. https://doi.org/10.1146/annurev.psych.57.102904.190038

van den Bergh K, Couckuyt D, Delarue E, D'haeseleer W (2015) Redispatching in an interconnected electricity system with high renewables penetration. Electric Power Systems Research 127:64–72. https://doi.org/10.1016/j.epsr.2015.05.022

Vucetie S, Tomsovic K, Obradovic Z (2001) Discovering Price-Load Relationships in California's Electricity Market. IEEE Power Eng. Rev. 21:63. https://doi.org/10.1109/MPER.2001.4311388

Weinhardt C, Gimpel H (eds) (2007) Market Engineering: An Interdisciplinary Research Challenge: Negotiation and Market Engineering. Ed.: N. Jennings. IBFI, Schloss Dagstuhl

Weinhardt C, Holtmann C, Neumann D (2003) Market-Engineering. Wirtschaftsinf 45:635–640. https://doi.org/10.1007/BF03250926

Weinhardt C, Neumann D, Holtmann C (2006) Germany: Computer-Aided Market Engineering. Commun. ACM 49:79. https://doi.org/10.1145/1139922.1139953

Wilson R (2002) Architecture of Power Markets. Econometrica 70:1299–1340. https://doi.org/10.1111/1468-0262.00334

Winkler R (2009) Now or Never: Environmental Protection Under Hyperbolic Discounting. SSRN Journal. https://doi.org/10.2139/ssrn.1726741

Wolak L (2019) Wholesale Electricity Market Design. https://web.stanford.edu/group/fwolak/cgi-bin/sites/default/files/wolak_November_2019.pdf

Henner Gimpel holds the chair for Digital Management in the Faculty of Business, Economics, and Social Sciences at the University of Hohenheim. He is a member of the Faculty of Mathematics, Natural Sciences, and Materials Engineering at the University of Augsburg, co-lead of the Research Center Finance & Information Management (FIM) and the Project Group Business & Information Systems Engineering of the Fraunhofer FIT. Henner received a diploma in Industrial Engineering and Management and a doctorate in Economics from the University of Karlsruhe. Christof Weinhardt was the supervisor of his doctoral studies and mentor during his time as a postdoctoral student at Karlsruhe. His current research interests include the analysis and design of digital markets and human-centered, behavioral information systems.

Lisa Hanny is a doctoral candidate at the Research Center Finance & Information Management (FIM) and the Project Group Business & Information Systems Engineering of the Fraunhofer

FIT. She holds a Master of Arts in International Economics from the University of Passau. Lisa's current research interests include electricity market design and regulation, as well as digital energy technologies.

Marion Ott is an advanced researcher in the Department "Market Design" at the ZEW Mannheim. She received a diploma in Industrial Engineering and Management and a doctorate in Economics from the University of Karlsruhe. She was a junior professor of game theory and behavioral economics at RWTH Aachen University before moving to the ZEW. Her research interests lie in the design and analysis of all kinds of markets, in particular auctions. Using game theory and experiments, she analyzes, for example, auctions for multiple heterogeneous goods.

Jonathan Wagner is a doctoral candidate at the Research Center Finance & Information Management (FIM) and the Project Group Business & Information Systems Engineering of the Fraunhofer FIT. He holds a Master of Science in Economics from the University of Bayreuth. Jonathan's current research interests include market design and digital energy.

Martin Weibelzahl leads an energy research group at the Research Center Finance & Information Management (FIM) and the Project Group Business & Information Systems Engineering of the Fraunhofer FIT. Martin also serves as a lecturer at the University of Bayreuth and the University of Augsburg. In 2011, he completed his studies in quantitative economics at the Friedrich-Alexander University Erlangen-Nuremberg. He then began his doctorate at the Chair of Business Mathematics within the Elite Network of Bavaria, followed by a position as a postdoctoral fellow at RWTH Aachen University. In his research, he mainly focuses on digital energy and market design.

Martin Bichler is Associate Dean and has been a full professor in the Department of Computer Science of the Technical University of Munich since 2003. Previously, he was a research fellow at UC Berkeley, a research staff member at the IBM T.J. Watson Research Center in New York, and a postdoc at the Vienna University of Economics and Business. In recent years, he has been a visiting scholar at Cambridge University, Yale University, and Stanford University. In his research, Martin focuses on optimization, game theory, and market design. Martin was Editor-in-Chief of the *Business & Information Systems Engineering* journal until 2019 when Christof Weinhardt took over.

Steffi Ober is Head of the Department of Economy and Sustainable Research Policy at NABU, Germany's largest environmental organization. She is also founder and leader of the Civil Society Platform Forschungswende (Research Turnaround). Her research interests lie in the design and analysis of CO-Design and Stakeholder involvement processes to achieve socially robust science-based solutions for sustainable transformation.

Decision Analytics for Initial Public Offerings: How Filing Sentiment Influences Stock Market Returns

Jonas Krinitz and Dirk Neumann

Abstract Companies issuing stocks through an initial public offering (IPO) are obligated to publish relevant information as part of a prospectus. Besides quantitative figures from accounting, this document also contains qualitative information in the form of text. In this chapter, we analyze how sentiment in the prospectus influences future stock returns. In addition, we investigate the impact of pre-IPO sentiment in financial announcements on first-day returns. The results of our empirical analyses using 572 IPOs from US companies suggest a negative link between words linked to uncertainty and future stock market returns for up to 10 trading days. Conversely, we find that uncertainty expressed in pre-IPO announcements is positively linked to first-day stock returns. These insights have implications for research on IPOs by demonstrating that future stock returns are also driven by textual information from the prospectus and assist investors in placing their orders.

1 Introduction

Companies are increasingly turning to stock markets to raise expansion capital to monetize the investments of early private investors. An *initial public offering* (IPO) refers to a type of public offering where shares of stock in a company are sold to the general public, for the first time, on a securities exchange. As a result of regulatory publication requirements, firms must file a prospectus with, e.g., the Securities and Exchange Commission (SEC) in the USA prior to its initial public stock offering (c.f. Kenney and Patton 2013a, Ritter and Welch 2002). Details of the proposed offering are disclosed to potential purchasers in the form of a detailed document known as a *prospectus*. This prospectus contains key figures from financial accounting, as well as information on current and future business

J. Krinitz · D. Neumann (✉)
Chair for Information Systems, University of Freiburg, Freiburg im Breisgau, Germany
e-mail: dirk.neumann@is.uni-freiburg.de

© The Author(s) 2021
H. Gimpel et al. (eds.), *Market Engineering*,
https://doi.org/10.1007/978-3-030-66661-3_3

models, potential opportunities, and risks threatening the business. The prospectus is used as an instrument to remove or at least alleviate disadvantages stemming from information asymmetries among different investor groups. Obviously, the prospectus plays a major role in the formation of IPO prices, which ultimately determines the amount of capital that accrues from the IPO. Thus, all involved stakeholders in the IPO may need to understand how the prospectus affects the final IPO prices. While the underwriting company has a natural incentive to cast a positive light on their company, investors have a need to decipher the text messages for relevant signals on the future performance of the company.

The theory of market microstructure may fill the bill in explaining the relationship between the prospectus and final IPO price as it refers to the branch of finance that is concerned with the details of how exchange occurs in markets. More specifically, market microstructure theory epitomizes *the study of the process and outcomes of exchanging assets under a specific set of rules* (O'Hara 1995). One crucial aspect refers to the role of information and how prices reflect them. Interestingly, market microstructure theory is still in its infancy, dealing with information which consists of text messages, such as the prospectus. The theory is, thus, nearly silent in explaining how text messages are processed into prices (c.f. Jegadeesh and Wu 2013, Loughran and McDonald 2011, Tetlock et al. 2008).

This is where *decision analytics*, as a subfield of Information Systems (IS) research, comes into play (Chen et al. 2012) in order to contribute to the understanding of how human agents process information when facing textual news. Besides quantitative information, such as quarterly earnings, the textual content obviously also provides valuable insights. Typically, the sentiment of financial news is utilized to analyze how information is processed (Siering 2013) as investors and analysts perceive novel information differently. Liebmann et al. (2012) come to the conclusion that investors rapidly translate novel information into transactions, whereas analysts wait to respond. Similarly, commodity markets seem to be mostly driven by negative news (Feuerriegel and Neumann 2013, Feuerriegel et al. 2014). Hence, information processing has been subject to many decision analytics research publications since problems span several dimensions, namely, volume, velocity, variety, and veracity (IBM 2013). Thus, these research questions are placed at the intersection between behavioral finance, Information Systems, and decision analytics, which has been receiving great attention lately (Chen et al. 2012).

Altogether, information from an IPO prospectus provides the basis for the decision-making process for potential investors. Thus, it is logical consequence to study the *information processing* of investors facing IPO filings in the context of efficient electronic markets. Though IPO filings consist of a few quantitative facts, a large proportion accounts for qualitative information. While prior research focuses on quantitative facts, such as the number of offered shares, knowledge of the textual components is rare. Hence, this paper examines the statistical relationship between sentiment in IPO filings and the subsequent stock market performance.

As a main contribution to Information Systems research, this chapter sheds some light on information processing along IPO filings. The soft data contained in these filings conveys insights and potentially valuable information that is absent in traditional quantitative numbers. A recent study by Ferris et al. (2013) points out that *the extent to which management is confident about the success of its issue and the implications that such beliefs have on IPO pricing are largely ignored in the literature*. To close this gap, individual research questions addressing the content of IPO prospectuses, as well as contributions, are as follows.

Confirmatory Analysis: To what extent are the stock market returns of firms driven by the sentiment of their IPO filings?

As a confirmatory analysis of previous research (Ferris et al. 2013, Loughran and McDonald 2013), we investigate how investors react to IPO prospectuses and analyze information processing empirically by exploiting sentiment analysis. We find that sentiment in IPO prospectuses correlates with first-day return. In fact, one standard deviation increase in the sentiment measure is negatively linked to an increase in first-day returns by an economically significant 10.56%.

Research Question 1: How persistent is the influence of filing tone on long-term returns?

According to our results, sentiment is not only positively correlated with returns in the short term, but the polarity of filings also affects the performance in the long term.

Research Question 2: How is the IPO performance affected by pre-IPO news sentiment?

The confirmatory analysis proves that IPO filings have an effect on the subsequent stock market returns. However, the media coverage of firms going public occurs in more depth, since journalists also report on the progress of the IPO, the previous performance of the firm, and the general outlook. Because of these reasons, we investigate the impact of pre-IPO news announcements on first-day returns and, finally, compare the influence of sentiment on IPO filings and news announcement in terms of strength.

The remainder of this chapter is structured as follows. In Sect. 2, we combine previous research on both initial public offerings and approaches for sentiment analysis in order to study literature on their intersection, which deals with the information processing theory of IPO filings. To gauge the sentiment of these IPO filings, we detail our research model in Sect. 3. Using this research model, Sect. 4 analyzes how the sentiment in an IPO prospectus is linked to the corresponding stock market performance and how information processing is influenced by pre-IPO news sentiment. Section 5 concludes the chapter with a summary and an outlook on future research.

2   Related Work

In this section, we present related literature grouped into two categories. First, we revisit literature covering different types of IPO filings. Second, we compare approaches for financial documents to measure their sentiment. Third, we review previous work on information processing of investors when facing IPO filings. All in all, the following references provide evidence that investigating the effect of sentiment on IPO filings across different time spans, as well as the impact of pre-IPO news sentiment, is both a novel and relevant research question to the Information Systems community.

To a large extent, market efficiency relies upon the availability of information (Fama 1965). Access to market information is promoted with ease in electronic markets, and because of straightforward access, decision-makers (i.e., consumers, suppliers, and intermediaries) can use more detailed information to make purchases and sales more beneficial (e.g., Granados et al. 2010). In fact, it is both native and crucial to IS research regarding how decision-makers process and act upon (qualitative) information in IPO filings. Though information processing has been extensively studied in capital markets, this is not the case when it comes to literature focusing on IPO filings: "An examination of the textual or soft information contained in prospectuses is less common" (Ferris et al. 2013).

2.1 IPO Filings

This section introduces the basic filing types required by US firms going public. For US firms, one of the first steps in going public is filing a Form S-1 on the Securities and Exchange Commission's (SEC) Electronic Data Gathering, Analysis, and Retrieval (EDGAR) system. Typically, the S-1 offers investors their first detailed glimpse of a firm's business model and financial statements. It is a pre-effective registration statement submitted when a company decides to go public. Hence, an investor can use its content to evaluate potential investment opportunity. If the S-1 is followed by a successful initial public offering, firms file a final prospectus (so-called Form 424), which is published via EDGAR on the day of or a few days following the IPO. Loughran and McDonald (2013) report a median time lag of 88 calendar days between S-1 and Form 424. According to the authors, more calendar time between the S-1 and 424 filings (the final IPO prospectus) is associated with significantly lower first-day returns. Companies with more problematic S-1 filings or facing adverse market conditions are often delayed in issuing stock. Some of the delay in going public could be due to the many days of management needed to properly respond to SEC concerns about the IPO document or a sharp decline in IPO market conditions. However, the overall tone of the S-1 is typically very similar to the tone of the final IPO prospectus. In fact, changes in tone between the S-1 and 424 filings seem to be unrelated to positive revisions in the offer price (Loughran and McDonald 2013).

2.2 Sentiment Analysis in the Finance Discipline

Methods that use the textual representation of documents to measure the positivity and negativity of the content are referred to as opinion mining or *sentiment analysis*. In fact, sentiment analysis can be utilized to extract subjective information from text sources, as well as to measure how market participants perceive and react upon financial materials. Here, one uses the observed price reactions following the financial text to validate the accuracy of the sentiment analysis routines. Based upon sentiment measures, one can study the relationship between financial documents and their effect on markets. For example, empirical evidence shows that a discernible relation between news content and its stock market reaction exists (e.g., Antweiler and Frank 2004, Tetlock 2007, among the first).

As sentiment analysis is applied to a broad variety of domains and text sources, research has devised various approaches to measure sentiment. For example, Pang and Lee (2008) provide a comprehensive domain-independent survey. Within finance, recent literature surveys (Minev et al. 2012, Mittermayer and Knolmayer 2006b) compare studies aimed at stock market prediction. For example, *dictionary-based approaches* are very frequently used in recent financial text mining research (cp. Demers and Vega 2010, Henry 2008, Jegadeesh and Wu 2013, Loughran and McDonald 2011, Tetlock et al. 2008). These methods count the frequency of predefined positive and negative words from a given dictionary—producing results that are straightforward and reliable. Similarly, *term-weighting methods* also rely upon positive and negative words, but these are classified based on word frequencies in a training set (i.e., the prior probabilities) to assign a weight to each term (Liebmann et al. 2012). *Machine learning approaches* (e.g., Antweiler and Frank 2004, Li 2010, Mittermayer and Knolmayer 2006a, Schumaker and Chen 2009) offer a broad range of methods but may suffer from overfitting (Sharma and Dey 2012).

In our research framework, we have only a few hundred IPO filings, each linked to a large text basis (i.e., a length of several thousand words) along with a continuous return value. Thus, we have experienced difficulties in achieving robust results with term-weighting as well as with machine learning approaches and focused, instead, on dictionary-based methods. In fact, we have tested all of the above dictionary-based metrics in combination with various dictionaries. In short, we find that dictionaries vary strongly in the strength of the link between sentiment and stock market reaction. Along with previous research on IPOs, the ratio of words labeled as *uncertainty* according to the Loughran and McDonald Financial Sentiment Dictionary (McDonald 2012) outperforms all other approaches.

2.3   Information Processing Theory of IPO Filings

This section provides an overview of related research investigating the information processing of IPO filings. First, we review other research studying the information processing of IPO, but without considering the polarity of the prospectus content.

- Arnold et al. (2010) examine the risk factors section of a prospectus. They not only count the number of risk factors disclosed in this section but also measure the number of words used to explain each of the risk factors. They find that the soft information is significantly related to both the initial and subsequent IPO returns, but not to ex post measures of investor sentiment.
- Hanley and Hoberg (2012) find that issuers trade off first-day returns and disclosure in amended filings (S-1/A) as a hedge against the risk of future law suits. The two authors show that IPOs having a higher risk of material omissions in their filings are more likely to hedge litigation exposure with higher levels of underpricing. A greater level of disclosure by issuers, as proxied by more meaningful revisions in their S-1/A filings during the bookbuilding period, lowers the probability of being sued by investors. The key assumption of Hanley and Hoberg (2012) is that an issuer with a large pre-IPO price adjustment (but having only revised their filings slightly) *is likely to have a material omission in the prospectus as the issuer did not disclose the information underlying the price change*.
- To evaluate disclosure style, Loughran and McDonald (2014) create a standardized statistic that aggregates a series of writing components specifically identified by the SEC. The six components are average sentence length, average word length, passive voice, legalese, personal pronouns, and negative/superfluous phrases. In the context of Form 424 filings, the authors find substantial differences in the content of IPO filings. This is a result of the 1998 rule implemented by the SEC requiring firms to use plain English in their prospectus filings.

Closest to our research are the approaches by Ferris et al. (2013), Hanley and Hoberg (2010), and Loughran and McDonald (2013), in terms of both research objectives and methodology. We individually address each of these papers as follows:

- Ferris et al. (2013) examine the effect that conservative or cautionary language (measured using negative tone) in the prospectus might have on IPO performance. As a result, greater conservatism in the prospectus is related to increased underpricing. The authors observe that this relation is stronger for technology than non-technology IPOs. Besides that, they study how conservative language evolves across time. In addition, they find a significant relationship between conservative language from the Loughran-McDonald dictionary and an average industry-adjusted return on assets for the 3 years following the IPO, but give no insights on how returns evolve through time.
- Hanley and Hoberg (2010) examine the information content of IPO initial prospectuses and its effect on pricing. The authors split the information contained in the S-1 into standard and informative components. Interestingly, they find that

IPOs with more informative content in their S-1 have lower offer price revisions and first-day returns. They argue that IPOs with more standard S-1 content would be more likely to solicit information from investors during bookbuilding.

- Liu et al. (2014) explore the effects of pre-IPO media coverage (in the Factiva database) measured by the number of newspaper articles. According to the authors, this news count correlates positively with the stock's long-term value, liquidity, analyst coverage, institutional investor ownership, and first-day returns. Overall, the paper provides evidence for a long-term role for media coverage, consistent with Merton's attention or investor recognition hypothesis.

- Loughran and McDonald (2013) study the relationship between S-1, as well as Form 424 filings, and the IPO first trading day returns. As a result, IPOs with a more uncertain or weak modal tone experience higher first trading-day returns. Moreover, the percentages of uncertain, weak modal, and negative words in the S-1 are much more powerful variables in explaining levels of underpricing than many commonly used IPO control variables, such as venture capital dummy, top-tier underwriter dummy, or trailing annual sales. In fact, the t-statistics are higher when using Form 424 instead of S-1. In addition, the tone is positively linked with higher volatility in a 60-day period following the offering, but there is no similar evidence for stock market returns.

Hence, information processing has been the subject of many IS research publications. However, the above research papers concentrate on a partial examination of prospectus sentiment, and, thus, many questions are left unanswered. All listed publications lack (1) an in-depth evaluation of how persistent the influence of filing content on long-term returns is and (2) a comparison between the reception of IPO filings and pre-IPO news sentiment. Consequently, an empirical study analyzing the effects of filing sentiment in the long term and in pre-IPO news seems to be an open research question. Consequently, we pursue a rigorous IS approach: First, we utilize sentiment analysis to extract the polarity of IPO filings. Second, we specify a model to measure the impact of prospectus sentiment empirically.

3   Research Methodology: Sentiment Analysis of IPOs

This section introduces our research methodology as depicted in Fig. 1. In a first step, only those IPO prospectuses and news announcements are filtered that fit our research focus. Then, each prospectus and each announcement is subject to *preprocessing* steps which transform the running text into machine-readable tokens. The frequencies of these tokens are aggregated to compute the corresponding *sentiment*.

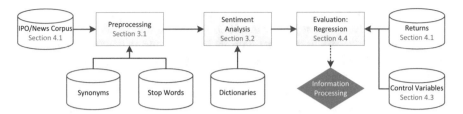

Fig. 1 Research model to study information processing using sentiment analysis of IPO filings

3.1 · Preprocessing IPO Filings

Before performing the actual sentiment analysis, several operations are involved in the preprocessing phase. The individual steps are as follows:

- **Cleaning.** We use the textual component of IPO filings only, and then, all HTML tags and XBRL syntax are removed. This is consistent with Ferris et al. (2013), as well as Loughran and McDonald (2013).
- **Tokenization.** Each announcement is split into sentences and single words named *tokens* (Grefenstette and Tapanainen 1994).
- **Negations.** Negations invert the meaning of words and sentences. According to Loughran and McDonald (2011), as well as Tetlock (2007), handling negations is an inevitable prerequisite to measure positive tone. However, in all previous papers, handling negations is neglected. To close this gap, we adopt the following approach (Dadvar et al. 2011): When encountering the word *no*, each of the subsequent three words (i.e., the object) is counted as words from the opposite dictionary. When other negating terms are encountered (*rather, hardly, couldn't, wasn't, didn't, wouldn't, shouldn't, weren't, don't, doesn't, haven't, hasn't, won't, hadn't, never*), the meaning of all succeeding words is inverted.
- **Stop word removal.** Words without a deeper meaning, such as *the, is, of,* etc., are named *stop words* and, thus, can be removed. We use a list of 571 stop words (Lewis et al. 2004).
- **Synonym merging.** Synonyms, though spelled differently, convey the same meaning. Thus, approximately 150 frequent synonyms are grouped and aggregated by their meaning—a method referred to as *pseudoword* generation (Manning and Schütze 1999).
- **Stemming.** Stemming refers to the process of reducing inflected words to their stem (Manning and Schütze 1999). Here, we use the so-called Porter stemming algorithm.

3.2 Method for Sentiment Analysis

As shown in a recent empirical evaluation on the robustness of sentiment analysis (Feuerriegel and Neumann 2013), the correlation between sentiment in financial materials and the corresponding stock market reaction varies strongly across different sentiment metrics. Out of the potential dictionaries, the ratio of words labeled as *uncertain*—according to the Loughran and McDonald Financial Sentiment Dictionary (McDonald 2012)—achieves the highest robustness, and, consequently, we rely upon this approach in the following evaluation.

Let us briefly recapitulate this sentiment analysis approach. Let $W_{total}(P)$ denote the total number of words in the prospectus P and $W_{uncertain}(P)$ denote the number of *uncertainty* words in the prospectus P. Then, the sentiment is defined by

$$Sentiment(P) = \frac{W_{uncertain}(P)}{W_{total}(P)} \in [0, 1]. \tag{1}$$

Thus, the sentiment variable *Sentiment*(P) measures the number of *uncertainty* words normalized by the number of total words. We improve the metric, in contrast to Ferris et al. (2013), as well as Loughran and McDonald (2013), by using rules to invert the meaning when encountering negations. Thus, tokens following a negation are not counted as *uncertainty* words. This allows us to further boost the accuracy.

4 Empirical Evaluation: Analyzing Sentiment of IPO Filings

Having discussed the steps to compute sentiment values, we apply the sentiment analysis to investigate how stock market returns of initial public offerings are driven by their prospectus. Initially, we choose the IPO filing corpus and gain first insights by descriptive statistics. Then, we specify all control variables, which, ultimately, give the regression design that inspects information processing by linking returns with prospectus sentiment. By varying the time span of returns, we study the persistence of sentiment on stock market performance, and in addition to that, we analyze the reception of news covering initial public offerings.

4.1 IPO Filing Corpus, News Corpus, and Stock Market Data

A structured dataset of US initial public offerings is found in the so-called Kenney-Patton IPO database (Kenney and Patton 2013a;b). This database consists of all de novo firms going public on American exchanges and filed with the Securities and Exchange Commission (SEC), where we restrict the corpus to those initial public offerings between the years 2003 and 2010. This accounts for a total of 625 IPOs.

In a next step, we collect the final prospectus (i.e., Form 424) for each of these initial public offerings from the Electronic Data Gathering, Analysis, and Retrieval (EDGAR) system.[1] Filings are available online for the 621 out of 625 initial public offerings.

Afterward, we combine the Form 424 filings with their corresponding stock market performance. Here, we use the return after the n-th trading day, defined as

$$R(n) = (ShareClosingPrice_n - InitialSharePrice) / InitialSharePrice. \qquad (2)$$

Daily data from stock markets is (mostly) provided by Thomson Reuters Datastream where price data is available for 577 initial public offerings. As in Ferris et al. (2013) and Loughran and McDonald (2013), we require an initial offer price of at least \$5. In order to adjust for sector-specific differences like previous research (Ferris et al. 2013, Loughran and McDonald 2013), we introduce dummy variables for each industry. We use the dummies provided by the Thomson Reuters Business Classification (TRBC),[2] which are classified into 52 industry groups. Because of data availability, we use a total of 572 out of these 577 observations.

Our news corpus originates from the *Thomson Reuters News Archive* for Machine Readable News. We choose Reuters news deliberately because of three reasons: (1) Reuters conveys, in particular, news about stock markets. (2) Reuters news is a third-party content and, thus, gives a certain level of objectivity. (3) In contrast to newspapers, news agencies feature a shorter time lag and lack perturbations by edits. All announcements provided by Reuters arise from January 1, 2003, onward. The announcements come along with stock symbols denoting the firm the content it deals with. Based upon these labels, the news corpus is filtered such that we extract the announcements of firms going public.[3] In addition, we require announcements to be published during the 365 days prior to the IPO. All in all, this set of criteria filters a total of 1085 announcements covering initial public offerings. If no announcement on an IPO is available, we set the sentiment value to 0. If more than one announcement is available, we use the average sentiment value. Furthermore, we incorporate the number of news announcement linked to each IPO into a separate control variable *#News*. Examples of headlines are given

---

[1]US Securities and Exchange Commission (2013). *EDGAR Company Filings*. Web: http://sec. gov/edgar/searchedgar/companysearch.html, retrieved on June 17, 2013.

[2]Thomson Reuters (2014). *Thomson Reuters Business Classification (TRBC)*. Web: http:// thomsonreuters.com/business-classification/, retrieved on February 18, 2014.

[3]This is achieved by applying a set of filter criteria (Feuerriegel and Neumann 2013): (1) The language must be English. (2) The event type is *Story Take Overwrite* to guarantee that we do not yield an alert but the actual message. (3) Special types of announcements, such as alerts or tabular data, might have limited relevance, and we want to exclude these. Thus, we omit announcements that contain specific words (*advisory, chronology, feature, diary, instant view, analysts view, newsmaker, refile, rpt, schedule, table, service, alert, wrapup, imbalance, update*) in their headline. (4) In order to remove white noise, we require announcements to count at least 50 words.

Table 1 Examples of headlines from news used in news sentiment variable

Date and time	Stock symbol	Headline
Jan 2, 2003, 14:15	SCOR	Cardinal Health completes acquisition of Syncor
Jan 6, 2003, 10:49	CE	Council of Europe plans $750 mln 2010 bond Monday
Jan 7, 2003, 16:59	ONE	Bank One launches $1 billion 5-year note sale
Jan 7, 2003, 17:10	PATH	AmeriPath shareholder urges buyout rejection
Jan 7, 2003, 18:38	ONE	New Issue—Bank One sells $1 bln five-yr notes
Jan 8, 2003, 14:01	MGG	MGM Mirage says it will miss Wall St. profit estimates
Jan 8, 2003, 23:45	MGG	Park Place has not changed Q4 guidance-spokesman
Jan 9, 2003, 10:17	PRO	Provalis expects first annual pre-tax profit
...	...	...

Table 2 Descriptive statistics of sentiment, issued prices and returns after n trading days

Variable	Mean	Median	Min	Max	Std. Dev.	Skewness	Kurtosis
$Sentiment_{IPO}$	0.0173	0.0173	0.0125	0.0246	0.0017	0.2094	0.5365
$Sentiment_{News}$	0.0049	0.0000	0.0000	0.0476	0.0074	1.6724	3.1994
#News	2.2945	1.0000	0.0000	108.0000	8.2986	8.8609	90.7178
Issued price	14.2613	14.0000	4.0000	85.0000	6.5506	3.6347	29.3660
$R(1)$	0.4216	0.0842	−0.8558	35.0000	2.2441	10.5652	134.3806
$R(10)$	0.4124	0.1037	−0.8452	29.3000	2.0963	9.9248	116.7767
$R(21)$	0.4304	0.1114	−0.8337	30.8000	2.1816	9.7876	114.0889

in Table 1. From this table, we can see that the news not only reports that a firm is going public but states more insights of the pre-IPO activities.

4.2   Descriptive Statistics of Stock Market Returns

In our evaluation, we vary the time span of returns to study the persistence of prospectus sentiment. All descriptive statistics of issued share prices, as well as returns after the n-th trading day, are presented in Table 2. Accordingly, the initial issued prices range from $4.00 to $85.00, while the mean initial share price accounts for $14.2613 with a standard deviation of $6.5506. Furthermore, the returns after 21 trading days span approximately from −0.8337 to 30.8000, with a nonzero mean of approximately 0.4304. Interestingly, the kurtosis of 134.3806 on the first day of trading is substantially higher than 3, indicating the existence of heavy tails, which are probably caused by price spikes. Both characteristics of nonzero mean and a high kurtosis are consistent with related literature (cf. Jenkinson and Ljungqvist 2001, Ritter and Welch 2002, for recent reviews), where these effects are referred to as *underpricing*.

4.3   Control Variables

When isolating and extracting the effect of sentiment, we use a wide range of control variables. We control for the development of the stock market and, in addition to that, further control variables which comprise the number of shares, the share overhang, and the underwriter discount. The latter three variables are retrieved from the Kenney-Patton IPO database (Kenney and Patton 2013a;b), which we improved with additional corrections. Similar variables are used by a number of prior papers to explain first-day returns (see, e.g., Ferris et al. 2013, Loughran and McDonald 2013). Individual control variables are as follows:[4]

- *UpRevision* This control variable measures the percentage of the upward revision from the mid-point of the filing range if the offer price is greater than the mid-point; otherwise it is set to zero. As in Ferris et al. (2013) and Loughran and McDonald (2013), including this variable is crucial; when this variable is added last, many others are no longer significant.
- $\Delta Days_{S-1, IPO}$ To control for possible delays of IPOs, we include a variable measuring the logarithmized calendar days between S-1 and the initial public offering.
- $NASDAQ_{-15d}$ We include the general development of a stock market index to ensure that the stock market performance is driven by sentiment instead of the economic cycle or the general mood of investors. Thus, we choose the return of the NASDAQ-100 stock market index of the 15 days prior to the initial public offering. Here, values originate from Thomson Reuters Datastream.
- ln *Sales* This variable is defined as the logarithm of the number of shares sold to the public in the offering multiplied by the initial share price. Thus, the logarithm of all sales controls the volume of the initial public offering.
- *ShareOverhang* This variable indicates the number of shares retained divided by the number of shares in the initial offering. More precisely, it is defined as

$$ShareOverhang = \frac{S_{\text{outstand}}}{S_{\text{outstand}} + S_{\text{sold}}}, \tag{3}$$

where S_{outstand} is the number of shares outstanding after the offer and S_{sold} is the number of shares sold to the public in this offering.
- *UnderwriterDiscount* This variable includes the per share discounts and commissions taken by the underwriters.

By using these control variables, we want to assure that our results measure the impact that comes from the sentiment only and avoid perturbations by other causes, such as changes in fundamental variables or external events. Next, descriptive statistics of all variables are presented in Table 3. In addition to that, we incorporate

---

[4]Although many papers control if the firm is backed by venture capital. However, Loughran and McDonald (2013) find no evidence that this variable has a significant impact, and thus, we omit it.

Table 3 Descriptive statistics of control variables

Variable	Mean	Median	Min	Max	Std. dev.	Skewness	Kurtosis
UpRevision	6.0484	0.0000	0.0000	79.3103	10.2935	2.5742	8.8797
$\Delta Days_{S-1,\,IPO}$	3.1603	3.0201	0.0000	6.6201	0.8557	−0.0029	5.1859
$NASDAQ_{-15\,d}$	0.0065	0.0072	−0.1800	0.0979	0.0373	−0.4665	0.5743
ln *Sales*	18.3719	18.2869	15.5690	21.5984	0.8806	0.4368	0.9694
ShareOverhang	0.7699	0.7826	0.0004	0.9879	0.0908	−2.7661	16.7556
UnderwriterDiscount	0.9538	0.9100	0.0000	3.8400	0.3752	1.8949	10.6112

additional dummies into our model to adjust for both seasonal and sector-specific effects.

4.4 Regression Design

This section presents the corresponding regression design, i.e.,

$$
\begin{aligned}
R(n) = \alpha &+ \beta_1 \, Sentiment_{IPO} + \beta_2 \, UpRevision + \beta_3 \, \Delta Days_{S-1,\,IPO} + \beta_4 \, NASDAQ_{-15\,d} \\
&+ \beta_5 \, \ln Sales + \beta_6 \, ShareOverhang + \beta_7 \, UnderwriterDiscount \\
&+ \sum_j \beta_j \, Dummy_j + \epsilon,
\end{aligned}
\tag{4}
$$

where n specifies the n-th day of trading, β_i are coefficients to be estimated, and ϵ is the error term. Dummies are added for each sector, as well as year, to consider additional external events not covered by the control variables and to handle non-seasonally adjusted time series. The correlation of sentiment values and first-day returns is depicted in Fig. 2. This diagram also features a so-called LOWESS trend line, which is a locally weighted scatterplot smoothing calculated via local regressions. From this LOWESS trend line (smoothing parameter f set to 2/3), we can identify a visible relationship between the sentiment variable and stock market returns. Finally, we give justice to extreme stock price effects and remove outliers at the 0.05% level at both ends.

4.5 Results: Linking Sentiment and Stock Market Performance

In this section, we investigate how investors react to IPO prospectuses and analyze the information processing empirically. To succeed in this goal, we exploit sentiment analysis to measure the relationship between investor behavior and the content of IPO filings.

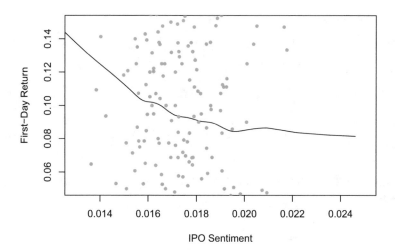

Fig. 2 Scatterplot of first-day returns and sentiment values with the LOWESS trend line

Confirmatory analysis: To what extent are stock market returns of firms driven by the sentiment of their IPO filings?

We use the above regression design from Eq. (4) to measure the impact of sentiment in prospectuses on IPO underpricing. We tested for heteroskedasticity, constant variance, serial correlation, and normally distributed residuals at the 0.01% level to ensure that the results are not confounded. When checking variance inflation factors, we also see no indication of multicollinearity. Independence across IPO filings is given as long as all prospectuses are entirely novel and not based on an interrelated course of events. Under the assumption that first-day returns are jointly multivariate normal, as well as independently and identically distributed through time, the model can be estimated using ordinary least squares (OLS).

Regression results are given in Table 4. According to this table, we observe that prospectus sentiment influences first-day returns significantly. The corresponding t-value accounts for -2.505 with a p-value of 0.013. Furthermore, we find that one standard deviation increase in the sentiment measure is negatively linked to an increase in first-day returns by an economically significant 10.56%. When additionally comparing the coefficients of the fundamental variables and sentiment, we find that the sentiment coefficient (accounting for -61.879) exceeds all other coefficients originating from the fundamental variables greatly. In addition to that, none of the control variables are, except for *UpRevision*, significant at the 10% level. Altogether, these results provide evidence that the sentiment in IPO prospectuses correlates significantly with first-day returns.

Table 4 OLS regression linking sentiment and first-day returns

	(a)	(b)	(c)	(d)	(e)	(f)	(g)
$Sentiment_{IPO}$	−47.969*	−45.915	−43.319	−41.023	−54.558*	−54.897*	−61.879*
	(−2.046)	(−1.954)	(−1.842)	(−1.740)	(−2.225)	−2.235	−2.505
UpRevision		0.005	0.005	0.006	0.008	0.008	0.009*
		(1.253)	(1.255)	(1.427)	(1.866)	(1.789)	(1.998)
$\Delta Days_{S-1, IPO}$			−0.073	−0.073	−0.083	−0.081	−0.079
			(−1.604)	(−1.612)	(−1.811)	(−1.777)	(−1.729)
$NASDAQ_{-15d}$				−1.341	−1.445	−1.408	−1.252
				(−1.253)	(−1.351)	(−1.309)	(−1.162)
ln Sales					−0.101	−0.099	−0.081
					(−1.940)	(−1.900)	(−1.434)
ShareOverhang						0.151	0.184
						(0.343)	(0.414)
Underwriter Discount							−0.133
							(−0.969)
Intercept	0.601	0.549	0.755	0.726	2.872*	2.733*	2.636*
	(1.102)	(1.006)	(1.347)	(1.295)	(2.317)	(2.094)	(1.972)
AIC	1469.705	1470.004	1469.213	1469.506	1467.41	1469.282	1470.776
BIC	1660.134	1664.761	1668.298	1672.919	1675.151	1681.351	1687.172
Multiple R^2	0.081	0.084	0.089	0.091	0.098	0.098	0.099

Stated: Coef. and t-stat. in parentheses   Dummies: Year, sector   Obs.: 572   Signif.: ***0.001, **0.01, *0.05

4.6 Results: Analyzing the Persistence of Sentiment Impact Over Time

Having discussed the regression design, we proceed to analyze how the sentiment affects n-th trading day returns after the initial public offering.

Research Question 1: How persistent is the influence of filing sentiment on long-term returns?

Thus, we vary the time span of returns across 10 and 21 days of trading, which is equivalent to 2 weeks and 1 month, respectively. The corresponding regression results are presented in Tables 5 and 6. Again, we checked for heteroskedasticity, constant variance, serial correlation, and normally distributed residuals and multi-collinearity to ensure that we can estimate the model using OLS. In short, the results can be summarized as a declining influence of sentiment for longer time lags.

In more detail, the coefficients indicating the sentiment reception start at −61.879 for first-day returns but change slightly to −54.302 after the 10th day of trading. Similarly, the t-statistic of the sentiment variable drops from −2.505 for first-day returns to −2.266 after the 10th day of trading. Its value shrinks further down to −1.033 when looking at returns after the 21st day of trading. The influence of sentiment on both the first and the 10th day of trading is significant at the 5%

Table 5 OLS regression linking sentiment and returns after the 10th day of trading

	(a)	(b)	(c)	(d)	(e)	(f)	(g)	(h)
$Sentiment_{IPO}$	−38.937	−36.711	−33.393	−32.095	−48.438*	−48.578*	−52.406*	−54.302*
	(−1.705)	(−1.605)	(−1.462)	(−1.400)	(−2.035)	(−2.037)	(−2.186)	(−2.266)
$UpRevision$		0.005	0.005	0.006	0.008*	0.008*	0.010*	0.009*
		(1.394)	(1.400)	(1.491)	(2.048)	(1.999)	(2.195)	(2.158)
$\Delta Days_{S-1,IPO}$			−0.093*	−0.094*	−0.105*	−0.104*	−0.103*	−0.104*
			(−2.11)	(−2.113)	(−2.365)	(−2.344)	(−2.303)	(−2.334)
$NASDAQ_{-15d}$				−0.758		−0.868	−0.788	−0.761
				(−0.728)		(−0.831)	(−0.754)	(−0.730)
$\ln Sales$					−0.122*	−0.121*	−0.102	−0.103
					(−2.413)	(−2.388)	(−1.851)	(−1.867)
$ShareOverhang$						0.063	0.111	0.174
						(0.147)	(0.257)	(0.402)
$UnderwriterDiscount$							−0.126	−0.130
							(−0.947)	(−0.980)
$NASDAQ_{10d}$								2.131
								(1.671)
Intercept	0.442	0.386	0.648	0.632	3.224**	3.166*	2.975*	2.990*
	(0.832)	(0.726)	(1.191)	(1.159)	(2.679)	(2.498)	(2.293)	(2.309)
AIC	1439.971	1439.864	1437.044	1438.466	1434.144	1436.12	1437.497	1436.437
BIC	1630.400	1634.622	1636.129	1641.879	1641.885	1648.189	1653.893	1657.162
Multiple R^2	0.057	0.060	0.068	0.069	0.080	0.080	0.081	0.086

Stated: Coef. and t-stat. in parentheses   Dummies: Year, sector   Obs.: 572   Signif.: ***0.001, **0.01, *0.05

Table 6 OLS regression linking sentiment and returns after the 21st day of trading

	(a)	(b)	(c)	(d)	(e)	(f)	(g)	(h)
$Sentiment_{IPO}$	−14.800	−12.015	−8.333	−7.667	−19.863	−19.996	−23.378	−26.104
	(−0.617)	(−0.501)	(−0.348)	(−0.319)	(−0.792)	(−0.796)	(−0.925)	(−1.033)
$UpRevision$		0.007	0.007	0.007	0.009*	0.008*	0.010*	0.010*
		(1.615)	(1.624)	(1.660)	(2.028)	(1.982)	(2.108)	(2.134)
$\Delta Days_{S-1,IPO}$			−0.103*	−0.103*	−0.111*	−0.110*	−0.109*	−0.110*
			(−2.220)	(−2.220)	(−2.389)	(−2.369)	(−2.335)	(−2.362)
$NASDAQ_{-15d}$				−0.409	−0.505	−0.492	−0.423	−0.248
				(−0.376)	(−0.464)	(−0.449)	(−0.386)	(−0.226)
$lnSales$					−0.089	−0.089	−0.073	−0.074
					(−1.69)	(−1.67)	(−1.266)	(−1.281)
$ShareOverhang$						0.056	0.094	0.162
						(0.125)	(0.208)	(0.358)
$UnderwriterDiscount$							−0.104	−0.117
							(−0.746)	(−0.835)
$NASDAQ_{21d}$								1.716
								(1.810)
Intercept	0.039	−0.030	0.257	0.249	2.156	2.105	1.956	1.898
	(0.070)	(−0.054)	(0.452)	(0.437)	(1.705)	(1.582)	(1.436)	(1.396)
AIC	1489.858	1489.035	1485.702	1487.548	1486.441	1488.424	1490.481	1488.897
BIC	1680.287	1683.792	1684.787	1690.961	1694.182	1700.493	1706.878	1709.622
Multiple R^2	0.052	0.056	0.065	0.066	0.071	0.071	0.071	0.077

Stated: Coef. and t-stat. in parentheses   Dummies: Year, sector   Obs.: 572   Signif.: ***0.001, **0.01, *0.05

level, while the sentiment coefficient after 21 trading days becomes not significant at common significance levels. Altogether, this supports the hypothesis of a declining influence of sentiment on longer time spans.

4.7 Results: Prospectus Sentiment Versus News Sentiment

While the previous sections analyzed the influence of news, the question regarding the relevance of the general news coverage is left unanswered.

Research Question 2: How is the IPO performance affected by pre-IPO news coverage?

We extend the regression of Eq. (4) by an additional variable measuring the sentiment of news announcements related to that initial public offering. Out of all 572 initial public offerings, we find at least one announcement in the news corpus for 207 firms, i.e., 39.6%. We tested for autocorrelation, heteroskedasticity, constant variance, serial correlation, and normally distributed residuals at the 0.01% level to ensure that the results are not confounded. When checking for variance inflation factors, we also see no indication of multicollinearity. Thus, the model can be estimated using ordinary least squares (OLS). The regression results are presented in Table 7. The influence of IPO sentiment remains similar with a coefficient of -66.045 and a corresponding t-value of -2.456. However, the influence of news announcements seems much stronger. Here, the news sentiment accounts for a coefficient of 20.907 with a P-value of 0.000 48 and a t-value of 3.518.

This is interesting for two reasons. First, a higher t-value indicates a significant link between returns and news, even stronger than the IPO sentiment. Second, while more *uncertainty* words in the prospectus lower the first-day returns, this does not hold for the news announcements. The more *uncertainty* words in the news announcements, the higher the first-day return. While one standard deviation increase in the IPO sentiment measure is linked to a decrease in first-day returns by an economically significant 11.30%, the news sentiment behaves differently. Here, one standard deviation change in news sentiment correlates with an increase in first-day returns by 14.72%. Furthermore, the number of news announcements (given by #*News*) has no impact on IPO prices at any common significance level. Astonishingly, the effect shows a larger magnitude, and at the same time, the more negative the pre-IPO news coverage, the higher the first-day returns.

A possible explanation can be attributed to the investors' psychological constraints in information processing—the processing depends on the attention different information receives. This phenomenon is already addressed in accounting literature (Hirshleifer et al. 2011): Limited investor attention theory for earning announcements suggests that investors neglect information about future earnings in current-period announcements creating a post-earning announcement drift. Subsequently, this mispricing is corrected over time. The same explanation may apply to IPO prospectuses, where mainly the risks of the company are recognized, which may entail the negative coefficient of our IPO sentiment variable. Underestimating

Table 7 OLS regression comparing influence of sentiment in IPO filings and news

	(a)	(b)	(c)	(d)	(e)	(f)	(g)	(h)	(i)
$Sentiment_{IPO}$	−46.617	−44.120	−44.066	−42.432	−39.287	−36.993	−56.361*	−56.439*	−66.045*
	(−1.813)	(−1.732)	(−1.735)	(−1.667)	(−1.540)	(−1.446)	(−2.113)	(−2.113)	(−2.456)
$Sentiment_{News}$		18.654**	20.021***	19.994***	19.488**	19.176**	20.76***	20.727***	20.907***
		(3.167)	(3.385)	(3.381)	(3.294)	(3.238)	(3.503)	(3.489)	(3.518)
#News			−0.010	−0.010	−0.009	−0.009	−0.010	−0.010	−0.010
			(−1.937)	(−1.857)	(−1.777)	(−1.754)	(−1.905)	(−1.905)	(−1.905)
UpRevision				0.005	0.005	0.005	0.008	0.008	0.010*
				(1.065)	(1.086)	(1.232)	(1.825)	(1.781)	(1.969)
$\Delta Days_{S-1,IPO}$					−0.074	−0.074	−0.086	−0.086	−0.084
					(−1.452)	(−1.455)	(−1.69)	(−1.681)	(−1.631)
$NASDAQ_{-15d}$						−1.279	−1.372	−1.356	−1.173
						(−1.117)	(−1.204)	(−1.181)	(−1.020)
ln $Sales$							−0.136*	−0.135*	−0.120*
							(−2.430)	(−2.407)	(−1.966)
ShareOverhang								0.053	0.070
								(0.113)	(0.146)
UnderwriterDiscount									−0.130
									(−0.890)
Intercept	0.723	0.566	0.551	0.515	0.709	0.681	3.561**	3.511*	3.507*
	(1.263)	(0.995)	(0.972)	(0.905)	(1.216)	(1.167)	(2.699)	(2.518)	(2.457)
AIC	1385.908	1377.069	1374.979	1375.735	1375.423	1376.05	1371.573	1373.559	1375.057
BIC	1568.072	1563.47	1565.615	1570.608	1574.533	1579.396	1579.155	1585.377	1591.112
Multiple R^2	0.086	0.105	0.112	0.114	0.118	0.121	0.132	0.132	0.133

Stated: Coef. and t-stat. in parentheses   Dummies: Year, sector   Obs.: 523   Signif.: ***0.001, **0.01, *0.05

future opportunities may create a post-prospectus announcement drift that was visible in our previous analysis. News announcements prior to the IPO are obviously less suspect to the companies' risks. On the contrary, the positive coefficient suggests that more emphasis is put on the companies' opportunities. Apparently, the degree of investor attention depends on the specific type of information.

5   Conclusion

Before shares of a company are sold to the general public on a security exchange for the first time, regulatory publication requirements force US firms to file an initial public offering prospectus. Studying the information processing of investors facing these filings is an active research question in the context of efficient electronic markets, though knowledge is rare (e.g., Liebmann et al. 2012): "While the accounting numbers in IPO prospectuses are closely studied by investors, analysts, and others involved in the equity issuance process, an examination of the textual or soft information contained in prospectuses is less common" (Ferris et al. 2013). To close this gap, research must harness decision analytics in order to explain the relationship between the textual content of filings and final IPO prices.

In this paper, we address information processing in IPO filings by analyzing how the sentiment in prospectuses influences stock market performances. Using the final filings of 572 US initial public offerings (Form 424) between 2003 and 2010, we can identify soft content as a major driver of stock returns. All in all, we can empirically establish a relationship between sentiment in IPO filings and stock market reaction. One standard deviation increase in the sentiment measure correlates negatively with a change in first-day returns by an economically significant 10.56%. This dependency appears not only on the first day of trading but also for longer phases of up to 10 days of trading. Apparently, "soft information can offer context to financial numbers and share values, provide insight into managerial expectations, and identify important qualifiers or caveats that are absent from purely numerical data" (Ferris et al. 2013). As an explanation, we find supporting evidence that we can expect initial public offerings with substantial uncertain language to have, on average, lower preliminary offer prices. This effect occurs due to the need for bankers to compensate investors for their information production (Loughran and McDonald 2013). According to Ferris et al. (2013), the findings "suggest that when hard information is noisier, textual information is seen as having greater usefulness and is more likely to be factored into IPO pricing." However, a much stronger impact on stock market prices happens not through the IPO prospectus, but comes from the pre-IPO news sentiment. Interestingly, the more uncertainty words that appear in pre-IPO news, the higher the following first-day stock market return. Consequently, this uncertainty puzzle must be resolved. It seems that investors mainly focus on the chances of a company rather than on the risks. This stands in contrast to the prospectus where risk considerations play a major role.

The work presented in this chapter opens several avenues for future research. First, a pooled regression can be utilized to analyze possible differences between *no crisis* and *crisis* periods where investors change their information processing to more cautious behavior. Second, further effort is needed to validate our approach in terms of robustness, and, thus, we plan to extend our analysis further to filings, such as S-1 or, alternatively, transcripts of court decisions. Third, an obvious next step is to bridge the gap between explanatory regression models and a prediction model (Shmueli and Koppius 2011) that can estimate expected stock market returns from IPO filings.

Acknowledgment   We thank Stefan Feuerriegel for his valuable contributions.

References

Antweiler W, Frank MZ (2004) Is All That Talk Just Noise? The Information Content of Internet Stock Message Boards. The Journal of Finance 59(3):1259–1294

Arnold T, Fishe RPH, North D (2010) The Effects of Ambiguous Information on Initial and Subsequent IPO Returns. Financial Management 39:1497–1519

Chen H, Chiang RRL, Storey VC (2012) Business Intelligence and Analytics: From Big Data to Big Impact. MIS Quarterly 36(4):1165–1188

Dadvar M, Hauff C, de Jong F (2011) Scope of Negation Detection in Sentiment Analysis. In: Proceedings of the Dutch-Belgian Information Retrieval Workshop (DIR 2011), pp 16–20

Demers EA, Vega C (2010) Soft Information in Earnings Announcements: News or Noise? INSEAD Working Paper No. 2010/33/AC. SSRN Electronic Journal

Fama FE (1965) The Behavior of Stock-Market Prices. The Journal of Business 38(1):34–105

Ferris SP, Hao Q, Liao MY (2013) The Effect of Issuer Conservatism on IPO Pricing and Performance. Review of Finance 17(3):993–1027

Feuerriegel S, Neumann D (2013) News or Noise? How News Drives Commodity Prices. In: Proceedings of the International Conference on Information Systems (ICIS 2013), Association for Information Systems

Feuerriegel S, Lampe MW, Neumann D (2014) News Processing during Speculative Bubbles: Evidence from the Oil Market. In: 47th Hawaii International Conference on System Sciences (HICSS)

Granados N, Gupta A, Kauffman RJ (2010) Research Commentary–Information Transparency in Business-to-Consumer Markets: Concepts, Framework, and Research Agenda. Information Systems Research 21(2):207–226

Grefenstette G, Tapanainen P (1994) What is a word, What is a sentence? Problems of Tokenization. Meylan and France, http://citeseerx.ist.psu.edu/viewdoc/summary?doi=10.1.1.28.5162

Hanley KW, Hoberg G (2010) The Information Content of IPO Prospectuses. Review of Financial Studies 23(7):2821–2864

Hanley KW, Hoberg G (2012) Litigation risk, strategic disclosure and the underpricing of initial public offerings. Journal of Financial Economics 103(2):235–254

Henry E (2008) Are Investors Influenced By How Earnings Press Releases Are Written? Journal of Business Communication 45(4):363–407

Hirshleifer D, Lim SS, Teoh SH (2011) Limited Investor Attention and Stock Market Misreactions to Accounting Information. Review of Asset Pricing Studies 1(1):35–73

IBM (2013) The Four V's of Big Data. http://www.ibmbigdatahub.com/infographic/four-vs-big-data

Jegadeesh N, Wu D (2013) Word Power: A New Approach for Content Analysis. Journal of Financial Economics 110(3):712–729

Jenkinson T, Ljungqvist A (2001) Going Public: The Theory and Evidence on how Companies Raise Equity Finance, 2nd edn. Oxford University Press, Oxford

Kenney M, Patton D (2013a) Firm Database of Initial Public Offerings (IPOs) from June 1996 through 2010. Davis and CA

Kenney M, Patton D (2013b) Guide to the Firm Database of Initial Public Offerings (IPOs) from June 1996 through 2010. Davis and CA

Lewis DD, Yang Y, Rose TG, Li F (2004) RCV1: A New Benchmark Collection for Text Categorization Research. Journal of Machine Learning Research 5:361–397

Li F (2010) The Information Content of Forward-Looking Statements in Corporate Filings: A Naïve Bayesian Machine Learning Approach. Journal of Accounting Research 48(5):1049–1102

Liebmann M, Hagenau M, Neumann D (2012) Information Processing in Electronic Markets: Measuring Subjective Interpretation Using Sentiment Analysis. In: George JF (ed) Proceedings of the International Conference on Information Systems (ICIS 2012), Association for Information Systems

Liu LX, Sherman AE, Zhang Y (2014) The Long-Run Role of the Media: Evidence from Initial Public Offerings: (in press). Management Science

Loughran T, McDonald B (2011) When Is a Liability Not a Liability? Textual Analysis, Dictionaries, and 10-Ks. The Journal of Finance 66(1):35–65

Loughran T, McDonald B (2013) IPO first-day returns, offer price revisions, volatility, and form S-1 language. Journal of Financial Economics 109(2):307–326

Loughran T, McDonald B (2014) Regulation and financial disclosure: The impact of plain English. Journal of Regulatory Economics 45(1):94–113

Manning CD, Schütze H (1999) Foundations of statistical natural language processing. MIT Press, Cambridge and Mass

McDonald B (2012) Loughran and McDonald Financial Sentiment Dictionary. http://www3.nd.edu/mcdonald/Word_Lists.html

Minev M, Schommer C, Grammatikos T (2012) News and stock markets: A survey on abnormal returns and prediction models. Luxembourg, http://publications.uni.lu/record/9947/files/TR.Survey.News.Analytics.pdf

Mittermayer MA, Knolmayer GF (2006a) NewsCATS: A News Categorization and Trading System. In: Sixth International Conference on Data Mining (ICDM'06), pp 1002–1007

Mittermayer MA, Knolmayer GF (2006b) Text Mining Systems for Market Response to News: A Survey. Bern and Switzerland, http://pdf.aminer.org/000/246/869/forecasting_intraday_stock_price_trends_with_text_mining_techniques.pdf

O'Hara M (1995) Market Microstructure Theory. Wiley-Blackwell, Oxford and MA

Pang B, Lee L (2008) Opinion Mining and Sentiment Analysis. FNT in Information Retrieval (Foundations and Trends in Information Retrieval) 2(1–2):1–135

Ritter JR, Welch I (2002) A Review of IPO Activity, Pricing, and Allocations. The Journal of Finance 57(4):1795–1828

Schumaker RP, Chen H (2009) Textual analysis of stock market prediction using breaking financial news. ACM Transactions on Information Systems 27(2):1–19

Sharma A, Dey S (2012) A comparative study of feature selection and machine learning techniques for sentiment analysis. In: Cho Y, Computing ASIGoA (eds) Proceedings of the 2012 Research in Applied Computation Symposium (RACS 2012), ACM, pp 1–7

Shmueli G, Koppius O (2011) Predictive Analytics in Information Systems Research. MIS Quarterly 35(3):553–572

Siering M (2013) Investigating the Impact of Media Sentiment and Investor Attention on Financial Markets. In: Aalst W, Mylopoulos J, Rosemann M, Shaw MJ, Szyperski C, Rabhi FA, Gomber P (eds) Enterprise Applications and Services in the Finance Industry, Lecture Notes in Business Information Processing, vol 135, Springer Berlin Heidelberg, Berlin and Heidelberg, pp 3–19

Tetlock PC (2007) Giving content to investor sentiment: The role of media in the stock market. The Journal of Finance 62(3):1139–1168

Tetlock PC, Saar-Tsechansky M, Macskassy S (2008) More than words: Quantifying Language to Measure Firms' Fundamentals. The Journal of Finance 63(3):1437–1467

Taxonomy Development for Business Research: A Hands-On Guideline

Dennis M. Steininger, Manuel Trenz, and Daniel J. Veit

Abstract Classification schemes are important groundwork for research on many topics of different business disciplines such as information systems (IS). They make investigating topics manageable by allowing researchers to delimit their work to certain taxa or types (e.g., of artifacts or firms) and provide a basis for generalization. Opposed to theoretically grounded typologies, taxonomies are empirically derived from entities of a phenomenon and therefore have several advantages, such as more detailed and exhaustive coverage. Initial guidelines for developing taxonomies in business have been proposed; however, research is still missing a clear set of applicable procedures to empirically build taxonomies. We tackle this topic by suggesting an inductive approach based on the procedures of content and cluster analysis. Each of the proposed six steps is amended with comprehensive state-of-the-art guidelines, suggestions, and formative measures of reliability and validity.

1   Introduction

Originally stemming from biology to differentiate animals or plants, classification schemes allow the systematic ordering or sorting of phenomena into similar groups or classes (e.g., business models, Veit et al. 2014). They are of fundamental importance for science and academic research in business (Kantor 1953; Kemeny 1959; Nickerson et al. 2013). Wolf (1926) emphasizes this importance by explaining the links and stating that verification of laws of science may only succeed after classification has been completed since it is "the first and last method employed by science." Hence, classification schemes such as taxonomies make investigating

D. M. Steininger · D. J. Veit (✉)
University of Auzsburg, Augsburg, Germany
e-mail: dennis.steininger@wiwi.uni-augsburg.de; veit@wiwi.uni-augsburg.de

M. Trenz
University of Göttingen, Göttingen, Germany
e-mail: trenz@uni-goettingen.de

© The Author(s) 2021   69
H. Gimpel et al. (eds.), *Market Engineering*,
https://doi.org/10.1007/978-3-030-66661-3_4

phenomena manageable by allowing researchers to delimit their work to certain classes (i.e., taxa or types), such as IS technologies or firms, and also provide a basis for generalization. This allows the building of theories that apply to certain classes of developed schemes. When classifying an area of investigation, two different approaches can be used: typologies or taxonomies. Typologies are created deductively by classifying objects into predefined groups that are created based on intuition or previously existing knowledge and theory (Bailey 1994). Especially when examining an unexplored area of research, as often done with new technologies, there is a risk of researcher bias or general misconception, since existing theory is limited. Unlike theoretically grounded typologies, taxonomies are derived inductively from empirical data (i.e., entities of a phenomenon under investigation) and therefore have several advantages, such as more detailed and exhaustive coverage and mutual exclusiveness of classes. Despite some foundational work (e.g., Nickerson et al. 2013; Oberländer et al. 2019), business research is still missing a clear set of rigorous procedures on how to empirically build taxonomies of firms, artifacts, systems, user behavior, or processes. Especially in fast-moving areas such as IS, it is important to be able to describe new phenomena rigorously and quickly by applying systematic actions. Building on these thoughts, we propose the following research question for this work:

> How can taxonomies be developed in business research from empirical entities using content analysis?

We tackle this question by suggesting an inductive empirical approach based on the procedures of content and cluster analysis. Content analysis allows a systematic and rigorous analysis of entities to get a first grasp of their characteristics, associated manifestations and densities. Based on these results, procedures of cluster analysis can be applied to derive final classes. The remainder of this chapter is structured as follows. In the second section we propose six steps to build taxonomies. Each of these steps is amended with state-of-the-art guidelines, alternatives, and measures of reliability and validity. Summative measures of taxonomic quality are also depicted for evaluating final taxonomic constructs. In the last section we sum up our findings, address the usefulness of taxonomic outcomes, and identify interesting topics in IS that might be investigated by using the introduced method.

2 The Process of Taxonomy Building

We introduce detailed steps and procedures to build taxonomies in IS and management-related phenomena using content and cluster analysis. The process is based on Steininger et al. (2011b), who use clustering and content analysis to inductively build a taxonomic framework of Web 2.0 characteristics. This chapter can be seen as a working example. We added inspirations from the articles of Nag et al. (2007), defining strategic management via content analysis and clustering; Al-Debei and Avison (2010), developing a business model framework through content analysis; and the seminal work of Nickerson et al. (2013). Content analysis is a technique to gain "replicable and valid inferences from text" (Krippendorff 2004a, p. 18) and thereby find trends, characteristics, patterns, and densities. The material for analysis might include written or spoken texts as transcripts from various sources (for a list of potential sources see: Steininger 2019). The objectivity, validity, and reliability of the outcomes are obtained through rigorous rules and systematic procedures, which have been refined and adapted to the various needs of different disciplines over time (Angelmar and Stern 1978; Abbasi and Chen 2008; Steininger et al. 2011a, b) and distinguish content analysis from regular critical reading. The aforementioned potential to reliably and systematically uncover characteristics and patterns is of high relevance for constructing taxonomies. Hence, we adapt state-of-the-art procedures of inductive and deductive content analysis for major parts of the taxonomy-building process. The outline of our idea is to define a phenomenon of investigation and collect examples resembling the phenomenon as entities of investigation. We then inductively develop the characteristics of the phenomenon from these entities and deductively measure the manifestation of the characteristics for each entity.

We finally propose to cluster the entities into classes (i.e., taxa) by analyzing their manifestations and densities of characteristics. The entire process is depicted in Fig. 1, highlighted for one entity (marked with black ink). It starts with a definition of the phenomenon under investigation (e.g., electronic business models). This entails a clear statement of the research question (e.g., What classes of electronic business models do exist?). After these initial specifications, a set or population of entities and their textual descriptions resembling the phenomenon (e.g., examples of existing electronic business models) is required as a basis for analysis, which is addressed in our first suggested step on the selection and sampling of entities.

To proceed with building the taxonomy, it is necessary to analyze the manifesta-tion of the phenomenon's characteristics for each entity. Since we assume missing theoretical foundations on the characteristics of the phenomenon, we describe procedures on how to inductively derive raw characteristics from selected entities by using content analysis (step 2). Raw characteristics are subsequently reduced to main characteristics of the phenomenon under investigation (e.g., characteristics of electronic business models) by applying cluster analysis (step 3). These two steps might be skipped if our assumption does not hold true and there are already existing and exhaustive definitions of characteristics for the phenomenon in theory, which can be utilized for the fourth step. In this fourth step we suggest deductive content analysis procedures to measure the manifestations and densities of the characteristics for each entity (e.g., how often is a characteristic mentioned in the textual material for one entity). This can be reached through analyzing the entities by applying a coding scheme of characteristics, which might be constructed from the inductively developed (cf. steps 2/3) or aforementioned theoretically derived characteristics. The classes of similar entities for the taxonomy (e.g., virtual shopping malls) are then built by suggested procedures of cluster analysis on the resulting manifestations (step 5). We amend this penultimate step with propositions and guidelines on measures for taxonomic quality (e.g., mutual exclusiveness).

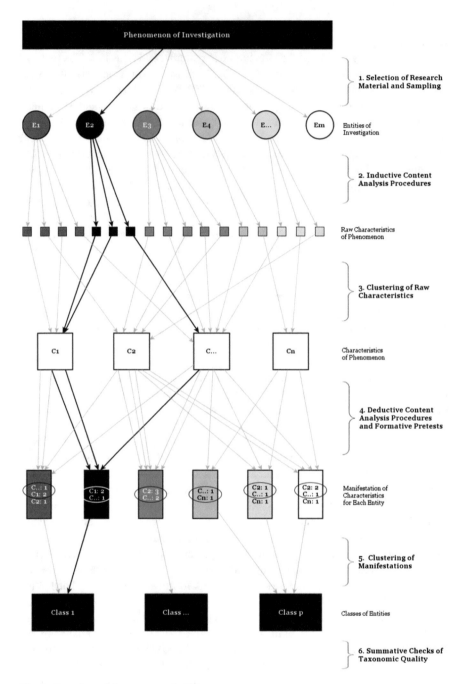

Fig. 1 Overview of the taxonomy-building process

Details and guidelines for each of our suggested steps are introduced in the following sections.

2.1 Selection of Research Material and Sampling

Entities of investigation (e.g., firms using an electronic business model) are needed as empirical research material to develop and retrieve characteristics, manifestations, and final classes (i.e., taxa) for a phenomenon. We explain procedures for selecting and sampling these entities throughout this section and amend them with hints on data sources and data collection techniques to gain rich data on the selected entities.

A representative sampling of entities might be used but, in many cases, may be neither manageable nor required. Instead, we propose to follow a theoretical sampling approach as suggested by Eisenhardt (1989). This means broadly choosing the entities of investigation for variation, heterogeneity (i.e., unique cases), or replication instead of random selection (Yin 2009). The availability of existing textual (e.g., case descriptions, annual or mission statements, product descriptions, websites, directories) or transcribable (e.g., interviews) descriptions for the entities might also be taken into account as a factor of selection during this sampling process. We suggest collecting descriptive data of the entities by following the sources of evidence given in Table 1.

It is recommended to use similar sources of evidence for all entities. Triangulation of more than one source might enrich the descriptions and lead to more robust results (cf. Yin 2009). We suggest listing derived entities in a longlist (LL). If entities are gained from different sources, this list should be cleaned of possible duplicates. The introduction of a selection factor (SF) can help to prepare the LL for further proceedings (Steininger et al. 2011b). This selection factor might encompass extra credit points for criteria such as an entity being a unique or extreme case, certain keywords within the name of an entity for restriction to a specific area of interest, or the availability of evidence for an entity. In a final step the LL has to be sorted in descending order by SF. Entities at the lower end of the list not reaching a certain selection factor might now be truncated, which results in shortlist (SL). Different approaches to gaining this shortlist might also be applied (i.e., taking a sample of entities from an existing journal paper on the phenomenon). The SL should be amended with an ascending research material ID (i) for each entity in a finalizing step.

2.2 Inductive Content Analysis Procedures

In this second step of our approach, we present a set of procedures and guidelines on how to inductively develop raw characteristics from textual descriptions of the selected entities from the preceding section.

Table 1 Data sources for entity description (Myers 2008; Yin 2009)

Name	Application	Advantages	Disadvantages
Documentation and Archival Records	Usually available in written form	Stable Unobtrusive	Bias of author unknown Retrievability and access
Web, Databases, and Social Media	Usually available in written and retrievable form	Relatively stable	Bias of author unknown Usage restrictions
Interviews	Transcription by person independent from interviewer. Final approval of transcript by interviewee	Targeted Insightful	Poor question bias Response bias Reflexivity
Fieldwork	Written memos of direct or participant observation Final check of memos by participants	Real-time coverage Contextual Insightful into behavior and motives	Time-consuming Observer bias Reflexivity
Physical Artifacts	Use of existing descriptions or composition of descriptive memos by two independent authors	Insightful into cultural features and technical operations	Selectivity Availability Access

After specification of the entities and their sampling as research material, the unit of analysis needs to be subsequently defined. This addresses the issue of "the basic unit of text to be classified" (Insch et al. 1997, p. 10) such as paragraphs or words into the categories of characteristics derived in succeeding steps. The configuration of this unit has a considerable impact on the quality and reliability of research results. Choosing a smaller unit (e.g., word) usually leads to higher reliability and possible automation but might corrode results which focus on larger meanings than transported by single words (Saris-Gallhofer et al. 1978). Following Kassarjian (1977), the "theme" is usually suggested for this type of taxonomic method, ensuring the capture of word- or sentence-spanning ideas especially within the inductive phase of building raw characteristics. To stabilize the results and reliabilities, entire sentences should be used as the operationalized coding unit, which leads to solely coding a category once within one sentence (Steininger et al. 2011b). In the suggested approach, the raw characteristics should be developed inductively from the selected research material (i.e., entities of investigation). This is done to initially capture the characteristics of the phenomenon of investigation, which are needed as groundwork for further analysis.

Based on raw characteristic-building rules (Mayring 2002), the research material should be worked through consecutively, and raw characteristics are defined beginning with the first selected entity of investigation. Each occurrence of a new or additional raw characteristic-building incident should be marked and uniquely

Table 2 Units of analysis (adapted from Kassarjian 1977)

Unit	Description	Advantages	Disadvantages
Word	Analysis of single words such as key symbols or value-laden terms	Ease of coding Ease of automation Highest reliabilities	Loss of context Loss of word-spanning ideas
Sentence	Analysis of entire sentences	Relative ease of coding Clear demarcation of unit borders	Loss of sentence-spanning ideas
Theme	Analysis of single assertions about a subject	Capturing of entire subjects of investigation Very useful in most content analyses	Ambiguous unit borders Difficult coding Lower reliabilities
Item	Entire documents such as speeches, letters, manuals	Useful in classifying entire documents	Often too gross for most research
Character	Mostly used in the analysis of streaming media or commercials to analyze heroes, bad guys, etc.	Useful in the analysis of behavior or communication of actors Might be of interest to develop taxonomies of user behavior in IS	Sometimes ambiguous unit borders Context might not be captured
Space and time	Analysis by column (e.g., newspaper), line, paragraph, or minute	Useful for historical timeline analysis and longitudinal taxonomies Clear demarcation of unit borders	Loss of unit-spanning ideas and context

numbered using the research material ID i (cf. Sect. 2.1). If the marked and colored occurrence in the text defines a nonexistent characteristic, a new and unique raw characteristic ID (r) is hyphenated (e.g., $i.1$-r). If the occurrence matches an existing raw characteristic and only adds richness to the description of the characteristic, that existing characteristic number should be used instead, and the mark is suggested to be set in a different color (e.g., dark blue). All raw characteristics categories are summoned in a list (RcL). This process should be continued until saturation is reached (i.e., no new raw characteristics can be derived from the research material entities) (Mayring 2008).

2.3 Clustering of Raw Characteristics

In this section we develop a set of guidelines on how to reduce and cluster the raw characteristics developed through the procedures outlined above. The goal of this step is to reach a generalizable and manageable set of main characteristics of the phenomenon of investigation, which can be used for further analysis.

As suggested by Mayring (2008), the entire list of raw characteristics has to be iteratively reduced and qualitatively bundled until the main characteristics emerge. We depict some of the approaches available to operationalize this task in the following. A first approach is suggested by Eisenhardt and Bourgeois (1988) in iteratively comparing within-group similarities (i.e., groups of similar raw characteristics) and intergroup differences. The technique can be advanced by using matrices and introducing continuous measurement scales for comparison (Eisenhardt and Bourgeois 1988). As an alternative approach an iterative comparison of pairs can be used by listing similarities and differences for each pair (Eisenhardt 1989). Another way to operationalize the task of grouping the raw characteristics into categories of main characteristics might be based on the approach of Steininger et al. (2011b). They suggest having at least two independent researchers who are familiar with the topic judge proximities of paired raw characteristics in a matrix ranging from 100 to show perfect similarity to zero reflecting complete independence. Whichever approach is finally used, each of the resulting main characteristics should be labeled with a descriptive name, which is ideally developed inductively from associated bundles of raw characteristics (Mayring 2008). From these grouped resulting main characteristics of the phenomenon under investigation, a category or coding scheme of characteristics needs to be developed. This is reached through amending each main characteristic with explanations, "anchor examples" from the associated and coded raw characteristics and coding rules (i.e., rules regarding when an occurrence of a characteristic should be coded or excluded during analysis). For quality assurance the scheme might be tested by three or four judges following the suggestions of Moore and Benbasat (1991).

2.4 Formative Pretests and Deductive Content Analysis Procedures

In the following, we depict the deductive content analysis of the sampled entities based on the main characteristics coding scheme developed in the preceding steps. This is needed to ensure formative quality and reliability of the coding scheme and to find manifestations and densities of characteristics for each entity. A content analytical core component is the classification of the aforementioned units of analysis into the categories of characteristics by independent researchers. This process is typically referred to as "coding" (Scott 1955) and requires the category scheme of characteristics developed above. To capture word-spanning meanings and stabilize the results and reliabilities, we suggested the theme as the coding unit and entire sentences as the operationalized coding unit in this study, which leads to only coding a certain category once within one sentence (Kassarjian 1977). The finalized category scheme of characteristics (also referred to as coding scheme) is iteratively used and adjusted for an extensive training of coders. At least a second independent coder should be employed to ensure stable results and calculate intercoder reliabilities (Mayring 2000). The coder(s) should be trained using research materials from *LL* with the lowest *SF*. The coding scheme and rules should be adjusted iteratively to sort out ambiguities through discussion of nonmatching codings. The procedure is repeated with different materials until the overall agreement (reliability) of all coders is calculated above 0.8 (cf. Moore 2000). This ensures intersubjectively comprehensible results and verifies the decency of the main characteristics coding scheme. Clearly distinguishable and exclusive categories of main characteristics are thereby ensured. We suggest using Krippendorf's Alpha (Hayes and Krippendorff 2007) for a sensitive and advanced measurement or the most commonly used simple "percent agreement" reliability measure of Holsti (1969). More details on possible measures, their mathematical references, advantages, and disadvantages are given in Table 3. All calculated reliabilities, discussions, and adjustments made to the coding scheme or the coding rules should be collected and given in a transparent and comprehensive manner for reproducibility (e.g., "If there are two occurrences of the same subcategory within one sentence, only the first occurrence should be

Table 3 Frequently cited measures of reliability for content analysis

Name	Advantages	Disadvantages
Krippendorf's Alpha (2007)	Allows any number of coders Takes into account agreements by chance Takes into account low coding numbers Takes into account number of categories Allows binary, nominal, ordinal, interval, ratio, polar, and circular data Allows measuring of incomplete data	Complex application Extensive details of data regarding coded occurrences needed
Holsti's Percent Agreement (1969)	Very facile and quick application Basic calculations	Does not take into account variables such as the number of categories, number of correct codings on incident, etc.
Scott's Pi (Scott 1955)	Relatively facile and quick application	Only allows nominal data Assumes same distribution of coder responses
Fleiss' Kappa (1971)	Relatively facile and quick application Extends Scott's Pi by allowing multiple coders	Only allows nominal data Assumes same distribution of coder responses
Cohen's Kappa (1960)	Takes into account agreements occurring by chance Does not assume same distribution of coder responses	Sometimes considered a too conservative measure Only allows measuring of two coders

coded, counted and marked"). Density results of the materials used for training shall be discarded after calculation of agreements and not be used for the building of final classes.

After finishing the aforementioned amendments to the coding scheme during the training session, the main coding process for all of the research material entities is initiated. This is done by analyzing all of the evidence of each entity for occurrences (i.e., manifestations) of the main characteristics categories. All manifestations should be marked and counted within the materials by category and entity. They are individually deemed as belonging to a certain category of characteristics. Finally, all manifestations in the evidence of each entity should be counted separately for every category. We suggest transforming these results into relative numbers (i.e., relative manifestations) and thereby making them comparable through dividing them by the number of averaged sentences in the sources of evidence for each entity. This number is calculated by counting the words of an entity's sources of evidence and dividing the results by 22. The number 22 is the average of words contained within a sentence in English texts reported by Charniak (1996). For readability reasons, the averaged sentences are interchangeably referred to as "sentences" in the following. No further refinements to the coding scheme and coding rules within this main coding process should be made. Results are not to be exchanged or discussed by the coders during this main phase to avoid introducing any biases (Mayring 2000). It is suggested that coders be employed independently from the ones used for adjusting the coding scheme if possible. After finishing the coding process for all of the research material, the summative reliabilities should be calculated for the resulting manifestations. Pavlou and Dimoka (2006) suggest also calculating intra-coder reliabilities by having each coder re-code a sample after a certain time. There is no common absolute number of these agreements, which is found to be satisfactory in the academic discussion on reliabilities. This is due to large differences especially in the units of analysis and coding but also in category systems, complexity of the evaluated contents, and coder experience with the phenomenon. Nevertheless, a reliability of at least 0.7–0.85 is seen as acceptable and reachable by many authors (e.g., Mayring 2000; Krippendorff 2004a; Frueh 2007) for the "theme" as the unit of analysis that we suggest for this type of study.

2.5   Quantitative Clustering of Manifestations

Verifying the manifestations of the characteristics of each entity enables us to group the different entities. Thereby a set of classes (of entities) within the phenomenon of investigation can be identified. These classifications have usually been performed subjectively based on researchers' ideas or intuition. Using our empirically derived and standardized densities instead leads to more objective classifications. Following the inductive procedure, again, no classes were predefined but instead derived inductively from the data sources.

Table 4 Manifestation matrix of entities and characteristics (cf. Steininger et al. 2011b)

Characteristics entities	C_1	C_2		C_n
E_1	x_{11}	x_{12}	...	x_{1n}
...		...	...	...	...
E_m	x_{m1}	x_{m2}	...	x_{mn}

Table 5 Distance matrix of entities

Entities	E_1	E_2	E_3	...	E_{m-1}
E_1	$d_{21} = d_{12}$				
E_2	d_{13}	d_{23}			
E_3	d_{14}	d_{24}	d_{34}		
...	...	...	...	...	
E_m	d_{1m}	...	...	...	$d_{(m-1)m}$

The main goal of this step is to identify classes that are mutually exclusive and collectively exhaustive. This means that there must be an appropriate class for each entity and each entity must fit into one class only (Bailey 1994). Furthermore, the classification should be generally applicable. The latter requirement is met by the extensive sampling method applied earlier, which ensures that the data used appropriately represents the phenomenon. The former two requirements are addressed by cluster analysis. Cluster analysis generally aims at finding classes such that entities within the same group are similar to each other while entities in different groups are as dissimilar as possible. The five typical steps of cluster analysis are outlined based on our problem (Aldenderfer and Blashfield 1984): (1) selection of a sample to be clustered, (2) definition of a set of variables on which to measure the entities in the sample, (3) computation of similarities among the entities, (4) use of a cluster analysis method to create groups of similar entities, and (5) validation of the resulting cluster solution.

The first step, selecting the sample, has already taken place. Regarding the selection of the cluster variables, which is usually a complex procedure (Fowlkes et al. 1988), it is again very helpful that we have already identified and reduced the relevant characteristics in the previous qualitative steps. Therefore, we can directly create the data matrix containing the densities of the characteristics that correspond to the different entities (see Table 4). In the next step, the similarity calculation takes place. Due to the standardized scale of manifestations (i.e., relative manifestations), the Minkowski distance[1] can be used to calculate these values without having to compute weights for the different characteristics (Kaufman and Rousseeuw 1990) (cf. Table 5). The elimination of potential single outliers that exhibit a large distance to all other entities should be checked manually by an in-depth analysis of the underlying data of this entity. Rash elimination of entities can lead to problems in the validity of the resulting taxonomy and should be avoided.

---

[1] $d(i,j) = (|x_{i1} - x_{j1}|^q + |x_{i2} - x_{j2}|^q + |x_{i3} - x_{j3}|^q + \ldots |x_{in} - x_{jn}|^q)^{1/q}$, where q is a natural number larger or equal to 1, and describes the distance between the entities i and j. Most algorithms use Manhattan distances ($q = 1$) or Euclidian distances ($q = 2$).

Many different analysis techniques can be applied in order to derive clusters from this data. Generally, partitioning methods like K-Means (Howard and Harris 1966) have been shown to be superior to hierarchical methods in this case (Punj and Stewart 1983). Nevertheless, these methods need a priori information about the starting points and the number of clusters, which may not be available when investigating a new phenomenon inductively. In this case, it might be useful to apply Ward's minimum variance method (Ward 1963) to derive preliminary clusters. Their center can then be used in a partitioning algorithm like K-Means (Punj and Stewart 1983). Common software packages such as SPSS or SAS can be used to process steps 3 and 4.

Despite the importance of exhaustiveness and mutual exclusiveness, further quality indicators can be addressed. Checking the quality of classifications has been discussed in detail by Aldenderfer and Blashfield (1984). They suggest two major techniques that are relevant to our procedure: significance tests and replication. Multivariate analysis of variance (MANOVA) or discriminant analysis can be used to check the significance of the clusters. However, this method has been criticized for indicating high significance even for very bad clusters. A solution to this problem might be the inclusion of external variables, which is difficult when analyzing a new phenomenon (Aldenderfer and Blashfield 1984). The replication technique can be used to check for internal consistency of the classification. If the base of entities is large enough, the split-half method can be applied.

Two random sets of entities are clustered independently using the same clustering method. If the same classes occur across different subsets of entities, this indicates further generalizability of the classification. Another form of replication is to use different clustering methods with the same data. If the same clusters are derived, the results indicate a high validity of the classification (Aldenderfer and Blashfield 1984). After having the clusters validated, the different classes have to be interpreted. For better understanding, they should also be described verbally. This usually complex task can be accomplished using the codings and descriptions of the entities within one class. The distribution of these codings already describes the characteristics of a certain class. If the number of entities in one class is very high, the naming should be based on the characteristics of the entities in the center of the class. The clusters should then be named inductively out of the names and characteristics from their associated entities (Mayring 2008).

2.6   Summative Checks of Taxonomic Quality

As discussed earlier, checking taxonomic quality is a very challenging task. Mutual exclusiveness and collective exhaustiveness are the two major quality measures that a high-quality taxonomy has to meet (Bailey 1994). In order to increase and verify the validity of our method, we suggest performing an additional (optional) step to test discriminant validity of the classification via a sorting procedure (see: Davis 1989; Moore and Benbasat 1991). If additional entities that have not been used for the taxonomy-building process are available, these entities should be combined with the entities from the sample into a common pool. The additional entities can be coded using the deductive procedure outlined earlier and can then be sorted into the classes mathematically to also obtain their class affiliations for subsequent comparison. Three to four judges are given the names and verbal descriptions of the classes that have been derived in the previous steps. The judges now sort all entities from the pool into the classes. Two measures can be applied to the results of this sorting process.

The first one measures the inter-judge reliability and focuses on the question of judges sorting the same entities into the same classes. We again suggest Krippendorf's Alpha (Hayes and Krippendorff 2007) or Holsti's percent agreement (Holsti 1969) to measure the level of agreement between the judges and thereby determine whether or not the descriptions precisely define the classes. Reliabilities above 0.7 can be seen as satisfactory (Krippendorff 2004a). If this level is not reached, the descriptions of the classes should be enhanced iteratively. A lack of increased inter-judge reliability even with refined descriptions indicates a general problem regarding the mutual exclusiveness or the collective exhaustiveness. Furthermore, for each class, a cumulated overall measure of correctly placed entities can be calculated.[2] This differs from the previous measure since it challenges the strength of the different classes separately. No description of a reasonable score for this measure is described in the literature. As a rule of thumb, the interval between 0.7 and 0.85 discussed above (Mayring 2000; Krippendorff 2004b; cf. Frueh 2007) can also be applied as a good indicator for this measure. A high value points to high construct validity and reliability of the class. This method can also be used qualitatively to identify critical class definitions and borders between two classes that should be refined.

2.7 Limitations of the Method

Potential limitations regarding the procedures introduced throughout this chapter should be taken into account. They are given below and if countermeasures do exist, they are also depicted in the following. Overall, we have tried to keep the complexity of the process low. Nevertheless, it might inhibit broader use. The process of inductively constructing raw characteristics from the entities is continued until saturation (Glaser and Strauss 1967). This allows real knowledge and deep insights to be gained in classes. Nevertheless, theoretical saturation is critical to identify. This might lead to missing definitions of characteristics threatening the collective exhaustiveness. The probability seems low since we suggested measures to objectify

---

[2]The overall measure for the quality of the class is defined as $B(i) = \frac{\#E_c}{\#E} \in (0, 1)$, where $\#E_c$ is the number of correctly selected entities into class i by all judges and $\#E$ describes the number of entities supposed to be sorted into this class.

significant saturation within the inductive process. Inductively built categories might also be biased by a coder's world views or insights on the phenomenon. The likelihood of such a bias might be lowered through introducing more than one coder to inductively build the raw characteristics. Construction of main characteristics from raw characteristics might also be subject to the coder's bias since they are qualitatively clustered. Improvement within this area might be reached by applying large proximity matrices judged by more than one person and statistical cluster analysis for their entire set.

The method of using averaged sentences for comparability reasons might lead to excessive numbers of coded sentences since figures or tables within the sources of evidence might be handled as text. This is additionally fostered by the assumption during calculations that all sentences only contain one code, which must not hold true since the rules allow coding a sentence twice with two different categories. One major critique regarding cluster analysis is that it lacks a theoretical foundation. Therefore the identified clusters may simply be statistical artifacts that capitalize on random numerical variation across entities (Thomas and Venkatraman 1988). Furthermore, cluster analysis might also find classes in situations where no clusters exist (e.g., Aldenderfer and Blashfield 1984). Our approach tries to invalidate the criticisms partly because the clusters are directly named and described based on the densities of their characteristics and are therefore not artificial constructs (Mayring 2008). Another main critique of cluster analysis is the potential multicollinearity among characteristics that may lead to overweighting of certain aspects (Ketchen and Shook 1996). Using more advanced distance measures such as the Mahalanobis distance might solve this issue (Hair et al. 2005), but this measure is supported neither by Ward's minimum variance method (Ward 1963) nor by software such as SPSS and SAS. However, our approach addresses this issue early in the research process. Since the characteristics of the topic are inductively derived from the raw categories and by controlling for weakness of the single characteristics (Frueh 2007), the risk of multicollinearity issues is reduced.

3   Conclusion

Throughout this chapter, we outlined and developed a method of building taxonomic classification schemes for business disciplines. Although the importance of such classifications is seen as very high in the research community (Wolf 1926; Kantor 1953; Kemeny 1959; Lambert 2006), these classifications have usually been performed subjectively based on researchers' ideas or intuition. The delineated approach enables researchers to derive classifications empirically, leading to more objective classifications (Bailey 1994). In essence, we proposed six subsequent steps relying on content and cluster analysis. Especially the use of content analysis in this context enhances the available set of techniques within our field. The first step begins with the sampling of entities and their sources of evidence as instantiations or examples of the topic. Since our method focuses on new and unexplored topics of investigation, we assumed that no theoretical basis of the topic was available. Accordingly, the second and third steps proposed to develop the characteristics of the topic from selected entities by using inductive content analysis procedures.

Based on these results we proposed a fourth step of deductive content analysis to find manifestations and densities of the derived characteristics for each entity. Cluster analysis was then applied to identify specific classes in the research material, leading to a taxonomic classification scheme. Formative state-of-the-art procedures for quality assurance were suggested throughout all steps of the method. Additionally, summative measures of taxonomic quality for the resulting constructs were outlined. We hope that our results will help academics to develop empirically grounded rigorous taxonomies in their fields of research by applying our suggestions, guidelines, and depicted alternatives. Taxonomies are important vehicles in IS and management research since they allow investigations on a topic to be limited to certain subclasses or taxa, which makes research projects more manageable. Lastly, they are of high value for intra- and interclass generalization, enabling the development of theories through analysis of these classes and their generalizations. There are innumerable applications of our method in the field of business and technology research. New and upcoming phenomena such as cloud computing applications and crowdsourcing services might require taxonomic classification, but also long-standing nonempirically grounded typologies in areas such as outsourcing, operational application software systems, or electronic business model research might be revisited and updated by applying our method to the topic.

References

Abbasi A, Chen H (2008) Cybergate: A Design Framework and System for Text Analysis of Computer-Mediated Communication. MIS Q 32:811–837

Al-Debei MM, Avison D (2010) Developing a Unified Framework of the Business Model Concept. Eur J Inf Syst 19:359–376

Aldenderfer M, Blashfield R (1984) Cluster Analysis. Beverly Hills Sage Univ Pap

Angelmar R, Stern LW (1978) Development of a Content Analytic System for Analysis of Bargaining Communication in Marketing. J Mark Res 15:93–102

Bailey KD (1994) Typologies and Taxonomies: An Introduction to Classification Techniques. Sage Publications, Thousand Oaks

Charniak E (1996) Tree-Bank Grammars. In: Proceedings of the National Conference on Artificial Intelligence. pp 1031–1036

Cohen J (1960) A Coefficient of Agreement for Nominal Scales. Educ Psychol Meas 20:37–46. https://doi.org/10.1177/001316446002000104

Davis FD (1989) Perceived Usefulness, Perceived Ease of Use, and User Acceptance of Information Technology. MIS Q 13:319–340

Eisenhardt KM (1989) Building Theories from Case Study Research. Acad Manage Rev 14:532–550

Eisenhardt KM, Bourgeois LJ (1988) Politics of Strategic Decision Making in High-Velocity Environments: Toward a Midrange Theory. Acad Manage J 31:737–770. https://doi.org/10.2307/256337

Fleiss JL (1971) Measuring Nominal Scale Agreement Among Many Raters. Psychol Bull 76:378–382. https://doi.org/10.1037/h0031619

Fowlkes EB, Gnanadesikan R, Kettenring JR (1988) Variable Selection in Clustering. J Classif 5:205–228

Frueh W (2007) Inhaltsanalyse: Theorie und Praxis (in German), 6th edn. UVK Verlagsgesellschaft, Konstanz

Glaser BG, Strauss AL (1967) The Discovery of Grounded Theory: Strategies for Qualitative Research. Aldine, New York

Hair JF, Black B, Babin B (2005) Multivariate Data Analysis, 6th ed. Prentice Hall

Hayes AF, Krippendorff K (2007) Answering the Call for a Standard Reliability Measure for Coding Data. Commun Methods Meas 1:77–89

Holsti OR (1969) Content Analysis for the Social Sciences and Humanities. Addison-Wesley, Reading

Howard N, Harris B (1966) A Hierarchical Grouping Routine, IBM 360/65 Fortran IV program. Univ Pa Comput Cent

Insch GS, Moore JE, Murphy LD (1997) Content Analysis in Leadership Research: Examples, Procedures, and Suggestions for Future Use. Leadersh Q 8:1–25

Kantor JR (1953) The Logic of Modern Science. University of Akron Press, Akron

Kassarjian H (1977) Content Analysis in Consumer Research. J Consum Res 4:8–18

Kaufman L, Rousseeuw PJ (1990) Finding Groups in Data: An Introduction to Cluster Analysis. Wiley Online Library

Kemeny JG (1959) A Philosopher Looks at Science. Van Nostrand, Princeton

Ketchen DJ, Shook CL (1996) The Application of Cluster Analysis in Strategic Management Research: An Analysis and Critique. Strateg Manag J 17:441–458. https://doi.org/10.1002/(SICI)1097-0266(199606)17:6<441::AID-SMJ819>3.0.CO;2-G

Krippendorff K (2004a) Content Analysis: An Introduction to its Methodology, 2nd edn. Sage Publications, Thousand Oaks

Krippendorff K (2004b) Reliability in Content Analysis: Some Common Misconceptions and Recommendations. Hum Commun Res 30:411–433

Lambert S (2006) Do We Need a "Real" Taxonomy of e-Business Models? In: ACIS 2006 Proceedings. 17th Australasian Conference on Information Systems

Mayring P (2000) Qualitative Content Analysis. Forum Qual Soc Res 1:1–10

Mayring P (2002) Einführung in die qualitative Sozialforschung: Eine Anleitung zu qualitativem Denken (in German), 5th edn. Beltz Verlag, Weinheim

Mayring P (2008) Qualitative Inhaltsanalyse: Grundlagen und Techniken (in German), 10th edn. Beltz, Weinheim

Moore JE (2000) One Road to Turnover: An Examination of Work Exhaustion in Technology Professionals. MIS Q 24:141–168

Moore GC, Benbasat I (1991) Development of an Instrument to Measure the Perceptions of Adopting an Information Technology Innovation. Inf Syst Res 2:192–222

Myers MD (2008) Qualitative Research in Business & Management, illustrated edition. Sage Publications Ltd.

Nag R, Hambrick DC, Chen M-J (2007) What is Strategic Management, Really? Inductive Derivation of a Consensus Definition of the Field. Strateg Manag J 28:935–955. https://doi.org/10.1002/smj.615

Nickerson RC, Varshney U, Muntermann J (2013) A Method for Taxonomy Development and Its Application in Information Systems. Eur J Inf Syst 22:336–359. https://doi.org/10.1057/ejis.2012.26

Oberländer AM, Lösser B, Rau D (2019) TAXONOMY RESEARCH IN INFORMATION SYSTEMS: A SYSTEMATIC ASSESSMENT. Res Pap

Pavlou PA, Dimoka A (2006) The Nature and Role of Feedback Text Comments in Online Marketplaces: Implications for Trust Building, Price Premiums, and Seller Differentiation. Inf Syst Res 17:392–414. https://doi.org/10.1287/isre.1060.0106

Punj G, Stewart DW (1983) Cluster Analysis in Marketing Research: Review and Suggestions for Application. J Mark Res 20:134–148. https://doi.org/10.2307/3151680

Saris-Gallhofer IN, Saris WE, Morton EL (1978) A Validation Study of Holsti's Content Analysis Procedure. Qual Quant 12:131–145. https://doi.org/10.1007/BF00144066

Scott W (1955) Reliability of Content Analysis: The Case of Nominal Scale Coding. Public Opin Q 19:321–325. https://doi.org/10.1086/266577

Steininger DM (2019) Linking Information Systems and Entrepreneurship: A Review and Agenda for IT-Associated and Digital Entrepreneurship Research. Inf Syst J 29:363–407

Steininger DM, Huntgeburth JC, Veit D (2011a) Conceptualizing Business Models for Competitive Advantage Research by Integrating the Resource and Market-Based Views. In: AMCIS 2011 Proceedings. pp 1–12

Steininger DM, Huntgeburth JC, Veit DJ (2011b) A Systemizing Research Framework for Web 2.0. In: ECIS 2011 Proceedings. AISeL, Helsinki, Finland, pp 1–13

Thomas H, Venkatraman N (1988) Research on Strategic Groups: Progress and Prognosis. J Manag Stud 25:537–555. https://doi.org/10.1111/j.1467-6486.1988.tb00046.x

Veit D, Clemons E, Benlian A, et al (2014) Business Models: An Information Systems Research Agenda. Bus Inf Syst Eng 6:45–53. https://doi.org/10.1007/s12599-013-0308-y

Ward JH (1963) Hierarchical Grouping to Optimize an Objective Function. J Am Stat Assoc 58:236–244

Wolf A (1926) Essentials of Scientific Method. Macmillan, New York

Yin RK (2009) Case Study Research: Design and Methods, 4th edn. Sage Publications, Inc, Thousand Oaks

Dennis M. Steininger is an assistant professor of Information Systems and Digital Entrepreneurship at the Faculty of Business and Economics of the University of Augsburg, Germany. In addition, he is co-managing director of the Augsburg Center for Entrepreneurship as well as a research fellow and guest lecturer in the Institute for SME and Entrepreneurship Research at the University of Mannheim, Germany. He received his PhD in Business Information Systems from the University of Mannheim (2016), Germany, supervised by Professor Dr. Daniel J. Veit. His research focuses on the success factors and impacts of digital entrepreneurship and related business models. His work has been published in the *Journal of Management Information Systems*, *Information Systems Journal*, *Electronic Markets*, and *Technological Forecasting and Social Change*, among others. Dennis is currently serving as a guest editor of a special issue on digital entrepreneurship at *Business & Information Systems Engineering* and as track chair and associate editor at a number of leading information systems conferences.

Manuel Trenz is Chair of Interorganizational Information Systems at the Faculty of Business and Economics of the Georg-August-University of Göttingen, Germany. He received his PhD in Business Information Systems from the University of Mannheim (2014), Germany, and his habilitation from the University of Augsburg (2019), Germany, both supervised by Professor Dr. Daniel J. Veit. His research addresses the targeted use of information systems and digital innovations and their influence on organizations and individuals. In particular, he focuses on interactions with and the impact of digital services and platforms, as well as the intersections between physical and digital worlds. His work has been published in journals such as *Management Information Systems Quarterly*, the *Journal of Management Information Systems*, the *European Journal of Information Systems*, *Information & Management*, and *Business & Information Systems Engineering*. Manuel is currently serving as senior editor for *Internet Research*, as associate editor for the *Information Systems Journal*, and as a member of the editorial board of *Electronic Markets*. In addition, he frequently serves as a track and workshop chair at leading information systems conferences.

Daniel J. Veit currently a full professor and Chair of Information Systems and Management at the Department of Business Administration of the Faculty of Business and Economics of the University of Augsburg, Germany. He holds a PhD in Economics and Business Engineering (2002) as well as a habilitation degree in Business Administration (2006), both from the University of Karlsruhe (TH), Germany, supervised by Professor Dr. Christof Weinhardt. He is also a visiting professor of Information Systems at the Department of Digitalization at Copenhagen Business School, Denmark. His research focuses on the transformational effects of information systems and digitalization in society, with a specific focus on sustainability. His publications have appeared in outlets such as the *Management Information Systems Quarterly*, the *Journal of Management Information Systems*, the *European Journal of Information Systems*, the *Journal of Service Research, Information & Management, Internet Research, MIS Quarterly Executive*, the *Journal of Business Economics*, and *Business & Information Systems Engineering*. He serves as an Editorial Board Associate Editor for the *Journal of the Association for Information Systems*, as well as associate editor for the *Information Systems Journal*. In addition, he serves as a member of the distinguished board of advisors for *Internet Research*. In 2019 he received the "Outstanding Reviewer Award" of the *Journal of the Association for Information Systems*. He has frequently served as a track chair and associate editor for leading conferences in the information systems field. In 2014 he received the conference best paper award at the European Conference on Information Systems in Tel Aviv, Israel. In 2016 he served as a program co-chair of the European Conference on Information Systems in Istanbul, Turkey. He is the principal investigator of a German Federal Ministry of Education and Research grant awarded to study the impact of the sharing economy on German society. Earlier in his career he was admitted to the young researchers' promotion program of the Volkswagen Foundation. During the past 14 years he has served as Associate Dean for international affairs and Academic Director of the ESSEC & Mannheim Executive MBA Program at Mannheim Business School, Germany, among other positions.

Understanding Emotions in Electronic Auctions: Insights from Neurophysiology

Marc T. P. Adam and Jan Krämer

Abstract The design of electronic auction platforms is an important field of electronic commerce research. It requires not only a profound understanding of the role of human cognition in human bidding behavior but also of the role of human affect. In this chapter, we focus specifically on the emotional aspects of human bidding behavior and the results of empirical studies that have employed neurophysiological measurements in this regard. By synthesizing the results of these studies, we are able to provide a coherent picture of the role of affective processes in human bidding behavior along four distinct theoretical pathways.

1 Introduction

Electronic auctions (i.e., electronic auction marketplaces) are information systems that facilitate and structure the exchange of products and services between several potential buyers and sellers. In practice, electronic auctions have been employed for a wide range of goods and services, such as commodities (e.g., Internet consumer auction markets, such as eBay.com), perishable goods (e.g., Dutch flower markets, such as by Royal FloraHolland), consumer services (e.g., procurement auction markets, such as myhammer.com), or property rights (e.g., financial double auction markets such as NASDAQ). In this vein, a large share of our private and commercial economic activity is being organized through electronic auctions today (Adam et al. 2017; Ku et al. 2005).

Previous research in information systems, economics, and psychology has shown that the design of electronic auctions has a tremendous impact on the auction

M. T. P. Adam
College of Engineering, Science and Environment, The University of Newcastle, Callaghan, Australia
e-mail: marc.adam@newcastle.edu.au

J. Krämer (✉)
University of Passau, Passau, Germany
e-mail: jan.kraemer@uni-passau.de

© The Author(s) 2021
H. Gimpel et al. (eds.), *Market Engineering*,
https://doi.org/10.1007/978-3-030-66661-3_5

87

outcome, even—or particularly—when theory did not suggest that there should be differences. For example, the auction outcome was found to be affected by the interface design (Adam et al. 2016), the auction mechanism used (Hariharan et al. 2016), the speed at which prices are incremented or decremented (Carare and Rothkopf 2005; Katok and Kwasnica 2008), and other elements of time pressure inherent to auctions (Ariely and Simonson 2003; Ku et al. 2005). In seeking to better understand these effects, scholars increasingly recognize the role of the bidders' emotions, such as the "joy of winning" or the "fear of losing" (Delgado et al. 2008). Furthermore, a bidder's emotional state may also culminate in a state of "competitive arousal" that is elicited during auction participation (Ku et al. 2005).

Despite these important and insightful findings, previous research on the role of emotions in electronic auctions is rather scattered throughout the economic, psychology, and IS disciplines. In 2011, Adam et al. (2011b) proposed an integrative theoretical framework for emotional bidding that aimed to provide a unified view for the dynamic influence of emotions on human bidding behavior. Thereby, the authors not only considered the classical economic perspective on human bidding behavior but also the role that a bidder's immediate emotions (e.g., frustration, joy, regret) as well as their overall emotional state (i.e., overall level and valence of emotional processing) may play in bidding. Almost 10 years later, we map the propositions of this framework to findings from empirical research. Thereby, we specifically focus on results taking into account neurophysiological measurements (e.g., brain imaging, heart rate, skin conductance) due to their ability to provide unique insights into the unconscious processing of human emotion.

2 Theoretical Background

2.1 Affective Processing and Emotions

Affective processes and emotions play an important role in how users perceive and experience information systems. Information systems can trigger affective processes in the user, which through the vehicle of emotion shape the users' attitudes, beliefs, and response tendencies. With or without conscious awareness, these processes can ultimately have an influence on user behavior. As famously stated by Bradley (2007, p. 602), "it sometimes seems that there are as many definitions [of emotion] as there are investigators." Reflecting a rather general understanding of emotions in psychological literature, the term emotion can be roughly defined as a subjectively experienced state that can be described qualitatively and is accompanied by changes in feeling, physiology, and expression (Myers 2004). Thus, a subjectively experienced feeling is only a part of the broader concept of emotion, which also comprises objectively observable changes, for example, in neurophysiology.

In the present work, we build on the conceptualization by Rick and Lowenstein (2008) and distinguish between a person's (1) immediate emotions and (2) overall emotional state. Within this conceptualization, an *immediate emotion* refers to a short burst of emotional experience which is elicited by an internal (e.g., fear in response to thinking about an unpleasant event) and/or external stimulation (e.g., joy in response to learning about a discount). By contrast, the *emotional state* refers to a person's overall state of emotions and thereby canalizes the influence of emotional reactions. Importantly, while immediate emotions are transient, the emotional state is ongoing and "the individual is never *without* being in some emotional state" (Zajonc 1984, p. 21).

2.2 Framework for Emotional Bidding

In the context of electronic auctions, affective processes can be triggered by the design of the user interface as well as by the underlying auction mechanism. Adam et al. (2011b) introduced an integrative theoretical framework along with a set of specific propositions to conceptualize the emergence and impact of affective processes in electronic auctions (see Fig. 1). The framework builds on the previously mentioned conceptualization by Rick and Loewenstein (2008) that distinguishes between immediate emotions and a person's overall emotional state.

The top row (Auction System & Environment → Auction Outcome) depicts the traditional, economic cause-and-effect relationship of auction theory (McAfee and McMillan 1987). Assuming an emotionless *homo economicus*, who is fully rational and has the ability to assess all available information and possible strategic interactions, the (equilibrium) bidding strategy is determined ex-ante and depends only on the auction system and environment (i.e., the set of rules governing the auction, the number of competitors, etc.). The bidding strategy is a master plan for every possible contingency that may occur during the auction process, and thus,

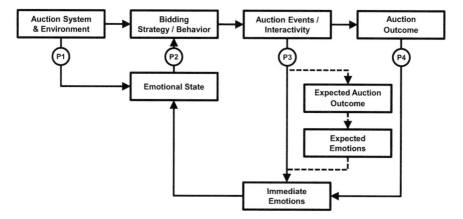

Fig. 1 Framework for emotional bidding (adapted from Adam et al. [2011b])

from a purely game-theoretic point of view, there is no need to modify the bidding strategy during the auction. Hence, under the traditional economic view, the cause-and-effect relationship between the auction system and environment and the auction outcome is unidirectional and does not contain feedback loops.

Below the top row, the framework takes into account the emergence and impact of affective processes on human bidding behavior and auction outcomes. In this vein, the framework explicitly takes into account psychological feedback loops that are not considered in the traditional economic perspective. In other words, the assumption of a *homo economicus* is thereby complemented by the assumption of a *homo emoticus* (Sigmund et al. 2002). The specific cause-and-effect relationships between a bidder's emotional state (i.e., their overall arousal and valence of affective processing) and their immediate emotions (e.g., joy of winning, frustration of losing) are made explicit by a set of theoretical propositions.[1] While the original framework contains a total of six propositions, in the present chapter we focus specifically on a simplified subset of four propositions:

Proposition 1 (P1): *The auction system and environment influences a bidder's overall emotional state.*

Proposition 2 (P2): *A bidder's current emotional state has an influence on their bidding behavior*

Proposition 3 (P3): *Auction events affect the emergence of immediate emotions*

Proposition 4 (P4): *The auction outcome affects the emergence of immediate emotions*

2.3 Neurophysiological Measurements

The field of NeuroIS draws upon the theories, methods, and tools in neurophysiology to advance the design, evaluation, and understanding of information systems (Riedl et al. 2014). This includes both techniques that measure brain activation such as functional magnetic resonance imaging (fMRI), electroencephalography (EEG), and positron emission tomography (PET) and physiological measurements such as electrocardiography (ECG), facial electromyography (EMG), and skin conductance (SC) measurements. By linking these neurophysiological measurements to users' perceptions and behaviors, researchers can investigate the role of human affective processing in human–computer interaction (Adam et al. 2011a; Hariharan et al. 2017; Jung et al. 2017).

---

[1]Specifically, the original framework also considers a more nuanced interplay between expected and immediate emotions. However, to the best of our knowledge, there is currently no research available that provides insight into these.

As for the context of affective processing, it is important to highlight that neurophysiological measures provide insight into two important dimensions of emotion: *valence* and *arousal*. According to the circumplex model of emotion (Russel 1980), the arousal dimension refers to the general intensity of emotion and ranges from calm to excited. In contrast, the valence dimension refers to whether the emotion is perceived as pleasant or unpleasant. By applying these measurements in the context of electronic auctions, this information provides important insights into a bidder's overall emotional state (e.g., the level of competitive arousal during auction participation) and the emergence of specific immediate emotions (e.g., the intensity of the joy of winning and the frustration of losing).

3   Empirical Results

In the following, we map the results of empirical studies to the four propositions of the framework shown in Fig. 1. Thereby, we particularly focus on evidence from studies employing neurophysiological measurements. Table 1 provides a summary of this mapping.

3.1   Impact of the Auction System and Environment on a Bidder's Current Emotional State (P1)

The auction system and environment includes a multiplicity of factors that may affect a bidder's emotional state. As noted by Adam et al. (2019), this could potentially even relate to seemingly irrelevant aspects such as whether the bidder had recently been to the gym or consumed an espresso. Conceptually, we can distinguish factors that are integral to the auction context and incidental factors that are outside the auction context. Providing support for P1, studies using neurophysiological measurements showed that both of these categories can affect a bidder's emotional state.

In terms of *integral* factors, one stream of literature has considered the speed of price changes in ascending and descending clock auctions. Specifically, it was shown that when increasing the clock speed from 5 s per price change to 0.5 s per price change, bidders exhibited higher heart rates (Adam et al. 2012, 2015). Further, research showed that competing with other human bidders instead of computerized bidders is another important driver for arousal in auctions (Adam et al. 2015; Teubner et al. 2015). In terms of *incidental* factors, research has shown that seemingly unrelated imagery in the auction environment affects a bidder's current emotional state. For instance, Adam et al. (2016) showed that competitive images (e.g., pictures of competitive sports) created a different emotional state in bidders than community images (e.g., pictures of family scenes).

Table 1 Mapping between propositions and empirical results

Proposition	Empirical result
P1: *The auction system and environment influences a bidder's overall emotional state*	Faster clock speeds in clock auctions are linked to higher arousal (heart rates) (Adam et al. 2012, 2015)
	Affective imagery in the auction environment increases bidders' overall arousal (Adam et al. 2016, 2019)
	Descending clock auctions induce higher arousal (heart rates) than ascending clock auctions (Smith and Dickhaut 2005)
P2: *A bidder's current emotional state has an influence on their bidding behavior*	Higher overall arousal (heart rates) is linked to higher (/lower) bids in ascending (/descending) clock auctions (Adam et al. 2012, 2015)
	Higher arousal in sealed-bid auctions is linked to higher (/lower) bids in common value (/private value) settings (Adam et al. 2019; Teubner et al. 2015)
P3: *Auction events affect the emergence of immediate emotions*	Submitting a sealed bid triggers skin conductance responses, the intensity of which is positively related to the amount of money at stake (Teubner et al. 2015)
	Placing a bid under high time pressure induces weaker immediate emotions than placing a bid under low time pressure (Adam 2010)
P4: *The auction outcome affects the emergence of immediate emotions*	Winning a sealed-bid auction induces stronger immediate emotions (brain activity, skin conductance) than losing it (Astor et al. 2013a; Teubner et al. 2015; van den Bos et al. 2013)
	Losing a descending clock auction induces a stronger skin conductance response than winning it (Adam et al. 2012)
	Losing a sealed-bid auction triggers stronger immediate emotions (brain activity in striatum) than losing an equivalent lottery removed from the auction context (Delgado et al. 2008)

3.2 Impact of a Bidder's Current Emotional State on Their Bidding Behavior (P2)

Researchers in psychology have long conjectured that factors in the auction system and environment may not only change a bidder's emotional state but that this change in the emotional state may also affect their bidding behavior (Ku et al. 2005; Murnighan 2002). In the literature, this impact of the emotional state on bidding behavior is often referred to as auction fever. Referring to the visceral nature of auction fever, Murnighan (2002, p. 63) conjectured that during auction fever bidders' "adrenaline starts to rush, their emotions block their ability to think clearly, and they end up bidding more than they ever envisioned." Providing support for P2, studies using neurophysiological measurements have linked changes in a bidder's emotional state to their bidding behavior.

Focusing on the role of clock speeds in ascending and descending clock auctions, Adam et al. (2015) and Adam et al. (2012) showed that the way in which the emotional state affects the bidding behavior depends on the auction mechanisms. While in ascending auctions higher arousal is associated with higher bids, the reverse is true for descending auctions. Here, higher arousal is associated with lower bids (Adam et al. 2012). Further research showed that the link between a bidder's emotional state and their bidding behavior does not only hold for dynamic auctions but also for static, sealed-bid auctions (Adam et al. 2016, 2019; Teubner et al. 2015). Importantly, however, these studies found that the direction of the relationship depends on the underlying value model. In sealed-bid settings, for instance, higher arousal was associated with higher bids in common value settings (Adam et al. 2019; van den Bos et al. 2013), whereas the reverse was true for independent private value settings (Adam et al. 2016; Teubner et al. 2015). These differences between ascending and descending and between common and private value settings, respectively, can be explained by the notion of arousal's risk-promoting effects. Placing higher bids in common value auctions is associated with a higher risk of paying too much. In first-price independent-private value auctions, risk-averse bidders would generally place higher bids, because, by definition, risk averseness means that a bidder is willing to accept a lower profit when the outcome is more certain. By bidding higher, winning the auction becomes more certain; in reverse, this means that a risk-taking bidder has a tendency to bid lower in a first-price auction, because this offers a higher profit in case the auction is won, but entails a higher risk of not winning the auction.

3.3 Immediate Emotions in Response to Auction Events (P3)

Only a few neurophysiological studies have investigated the emergence of immediate emotions in response to auction events. However, the limited studies that have been conducted provide support for the link expressed in P3. Specifically, Teubner et al. (2015) measured the bidders' skin conductance responses in response to submitting a bid and waiting for the result. Their results showed that both of these events trigger an immediate emotion, the intensity of which increases with higher amounts of money at stake. Complementarily, Adam (2010) found that placing a bid under high time pressure induces weaker immediate emotions in terms of skin conductance responses than placing a bid under low time pressure.

3.4 *Immediate Emotions in Response to Auction Outcome (P4)*

The announcement of the auction outcome is arguably the single most anticipated event in any auction. After all, the outcome of an auction provides clarity in terms of resource allocation (who gets what) and prices (who pays what). Providing support for P4, studies using neurophysiological measurements have shown that the announcement of the auction outcome can trigger a range of different immediate emotions with varying intensities.

While overall studies have shown that the emotions in response to winning an auction are experienced more strongly than those of losing an auction, both for sealed-bid (Astor et al. 2013a; Teubner et al. 2015; van den Bos et al. 2013) and ascending clock auctions (Adam et al. 2015), it is important to note that this is not the case for descending clock auctions. Specifically, Adam et al. (2012) found that in descending clock ("Dutch") auctions the skin conductance responses triggered in response to losing are stronger than those in response to winning. The authors explained this with the "click-to-win" characteristic of Dutch auctions, where losing comes as an unpleasant surprise. Further, pointing to the importance of the "social competition" (Delgado et al. 2008) inherent to auctions, immediate emotions in response to auction outcome are stronger when competing with a human opponent than they are when competing with computerized bidders (Adam et al. 2015; Teubner et al. 2015).

A different perspective on winning and losing is to consider whether the bidder *could* have achieved a more favorable result had they placed a slightly different bid. The immediate emotions associated with these ex-post considerations are referred to as winner regret and loser regret (Engelbrecht-Wiggans and Katok 2008). Winner regret refers to the notion that the bidder could have still won the auction but achieved a higher profit by placing a slightly lower bid. By contrast, loser regret refers to the notion that the bidder lost the auction but could have won the auction with a profit by placing a slightly higher bid. Note that such regret can only occur in first-price auctions, where bidders have to pay what they bid. Astor et al. (2011) were able to show based on skin conductance measurements that both of these events induce immediate emotions and that, as predicted by Engelbrecht-Wiggans and Katok (2008), loser regret is experienced more strongly than winner regret. However, the results of Astor et al. (2011) also show that the intensity of immediate emotions *increases* the closer the bidder's successful bid was to the second highest bid. This finding is in conflict with Engelbrecht-Wiggans and Katok's (2008) assumptions underlying the concept of *winner regret* and instead is more congruent with an emotion of *winner relief* (Astor et al. 2011).

4   Discussion

By facilitating the exchange of products and services, electronic auctions have become an important element of an increasingly digitized economy. In order to effectively utilize electronic auctions, system designers need to have a profound understanding of how the design of the auction environment affects human bidding behavior and auction outcomes. This requires taking into account not only the cognitive aspects of human bidding behavior but also aspects associated with human affect. The conceptual work by Adam et al. (2011b) attempted to capture how human affective processing may affect a bidder's emotional state and the emergence of immediate emotions during auction participation. Since then, a set of empirical studies have employed neurophysiological measurements to evaluate specific links in the emotional bidding framework for a range of different auction mechanisms.

In the present chapter, we have linked the results of these empirical studies back to the original framework and found support for its four main propositions. Specifically, studies found that both integral (e.g., clock speeds) and incidental factors (e.g., affective imagery) in the auction environment may affect a bidder's emotional state, which in turn affects their bidding behavior. Depending on the auction mechanisms and the type of product being sold, higher arousal may result in higher or lower prices. Further, placing a bid in an auction is an event that triggers immediate emotions, with higher amounts of money yielding stronger intensities. Finally, both winning and losing an auction trigger immediate emotions, the intensities of which depend on the auction mechanism, the type of interaction partner, and the amount of money at stake. Taken together, these findings show that the design of an electronic auction has a significant impact on the affective processes that bidders experience and the impact that this has on bidding behavior and auction outcomes.

Building on these insights, researchers have not only investigated how to design information systems in order to carry out auctions electronically, but also explored how to assist bidders during auction participation, e.g., by predicting auction outcomes based on psychophysiological measurements (Müller et al. 2016). Conceptually, user assistance systems in this context build on the notion of supporting bidders in regulating the emergence of arousal as well as its impact on decision making (Lux et al. 2018; Morana et al. 2020). For instance, system designers can employ biofeedback to support bidders in recognizing and regulating their own physiological arousal levels while participating in an auction (Astor et al. 2013b; Jerčić et al. 2012). There is reason to believe that these systems will become more effective with the increasing ability of machine learning to detect human emotional states based on biosensors. Specifically, the application of deep learning in affective computing has led to strong improvements in the automatic recognition of human emotions from a range of modalities (Rouast et al. 2020). It has also been shown that artificial intelligence can be used to identify psychophysiological features which contribute to a better prediction of bidding behavior (Müller et al. 2016). In this vein, leveraging the interplay of human and artificial intelligence, user assistance systems may support bidders in overcoming the detrimental impacts of auction fever.

References

Adam, M. T. P. (2010). *Measuring Emotions in Electronic Auctions*. Karlsruhe, DE: KIT Scientific Publishing.

Adam, M. T. P., Gamer, M., Krämer, J., & Weinhardt, C. (2011a). Measuring emotions in electronic markets. In *ICIS 2011 Proceedings* (pp. 1–19). Shanghai, CN.

Adam, M. T. P., Krämer, J., Seifert, S., & Weinhardt, C. (2011b). Understanding auction fever: A framework for emotional bidding. *Electronic Markets, 21*(3), 197–207. https://doi.org/10.1007/s12525-011-0068-9

Adam, M. T. P., Krämer, J., & Weinhardt, C. (2012). Excitement up! Price down! Measuring emotions in Dutch auctions. *International Journal of Electronic Commerce, 17*(2), 7–40. https://doi.org/10.2753/jec1086-4415170201

Adam, M. T. P., Krämer, J., & Müller, M. B. (2015). Auction fever! How time pressure and social competition affect bidders' arousal and bids in retail auctions. *Journal of Retailing, 91*(3), 468–485. https://doi.org/10.1016/j.jretai.2015.01.003

Adam, M. T. P., Astor, P. J., & Krämer, J. (2016). Affective images, emotion regulation and bidding behavior: An experiment on the influence of competition and community emotions in Internet auctions. *Journal of Interactive Marketing, 35*(1), 56–69. https://doi.org/10.1016/j.intmar.2015.12.002

Adam, M. T. P., Eidels, A., Lux, E., & Teubner, T. (2017). Bidding behavior in Dutch auctions: Insights from a structured literature review. *International Journal of Electronic Commerce, 21*(3), 363–397. https://doi.org/10.1080/10864415.2016.1319222

Adam, M. T. P., Ku, G., & Lux, E. (2019). Auction fever: The unrecognized effects of incidental arousal. *Journal of Experimental Social Psychology, 80*(1), 52–58. https://doi.org/10.1016/j.jesp.2018.07.009

Ariely, D., & Simonson, I. (2003). Buying, bidding, playing, or competing? Value assessment and decision dynamics in online auctions. *Journal of Consumer Psychology, 13*(1–2), 113–123. https://doi.org/10.1207/S15327663JCP13-1&2_10

Astor, P. J., Adam, M. T. P., Jähnig, C., & Seifert, S. (2011). Measuring regret: Emotional aspects of auction design. In *ECIS 2011 Proceedings* (pp. 1129–1140). Helsinki, FN.

Astor, P. J., Adam, M. T. P., Jähnig, C., & Seifert, S. (2013a). The joy of winning and the frustration of losing: A psychophysiological analysis of emotions in first-price sealed-bid auctions. *Journal of Neuroscience, Psychology, and Economics, 6*(1), 14–30. https://doi.org/10.1037/a0031406

Astor, P. J., Adam, M. T. P., Jerčić, P., Schaaff, K., & Weinhardt, C. (2013b). Integrating biosignals into information systems: A NeuroIS tool for improving emotion regulation. *Journal of Management Information Systems, 30*(3), 247–278. https://doi.org/10.2753/MIS0742-1222300309

Bradley, M. M. (2007). Emotion and motivation. In L. G. Tassinary & G. G. Berntson (Eds.), *Handbook of Psychophysiology* (pp. 602–642). Cambridge, UK: Cambridge Univ. Press.

Carare, O., & Rothkopf, M. (2005). Slow Dutch auctions. *Management Science, 51*(3), 365–373. https://doi.org/10.1287/mnsc.1040.0328

Delgado, M. R., Schotter, A., Ozbay, E. Y., & Phelps, E. A. (2008). Understanding overbidding: Using the neural circuitry of reward to design economic auctions. *Science, 321*(5897), 1849–1852. https://doi.org/10.1126/science.1158860

Engelbrecht-Wiggans, R., & Katok, E. (2008). Regret and feedback information in first-price sealed-bid auctions. *Management Science, 54*(4), 808–819.

Hariharan, A., Adam, M. T. P., Teubner, T., & Weinhardt, C. (2016). Think, feel, bid: The impact of environmental conditions on the role of bidders' cognitive and affective processes in auction bidding. *Electronic Markets, 26*(4), 339–355. https://doi.org/10.1007/s12525-016-0224-3

Hariharan, A., Adam, M. T. P., Dorner, V., Lux, E., Müller, M. B., Pfeiffer, J., & Weinhardt, C. (2017). Brownie: A platform for conducting NeuroIS experiments. *Journal of the Association for Information Systems, 18*(4), 264–296. https://doi.org/10.17705/1jais.00457

Jerčić, P., Astor, P. J., Adam, M. T. P., Hilborn, O., Schaaff, K., Lindley, C., ... Eriksson, J. (2012). A serious game using physiological interfaces for emotion regulation training in the context of financial decision-making. In *ECIS 2012 Proceedings* (pp. 1–14). Barcelona, ES.

Jung, D., Adam, M. T. P., Dorner, V., & Hariharan, A. (2017). A practical guide for human lab experiments in information systems research: A tutorial with Brownie. *Journal of Systems and Information Technology, 19*(3/4), 228–256. https://doi.org/10.1108/JSIT-06-2017-0049

Katok, E., & Kwasnica, A. M. (2008). Time is money: The effect of clock speed on seller's revenue in Dutch auctions. *Experimental Economics, 11*(4), 344–357. https://doi.org/10.1007/s10683-007-9169-x

Ku, G., Malhotra, D., & Murnighan, J. K. (2005). Towards a competitive arousal model of decision-making: A study of auction fever in live and Internet auctions. *Organizational Behavior and Human Decision Processes, 96*(2), 89–103. https://doi.org/10.1016/j.obhdp.2004.10.001

Lux, E., Adam, M. T. P., Dorner, V., Helming, S., Knierim, M. T., & Weinhardt, C. (2018). Live biofeedback as a user interface design element: A review of the literature. *Communications of the Association for Information Systems, 43*(1), 257–296. https://doi.org/10.17705/1CAIS.04318

McAfee, R. P., & McMillan, J. (1987). Auctions and bidding. *Journal of Economic Literature, 25*(2), 699–738.

Morana, S., Pfeiffer, J., & Adam, M. T. P. (2020). User assistance for intelligent systems. *Business & Information Systems Engineering,* 1–4. https://doi.org/10.1007/s12599-020-00640-5

Müller, M. B., Adam, M. T. P., Cornforth, D. J., Chiong, R., Krämer, J., & Weinhardt, C. (2016). Selecting physiological features for predicting bidding behavior in electronic auctions. In *HICSS 2016 Proceedings* (pp. 396–405). https://doi.org/10.1109/HICSS.2016.55

Murnighan, J. K. (2002). A very extreme case of the dollar auction. *Journal of Management Education, 26*(1), 56–69. https://doi.org/10.1177/105256290202600105

Myers, D. G. (2004). *Psychology* (7th ed.). New York, NY, USA: Worth Publishers.

Rick, S., & Loewenstein, G. (2008). The role of emotion in economic behavior. In M. Leis, J. M. Haviland-Jones, & L. F. Barrett (Eds.), *Handbook of Emotions* (pp. 138–156). New York, NY, USA: The Guilford Press.

Riedl, R., Davis, F. D., & Hevner, A. R. (2014). Towards a NeuroIS research methodology: Intensifying the discussion on methods, tools, and measurement. *Journal of the Association for Information Systems, 15*(10), i–xxxv.

Rouast, P. V., Adam, M. T. P., & Chiong, R. (2020). Deep learning for human affect recognition: Insights and new developments. *IEEE Transactions on Affective Computing,* 1–20. https://doi.org/10.1109/TAFFC.2018.2890471

Russel, J. (1980). A circumplex model of affect. *Journal of Personality and Social Psychology1, 39*(6), 1161–1178.

Sigmund, K., Fehr, E., & Nowak, M. A. (2002). The economics of fair play. *Scientific American, 286*(1), 82–87.

Smith, K., & Dickhaut, J. (2005). Economics and emotion: Institutions matter. *Games and Economic Behavior, 52*(2), 316–335. https://doi.org/10.1016/j.geb.2004.06.017

Teubner, T., Adam, M. T. P., & Riordan, R. (2015). The impact of computerized agents on immediate emotions, overall arousal and bidding behavior in electronic auctions. *Journal of the Association for Information Systems, 16*(10), 838–879. https://doi.org/10.17705/1jais.00457

van den Bos, W., Talwar, A., & McClure, S. M. (2013). Neural correlates of reinforcement learning and social preferences in competitive bidding. *Journal of Neuroscience, 33*(5), 2137–2146. https://doi.org/10.1523/JNEUROSCI.3095-12.2013

Zajonc, R. B. (1984). On the primacy of affect. *American Psychologist, 39*(2), 117–123.

Marc T. P. Adam is an associate professor of Computing and Information Technology at the University of Newcastle, Australia. In his research, he investigates the interplay of users' cognition and affect in human–computer interaction. In 2006, he completed an undergraduate degree in Computer Science from the University of Applied Sciences Würzburg-Schweinfurt, Germany. In 2010, he received a PhD in Information Systems from Karlsruhe Institute of Technology, Germany, supervised by Christof Weinhardt. He is a founding member of the Society for NeuroIS. His research has been published in top international outlets such as *IEEE Journal on Biomedical and Health Informatics*, *IEEE Transactions on Affective Computing*, the *Journal of the Association for Information Systems*, the *Journal of Management Information Systems*, and the *Journal of Retailing*.

Jan Krämer is a full professor of Information Systems and holds the chair of Internet and Telecommunications Business at the University of Passau, Germany. He is also an academic co-director at the Centre on Regulation in Europe (CERRE), a Brussels-based think tank. His current research interests include predominantly the regulation of telecommunications and Internet markets, as well as digital ecosystems and data-driven business models. Previously, he headed a research group on telecommunications markets at the Karlsruhe Institute of Technology (KIT), where he also obtained a diploma in Business and Economics Engineering (2005) with a focus on computer science, telematics, and operations research, and a PhD in Economics (2007), both with distinction. In 2013 he received a habilitation degree from KIT under the supervision of Christof Weinhardt. His research has been published in top-ranked scholarly journals of Information Systems, Marketing, and Economic Regulation, such as *Management Science*, *Information Systems Research*, the *Journal of Retailing*, and the *Journal of Industrial Economics*. Furthermore, he is the editor and author of several interdisciplinary books on the regulation of telecommunications markets, associate editor of the journal *Business & Information Systems Engineering*, and a member of the editorial board of the journals *Review of Network Economics* and *Telecommunications Policy*. Krämer has served as academic consultant for leading firms in the telecommunications and Internet industry, as well as for governmental institutions, such as the German Federal Ministry for Economic Affairs and the European Commission.

Studying Conceptual Modeling Processes: A Modeling Tool, Research Observatory, and Multimodal Observation Setup

Stefan Strecker, Kristina Rosenthal, and Benjamin Ternes

Abstract What do (non-)experienced modelers reason while conceptual modeling and how do they arrive at modeling decisions, which modeling and learning difficulties do they face and why, and how do they overcome these difficulties by tailored modeling tool support are questions of relevance and importance to practicing modelers and, likewise, to conceptual modeling research. For the past 7 years, we have been designing, developing, and evaluating a modeling tool integrating a research observatory aimed at studying individual modeling processes online, in the field, and under laboratory conditions—to contribute to a richer understanding of modeler reasoning and decision-making, to identify common modeling and learning difficulties, and, ultimately, to design tool support to mitigate difficulties and to improve assistance for (non-)experienced modelers. We present an overview of the modeling observatory and of a corresponding multimodal observation setup.

1 Conceptual Models and Conceptual Modeling

Conceptual models enable and empower us to shape the digital transformation of organizations—of small and medium businesses, large corporations, public administration, unions, clubs, and associations of all kinds. Without conceptual models, e.g., data models, object models, business process models, and more advanced (enterprise) models, of such enterprises and their social action systems in co-action with their computer information systems, we cannot understand the complex human-computer interactions that concern us and cannot fully seize their potential to address the problems of modern society and economy (Frank and Strecker 2021).

S. Strecker (✉) · K. Rosenthal · B. Ternes
FernUniversität in Hagen, Enterprise Modelling Research Group, Lehrstuhl für
Betriebswirtschaftslehre, insbes. Entwicklung von Informationssystemen, Fakultät für
Wirtschaftswissenschaft, Hagen, Germany
e-mail: stefan.strecker@fernuni-hagen.de; kristina.rosenthal@fernuni-hagen.de;
benjamin.ternes@fernuni-hagen.de

© The Author(s) 2021
H. Gimpel et al. (eds.), *Market Engineering*,
https://doi.org/10.1007/978-3-030-66661-3_6

Conceptual modeling—as an activity, e.g., when constructing a data model as Entity-Relationship diagram (Chen 1976)—involves an intricate array of cognitive processes and performed actions, including goal setting, abstracting, conceptualizing, associating and contextualizing, interpreting and sense-making, evaluating and judging, anticipating and envisioning and thinking ahead, drawing and visualizing, and, in group settings, communicating, discussing, and agreeing. The activity of conceptual modeling is, therefore, at one point in time, tool-mediated and based on interacting with modeling tools supporting conceptual modelers, e.g., by way of graphical modeling editors. Performing conceptual modeling is construed as a complex task based on codified and tacit knowledge, a task that requires mastering theoretical foundations, modeling languages (such as Entity-Relationship Model, Chen 1976), modeling methods, and modeling tools, applying them to practical problems, and, while performing a modeling process, critically thinking and reflecting upon an application domain in terms of the technical languages spoken in the targeted domain—the domain's technical terminology and its use in domain-specific technical languages, their imprecision, ambiguities, and related challenges—with the intention to (re-)construct the selected aspects of organizational reality and to reshape organizational reality by (re-)presenting a new perspective and reworked terminology and language embodied and conveyed by conceptual models (Frank et al. 2014).

The process (the actual "act") of conceptual modeling has for long received limited attention in conceptual modeling research (Hoppenbrouwers et al. 2005; 2006) but has recently seen increasing interest from researchers (e.g., Bera et al. 2019, Claes et al. 2015, Pinggera et al. 2015, Serral et al. 2016, Wilmont et al. 2017). How conceptual modeling is performed by modelers, how modeling processes proceed, which modeling challenges and difficulties modelers experience and why, and how to overcome these difficulties by tailored modeling support have been subject to studies on the cognitive processes and performed actions constituting conceptual modeling (e.g., Batra and Davis 1992, Bera 2011, Chaiyasut and Shanks 1994, Srinivasan and Te'eni 1995, Venable 1996). Still, further research on conceptual modeling processes is needed to understand the reasoning of modelers and their deliberations (e.g., about modeling decisions) and whether different (idealized) types of modelers can be identified, e.g., by determining the patterns of modeling processes and/or difficulties, and whether these modeler types benefit from modeling tool support tailored to overcome their difficulties. Similarly, further research is required to study how individuals learn conceptual modeling, how their learning progresses, and what their needs are for learning support and tool assistance (Rosenthal et al. 2019). Studying progressively more and more individual modeling processes under varying conditions, i.e., online and in the field and the laboratory, promises to shed further light on these open questions and, ultimately, to enable us to design targeted (tool) support for modelers at different stages of their learning and mastering of conceptual modeling.

Against this background, we pursue a research program to contribute to a richer and more complete understanding of individual modeling processes and of the learning of conceptual modeling—aiming for the overarching research objective of designing, implementing, and evaluating targeted tool support for modelers at different stages of their learning and mastering of conceptual modeling. In our pursuit of this research objective, we operate on the basic assumption that modelers' individual modeling processes demand a study from multiple complementary perspectives to account for the richness and complexity of conceptual modeling as a learning and performing task—following Berger and Luckmann's inspiring insight that "the object of thought becomes progressively clearer with this accumulation of different perspectives on it" (Berger and Luckmann 1967, p. 10). Ultimately, the research program aims to progressively add to the empirical and theoretical foundation of conceptual modeling research, e.g., by identifying modeling difficulties and by developing a taxonomic theory of such difficulties as a step toward advancing the body of knowledge to offer guidance for designing and implementing *targeted tailored* (tool) support for conceptual modelers. As part of this research program, we configure and validate a multimodal observation setup and corresponding analysis procedure that we realize by TOOL, a web browser-based modeling tool and research observatory implementing an array of observation and analysis features.

The subsequent Sect. 2 introduces the multimodal observation setup. Section 3 demonstrates how TOOL supports the observation setup, and Sect. 4 reports on a series of laboratory observations on individual modeling processes and concludes with lessons learned.

2 Multimodal Observation Setup

Observing conceptual modeling processes poses methodological challenges. For example, neither the reasoning of modelers nor the corresponding deliberations on modeling decisions are immediately accessible nor directly observable. Research on conceptual modeling processes has reverted to observable aspects of modeling processes such as modelers' interactions with software tools, modelers' eye movements, or their verbalizations of their own thought processes while modeling—as verbal protocols following the "think-aloud" method (Ericsson and Simon 1993, van Someren et al. 1994). Following this trajectory, we compile and arrange multiple complementary modes of observation for a multimodal observation setup (see Fig. 1). In particular, we combine four modes of observation:

1. Audio-taping think-aloud (verbal) protocols during conceptual modeling by a subject, i.e., while working on a modeling task, to obtain insights into the subject's cognitive processes during modeling, e.g., into the modeler's reasoning and deliberations toward modeling decision and also into difficulties the modeler encounters and expresses verbally
2. Tracking modeler interactions with the modeling canvas to observe specific modeling decisions, in particular, decisions with respect to placing a new model element on the modeling canvas (e.g., a rectangular graphical symbol representing an entity type, say "Customer," in an entity-relationship diagram), to

1. Tracking modeler interactions
   with modeling canvas

Intent: Observe modeling process
in terms of new & changed model
elements, element repositioning,
deletion of elements, renaming of
elements

2. Audio-taping think-aloud
   (verbal) protocols

Intent: Obtain insights into cognitive
processes during modeling, e.g,
modeler reasoning, modeling decisions

3. Surveying subjects pre
   and post modeling

Intent: Obtain information on prior
modeling experience, perceived
modeling difficulties, tool usability

4. Videotaping subjects
   (from an "over the shoulder" perspective)

Intent: Observe body language and movements
e.g. when switching media, interrupting modeling flow

Fig. 1 Complementary modes of observation

    change an existing model element, to element repositioning, to deletion of model elements, and to renaming a model element (giving it a new label)
3. Surveying subjects pre- and post-modeling to collect information on modeler demographics and to obtain self-disclosed information on modeling experience, perceived modeling difficulties, and tool usability, i.e., a post-modeling survey collects information about difficulties with using the tool's graphical editor, tool support, and overall user experience to evaluate TOOL as a design artifact
4. Videotaping subjects (e.g., from an "over-the-shoulder" perspective) to observe nonverbal cues on the individual modeling process, in particular on modeling difficulties, conveyed by body language and movement, e.g., when switching between media from the computer screen to paper and back or when interrupting the modeling flow as indicated by gestures

    The main rationale for combining these modes of observation lies in their complementarity (Rosenthal and Strecker 2019): The configured setup combines observation by think-aloud protocols and video recordings with modeler-tool interaction tracking and survey data to observe a wide range of facets about individual modeling processes including identifying modeling and learning difficulties expressed verbally by the modeler during and after modeling as well as nonverbally indicated through interactions with the modeling tool and its modeling canvas as well as by body language and movements. Specifically, analyzing think-aloud protocols has shown promising results for understanding the cognitive processes of subjects working on problem-solving tasks in general and on modeling tasks in particular (e.g., Batra and Davis 1992, Srinivasan and Te'eni 1995), and we consider verbalization of thoughts as the best available means of expression for achieving insights into modelers' reasoning as our spoken language provides a rich and flexible tool to express our thinking. However, to ask subjects to think aloud is a second-best approach, warranted only because it is not possible to directly access and capture cognitive processes and, thus, modeler reasoning while modeling. Modelers may have difficulties verbalizing their reasoning while modeling (Blech et al. 2019) on principle accounts (because verbalizing one's own thoughts can be difficult) or on modeling-related accounts (e.g., because of the difficulty of finding the right words to express oneself). Nonetheless, among all possible alternative modes of observation, think-aloud verbalization promises the richest insight into quintessential non-directly observable cognitive processes of an individual modeling process.

Modelers' reasoning, their chain of thought, and line of modeling arguments will, still, not always be observable from think-aloud protocols alone, since nonverbal information such as modelers' movements and gestures entail important additional cues about their perception of, for instance, modeling challenges and difficulties. Hence, the configured observation setup complements think-aloud protocols with videotaping modelers to allow for additional visual clues, e.g., regarding interaction with pen and paper or modelers' (e.g., erratic) movements during modeling plus modeler-tool interactions. Additionally, subjects are surveyed about their individual modeling process before and after they work on a (controlled) modeling task. Following Berger and Luckmann, this observation setup combines multiple perspectives on modeling processes and supports mixed methods research designs in which open (narratives, verbal protocols, video recordings) and closed (more) standardized (tracking data, survey data) modes of observation are combined to obtain a more complete picture of the phenomenon under investigation (Creswell and Plano Clark 2018).

3   Modeling Tool and Research Observatory

The multimodal observation setup is realized based on the modeling tool TOOL integrating a research observatory designed for observing and analyzing individual modeling processes (Ternes 2017, Ternes and Strecker 2018, Ternes et al. 2019). Resulting from a multi-year design science research project, the TOOL research prototype currently implements two graphical modeling editors (see Fig. 2): (1) an editor for a didactically adapted, simplified variant of the Entity-Relationship model (ERM) for data modeling and (2) an editor for a subset of the Business Process Model and Notation (BPMN 2) for business process modeling (Frank and Strecker 2021). For studying individual modeling processes under laboratory conditions, in the field, and in online settings, TOOL integrates a research observatory adapted to the multimodal observation setup (Ternes et al. 2020a;c). The modeling observatory presently features five modes of observation (as in-browser features):

1. Recording of tink-aloud (verbal) protocols via computer audio input (in addition to external audio recording used in laboratory settings; see Fig. 1)
2. Recording of the subject's computer screen to provide an additional video recording of the modeling process
3. Timed-discrete event tracking and recording of modeler interactions with the tool's modeling canvas
4. Tracking and recording of mouse pointer movement on the modeling canvas
5. Conducting and recording on-screen pre- and post-modeling surveys of subjects (as an alternative to printed surveys)

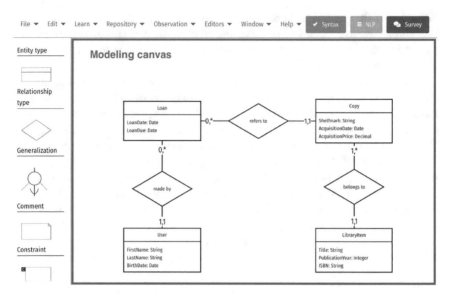

Fig. 2 Graphical editor for data modeling (with modeling canvas highlighted) (Ternes et al. 2020a)

The observatory also features data visualizations and analysis techniques for interpreting the recorded data: (a) Replay of the recorded modeler-tool interactions of a modeling process in real time or step by step, either as single replay or in comparison of up to four modeling processes shown concurrently over normalized time (see Fig. 3a): The step-by-step replay visually shows every step of the model construction, whereas the automatic replay shows model construction in real time, both allowing for additional visual inspection of the modeling process. (b) Replay with heat map overlays on mouse pointer position, dwell time, and mouse clicks (see Fig. 3b): Such heat maps allow insights into spatial areas of the modeling canvas in focus and into difficulties experienced with the modeling tool, e.g., indicated by uncontrolled mouse clicking. (c) Dot diagrams (see Fig. 3c), a data visualization inspired by PPMCharts (Claes et al. 2015) and dotted charts (Song and van der Aalst 2007): The vertical axis indicates the consecutively numbered model elements that are created (green circle), changed (blue circle), repositioned (gray), deleted (red circle), or relabeled (orange circle). The dot diagram visually differentiates the mentioned five types of specific modeling decisions (introduce new model element on canvas, change existing element, reposition an element, delete an element, relabel an element) and allows to clarify audio/video and tracking observations in cases when the observed modeling behavior is ambiguous. (d) Bar charts and related visualizations of survey data prepare for survey analysis, e.g., by visually representing results from closed-ended questions (see Fig. 3d). The visualizations and techniques (a–d) are used to further explore the observed situations identified as deviant or unclear in the audio and video protocol and to identify and clarify

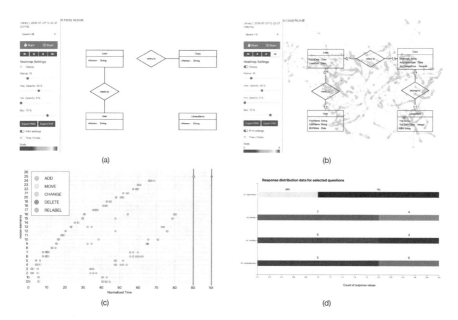

Fig. 3 Data visualization and analysis techniques (Rosenthal et al. 2020b). (**a**) Replay. (**b**) heat map, (**c**) dotted diagram, (**d**) survey results

anomalous modeling behavior by manual inspection. Additionally, the research observatory is adaptable to different research designs by selecting and combining modes of observation (1–5), by tailoring surveys, and by sequencing a corresponding observation workflow. A video demonstration of the research observatory is available at https://vimeo.com/441854796/5237d3782a.

From the outset run as a design science research project, two essential requirements drive the development of the TOOL research prototype: (1) platform independence and (2) ease of use and usability to the greatest extent economically viable. Further design considerations, requirements, and operating principles are outlined in Ternes (2017), Ternes and Strecker (2018), and Ternes et al. (2019; 2020a;c). In a nutshell, TOOL is designed and implemented as a web application with a JavaScript-driven web browser frontend and a Java EE (Enterprise Edition)-based server backend and, as a design artifact, also serves as a research laboratory for studying (web technology) software stacks and toolchains (see Fig. 4). The current working prototype sizes up to 55,000 lines of code (LoC) in the frontend and about 32,000 LoC in the server backend. TOOL has been applied to an initial test series, to pilot studies, as well as in a series of research studies on individual modeling processes at the University of Hagen, Germany; the Universitat Politècnica de València, Spain; and the Katholieke Universiteit Leuven, Belgium (see next section). Moreover, TOOL has supplemented our teaching of an undergraduate course on modeling business information systems where students use it for their assignments.

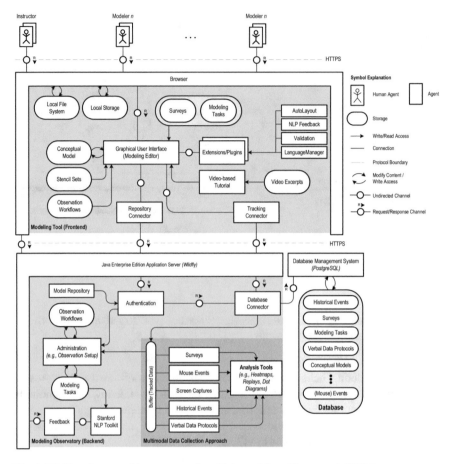

Fig. 4 TOOL software architecture overview (Enhanced from Ternes et al. 2020a)

4 Data Integration, Data Analysis, and Lessons Learned

A series of laboratory studies validates the multimodal observation setup in combination with the research observatory and modeling tool: For example, we have been studying individual modeling processes of experienced and non-experienced modelers to identify the modeling difficulties these modelers face while performing a data modeling task (Rosenthal and Strecker 2019, Rosenthal et al. 2020b). In a nutshell, subjects are provided with a natural language description of a data modeling task, receive instructions and an introduction to the graphical editor, and are then asked to think out loud while performing the modeling task. To achieve insights into the observed individual modeling processes, the collected data is purposefully integrated and analyzed to identify modeling difficulties and to understand modelers' reasoning: Each verbal think-aloud protocol is linked

Fig. 5 Coding audiovisual protocols (Screenshot from MAXQDA, VERBI Software 2018)

and time-synchronized to the video recording to produce an audiovisual protocol comprising the data from both modes of observation. To add structure to the data, we code these videos by systematically assigning codes to video segments/clips (following, e.g., Miles et al. 2014, pp. 81f.) using a qualitative data analysis software (see Fig. 5 for an example from a pre-test). Directly coding the audiovisual protocols rather than transcribing the verbalizations allows to benefit from the complementary angles provided by the respective mode of observation. Following problem-solving research (Newell and Simon 1972), we use the concept of cognitive breakdowns (e.g., Bera 2011) to identify modeling difficulties which modelers experience while constructing a conceptual model and, hence, use cognitive breakdown as deductive code. We define a cognitive breakdown as a cognitive difficulty which a modeler experiences when constructing a conceptual model based on a natural language description (Bera 2011, p. 4)—"when a line of thought fails" (Burton-Jones and Meso 2008, p. 768). Such a cognitive breakdown can manifest itself in a modeler explicitly verbalizing a difficulty while modeling or in interrupting or terminating a modeling activity, e.g., a modeling activity which is not completed, but instead the modeler switches to another activity (Bera 2011, p. 4). Segments in which a subject encounters a difficulty or an obstacle are initially marked with the code "cognitive breakdown," i.e., when the subject explicitly verbalizes a difficulty experienced during modeling or when the subject interrupts or terminates a modeling activity. This code is complemented with codes generally anticipated in think-aloud protocols as, e.g., talking about non-task-related issues, evaluation of the task at a meta-level, silent periods, and actions outside of the modeling tool (following, e.g., van Someren et al. 1994, p. 122). During coding, the coding scheme is complemented with emerging codes and sub-codes—allowing for refinements according to the actual behavior exhibited in the modeling processes. We supplement coding audiovisual protocols with analyzing timed modeler-tool interactions allowing us to identify peculiar situations. Segments identified as unclear in the videos are submitted for closer inspection by analyzing the recorded modeler-tool interactions in the respective time period to better understand the observed situation and to decide on assigning a code: Dot diagrams visualizing modeling processes and replays of model construction are used for further exploring situations identified as ambiguous or deviant in the audiovisual protocols. Vice versa, anomalous data in the recorded modeler-tool interactions is identified and further investigated through analyzing audiovisual protocols. Data integration is taken one step further by reviewing the pre- and post-modeling surveys and, thus, by supplementing another mode of observation (self-disclosed by the observed modeler). This coding step proved valuable especially as the individually perceived difficulties serve as indication for closer inspecting and deciding on assigning a code in the audiovisual protocols. We provide a more detailed description of the data analysis strategy and coding steps in Rosenthal and Strecker (2019, pp. 8–10).

Observations on individual modeling processes we performed so far led us to identify ten types of modeling difficulties the observed subjects faced while performing the data modeling task: The types of difficulties relate to different aspects of constructing conceptual data models, i.e., entity types, relationship types, attributes, and cardinalities. The majority of the difficulties encountered by the participants relate to modeling relationship types, i.e., deciding between modeling an entity type or a relationship type, developing sensible identifiers for relationship types, and determining cardinalities (Rosenthal and Strecker 2019, Rosenthal et al. 2020a). To overcome these modeling difficulties when formulating sensible identifiers (Breuker et al. 2016), we presently research and develop extensions to TOOL for automated modeler assistance based on natural language processing (NLP) (Manning et al. 2014) to provide tool-generated suggestions on labeling model elements at modeling time. To the best of our knowledge, this design science research is among the first to integrate a web-based data modeling tool with NLP to automatically process an arbitrary natural language description of a modeling task (in terms of its morphological structure) to identify words and phrases as suggestions for labels for model elements (Ternes et al. 2020b).

Conducting studies with experienced and non-experienced modelers demonstrates that the multimodal observation setup in combination with the research observatory opens entirely new paths for insights into conceptual modeling processes. Analyzing the collected data exemplifies that *only* the integration of the complementary observation modes allowed us to identify a wide range of modeling difficulties by identifying cognitive breakdowns and also to reason about the cause and type of difficulty observed: Supplementing the analysis of audiovisual protocols with analyzing tracked modeler-tool interactions enabled us to better understand ambiguous situations and to identify further deviant interactions, while reviewing the post-modeling survey proved especially valuable as the perceived difficulties served as indication for closer inspection of audiovisual protocols. Hence, our current findings suggest that combining multiple modes of observation to study individual modeling processes contributes to achieving a richer and more complete understanding of modeling processes and modeling difficulties encountered during model construction. Informed by these initial insights, we are preparing for further small-scale and large-scale studies aimed at deepening and substantiating our understanding of modeling difficulties and identifying patterns of modeling processes.

References

Batra D, Davis JG (1992) Conceptual data modelling in database design: Similarities and differences between expert and novice designers. International Journal of Man-Machine Studies 37(1):83–101

Bera P (2011) Situations That Affect Modelers' Cognitive Difficulties: An Empirical Assessment. In: Sambamurthy V, Tanniru M (eds) Proceedings of the 17th Americas Conference on Information Systems, AMCIS 2011, Detroit, Michigan, USA, August 4–8, 2011

Bera P, Soffer P, Parsons J (2019) Using Eye Tracking to Expose Cognitive Processes in Understanding Conceptual Models. MIS Quarterly 43(4)

Berger PL, Luckmann T (1967) The Social Construction of Reality. Anchor Books, New York, NY, reprint of the 1966 original published by Doubleday, Garden City, NJ

Blech C, Gaschler R, Bilalić M (2019) Why do people fail to see simple solutions? Using think-aloud protocols to uncover the mechanism behind the Einstellung (mental set) effect. Thinking & Reasoning

Breuker D, Matzner M, Delfmann P, Becker J (2016) Comprehensible predictive models for business processes. MIS Quarterly 40(4):1009–1034

Burton-Jones A, Meso P (2008) The Effects of Decomposition Quality and Multiple Forms of Information on Novices' Understanding of a Domain from a Conceptual Model. Journal of the Association for Information Systems 9(12):748–802

Chaiyasut P, Shanks GG (1994) Conceptual data modeling process: A study of novice and expert data modellers. In: Halpin TA, Meersman R (eds) Proceedings of the 1st International Conference on Object-Role Modeling, ORM-1, Magnetic Island, Australia, 4–6 July 1994, pp 310–323

Chen PPS (1976) The entity-relationship model—toward a unified view of data. ACM Transactions on Database Systems 1(1):9–36, https://doi.org/10.1145/320434.320440

Claes J, Vanderfeesten I, Pinggera J, Reijers HA, Weber B, Poels G (2015) A visual analysis of the process of process modeling. Information Systems and e-Business Management 13(1):147–190

Creswell JW, Plano Clark VL (2018) Designing and Conducting Mixed Methods Research, 3rd edn. Sage, Los Angeles, CA

Ericsson KA, Simon HA (1993) Protocol analysis: Verbal reports as data, 2nd edn. MIT Press, Cambridge, MA

Frank U, Strecker S (2021) Modellierung betrieblicher Informationssysteme : Einführung, theoretische Grundlagen und praktische Anwendungen. DeGruyter, Berlin, in preparation

Frank U, Strecker S, Fettke P, vom Brocke J, Becker J, Sinz EJ (2014) The Research Field "Modeling Business Information Systems" : Current Challenges and Elements of a Future Research Agenda. Business & Information Systems Engineering 6(1):39–43

Hoppenbrouwers SJBA, Proper HA, van der Weide TP (2005) A fundamental view on the process of conceptual modeling. In: Delcambre L, Kop C, Mayr HC, Mylopoulos J, Pastor O (eds) 24th International Conference on Conceptual Modeling (ER). Lecture Notes in Computer Science, Springer, Berlin, Heidelberg, vol 3716, pp 128–143

Hoppenbrouwers SJBA, Lindeman L, Proper HA (2006) Capturing modeling processes – towards the MoDial modeling laboratory. In: Meersman R, Tari Z, Herrero P (eds) On the Move to Meaningful Internet Systems 2006: OTM 2006 Workshops. Lecture Notes in Computer Science, Springer, Berlin, Heidelberg, vol 4278, pp 1242–1252

Manning CD, Surdeanu M, Bauer J, Finkel JR, Bethard S, McClosky D (2014) The Stanford CoreNLP natural language processing toolkit. In: Proceedings of the 52nd Annual Meeting of the Association for Computational Linguistics, ACL 2014, June 22–27, 2014, Baltimore, MD, USA, System Demonstrations, pp 55–60

Miles MB, Huberman AM, Saldaña J (2014) Qualitative Data Analysis: A Methods Sourcebook, 3rd edn. Sage, Thousand Oaks, CA

Newell A, Simon HA (1972) Human problem solving. Prentice-Hall, Englewood Cliffs, NJ

Pinggera J, Soffer P, Fahland D, Weidlich M, Zugal S, Weber B, Reijers HA, Mendling J (2015) Styles in business process modeling: an exploration and a model. Software & Systems Modeling 14(3):1055–1080

Rosenthal K, Strecker S (2019) Toward a Taxonomy of Modeling Difficulties: A Multi-Modal Study on Individual Modeling Processes. In: Krcmar H, Fedorowicz J, Boh WF, Leimeister JM, Wattal S (eds) Proceedings of the 40th International Conference on Information Systems, ICIS 2019, Munich, Germany, December 15–18, 2019

Rosenthal K, Ternes B, Strecker S (2019) Learning Conceptual Modeling: Structuring Overview, Research Themes and Paths for Future Research. In: vom Brocke J, Gregor S, Müller O (eds) 27th European Conference on Information Systems, ECIS 2019, Stockholm and Uppsala, Sweden, June 8–14, 2019

Rosenthal K, Strecker S, Pastor O (2020a) Modeling Difficulties in Data Modeling - Similarities and Differences Between Experienced and Non-experienced Modelers. In: Dobbie G, Frank U, Kappel G, Liddle SW, Mayr HC (eds) Proceedings of the 39th International Conference, ER 2020, Vienna, Austria, November 3–6, 2020, Springer, pp 501–511

Rosenthal K, Ternes B, Strecker S (2020b) Understanding individual processes of conceptual modeling: A multi-modal observation and data generation approach. In: Bork D, Karagiannis D, Mayr HC (eds) Proceedings of the Modellierung 2020, Vienna, Austria, February 19–21, 2020, Gesellschaft für Informatik e.V., Lecture Notes in Informatics, vol P-302, pp 77–92

Serral E, De Weerdt J, Sedrakyan G, Snoeck M (2016) Automating Immediate and Personalized Feedback: Taking Conceptual Modelling Education to a Next Level. In: 10th International Conference on Research Challenges in Information Science (RCIS), IEEE, Grenoble, France, pp 1–6

van Someren MW, Barnard YF, Sandberg JAC (1994) The Think Aloud Method: A Practical Guide to Modelling Cognitive Processes. Academic Press, London

Song M, van der Aalst WMP (2007) Supporting process mining by showing events at a glance. In: 17th Annual Workshop on Information Technologies and Systems (WITS), Montreal, Canada, pp 139–145

Srinivasan A, Te'eni D (1995) Modeling as Constrained Problem Solving: An Empirical Study of the Data Modeling Process. Management Science 41(3):419–434, https://doi.org/10.1287/mnsc.41.3.419

Ternes B (2017) Design and evaluation of a web-based modeling platform to support the learning of conceptual modeling and of studying the corresponding learning processes. In: Gulden J, Nurcan S, Reinhartz-Berger I, Guédria W, Bera P, Guerreiro S, Fellmann M, Weidlich M (eds) Joint Proceedings of the Radar tracks at the 18th BPMDS, and the 22nd EMMSAD, and the 8th International Workshop on Enterprise Modeling and Information Systems Architectures (EMISA) co-located with the 29th International Conference on Advanced Information Systems Engineering 2017 (CAiSE 2017), Essen, Germany, June 12–13, 2017, CEUR-WS.org, CEUR Workshop Proceedings, vol 1859, pp 138–142

Ternes B, Strecker S (2018) A web-based modeling tool for studying the learning of conceptual modeling. In: Schaefer I, Karagiannis D, Vogelsang A, Méndez D, Seidl C (eds) Modellierung 2018, Braunschweig, Germany, February 21–23, 2020, Gesellschaft für Informatik e.V., Lecture Notes in Informatics, vol P-280, pp 325–328

Ternes B, Strecker S, Rosenthal K, Barth H (2019) A browser-based modeling tool for studying the learning of conceptual modeling based on a multi-modal data collection approach. In: Ludwig T, Pipek V (eds) 14th International Conference on Wirtschaftsinformatik (WI 2019), Siegen, Germany, February 24–27, 2019, pp 1984–1988

Ternes B, Rosenthal K, Barth H, Strecker S (2020a) TOOL - modeling observatory & tool: An update. In: Michael J, Bork D, Fill H, Fettke P, Karagiannis D, Köpke J, Koschmider A, Mayr HC, Rehse J, Reimer U, Striewe M, Tropmann-Frick M, Ullrich M (eds) Companion Proceedings of Modellierung 2020 Short, Workshop and Tools & Demo Papers co-located with Modellierung 2020, Vienna, Austria, February 19–21, 2020, CEUR-WS.org, CEUR Workshop Proceedings, vol 2542, pp 198–202

Ternes B, Rosenthal K, Strecker S (2020b) Automated Assistance of Data Modelers: A Heuristics-Based Natural Language Processing Approach. Internal Working Paper. Enterprise Modelling Research Group, University of Hagen, Germany

Ternes B, Rosenthal K, Strecker S, Bartels J (2020c) TOOL—A Modeling Observatory & Tool for Studying Individual Modeling Processes. In: Michael J, Torres V (eds) ER Forum, Demo and Posters 2020 co-located with 39th International Conference on Conceptual Modeling (ER 2020), Vienna, Austria, November 3–6, 2020, CEUR-WS.org, CEUR Workshop Proceedings, vol 2716, pp 178–182

Venable JR (1996) Teaching novice conceptual data modellers to become experts. In: International Conference Software Engineering: Education and Practice, IEEE, Dunedin, New Zealand, pp 50–56

VERBI Software (2018) MAXQDA Standard 12. https://www.maxqda.com, accessed: 2020-11-12

Wilmont I, Hoppenbrouwers S, Barendsen E (2017) An Observation Method for Behavioral Analysis of Collaborative Modeling Skills. In: Metzger A, Persson A (eds) Advanced Information Systems Engineering Workshops. CAiSE 2017. Lecture Notes in Business Information Processing, vol 286, Springer, Cham, pp 59–71

Engineering Energy Markets: The Past, the Present, and the Future

Clemens van Dinther, Christoph M. Flath, Johannes Gaerttner, Julian Huber, Esther Mengelkamp, Alexander Schuller, Philipp Staudt, and Anke Weidlich

Abstract Since the beginning of the energy sector liberalization, the design of energy markets has become a prominent field of research. Markets nowadays facilitate efficient resource allocation in many fields of energy system operation, such as plant dispatch, control reserve provisioning, delimitation of related carbon emissions, grid congestion management, and, more recently, smart grid concepts and local energy trading. Therefore, good market designs play an important role in enabling the *energy transition* toward a more sustainable energy supply for all. In this chapter, we retrace how market engineering shaped the development of energy

C. van Dinther (✉)
ESB Business School at Reutlingen University, Reutlingen, Germany
e-mail: clemens.van_dinther@reutlingen-university.de

C. M. Flath
Julius-Maximilians-Universität Würzburg, Würzburg, Germany
e-mail: christoph.flath@uni-wuerzburg.de

J. Gaerttner
Siemens Digital Logistics, Karlsruhe, Germany
e-mail: johannes.gaerttner@siemens-logistics.com

J. Huber
FZI Forschungszentrum Informatik, Karlsruhe, Germany
e-mail: julian.huber@fzi.de

E. Mengelkamp
MK Consulting, Karlsruhe, Germany

A. Schuller
Audi AG, Ingolstadt, Germany

P. Staudt
Karlsruhe Institute of Technology, Karlsruhe, Germany
e-mail: philipp.staudt@kit.edu

A. Weidlich
Albert-Ludwigs-Universität Freiburg, Freiburg, Germany
e-mail: anke.weidlich@inatech.uni-freiburg.de

© The Author(s) 2021
H. Gimpel et al. (eds.), *Market Engineering*,
https://doi.org/10.1007/978-3-030-66661-3_7

113

markets and how the research focus shifted from national wholesale markets to more decentralized and location-sensitive concepts.

1 Introduction

Power markets rank among the most complex marketplaces operated at present. Several interrelated markets have evolved in many countries, which together facilitate efficient and reliable operation of the electricity system. Starting from wholesale power exchanges and control reserve procurement platforms, new products and trading platforms came into play, such as emission allowance exchanges, marketplaces for redispatch, and other flexibility products or local energy markets.

Following the postulation formulated by Roth (2002) or Weinhardt et al. (2003), among others, markets should be designed using engineering methods. The complexity of the electricity sector and its high importance for a competitive economy calls for modeling methods that help gain insights into the dynamics of power markets and that are capable of properly representing the relevant complex aspects. Computational methods and experiments are useful engineering tools that support analyses in the process of designing complex markets.

Figure 1 summarizes important periods and events of the energy market development. These can be seen as milestones on the way toward more sustainable energy systems. In the European Union, the vision of *Clean energy for all Europeans* nicely phrases the direction into which the energy system is planned to evolve, and it relies to a large extent on markets to ensure efficiency, facilitate emissions management, and allow consumers to actively participate in energy system operation.

This contribution recaps the history of the most prominent research topics in energy market engineering. The methods applied are reflected in the context of these research questions. It is shown how the market engineering framework (Weinhardt et al. 2003) contributes valuable elements to power market design. Finally, an outlook on the most urgent research challenges in the next years is given.

2 Energy Sector Developments

In the following, some prominent market design questions related to energy sector developments are recapped, and the methods applied in the respective context are reviewed. As sketched in Fig. 1, the development starts with market liberalization (Sect. 2.1) and the later introduction of carbon trading (Sect. 2.2). It continues with integrating the demand side and flexibility (Sect. 2.3) and with managing congestion in highly renewable energy systems (Sect. 2.4). A very recent focus, finally, is peer-to-peer energy trading (Sect. 2.5), which fosters consumer/prosumer participation.

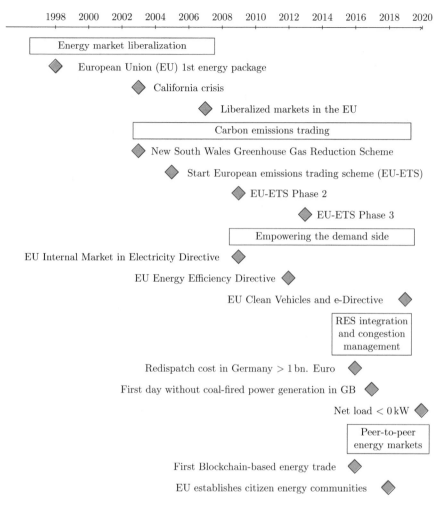

Fig. 1 Periods and milestones in the international energy sector development

2.1 Emergence of Power Markets

For the power sector, the 1990s were marked by deregulation policies. In many regions, formerly state-owned energy suppliers were transformed into private companies, network and generation were separated, and the networks were placed under state supervision by regulatory authorities. In this way, a market economy framework was created, which also characterizes the current structure of the energy sector. All this was done with the aim of increasing cost efficiency.

One important development after electricity sector liberalization was the establishment of open electronic power exchanges, which broadened and gradually replaced the formerly prevalent mutual exchange of electric energy among vertically integrated utilities (Strecker and Weinhardt 2001). The double-auction format became the dominant market institution for electricity trading. In a sealed-bid double auction, both buyers and sellers submit bids specifying the prices at which they are willing to buy or sell a certain good. Buying bids are then ranked from the highest to the lowest, selling bids from the lowest to the highest bid price. The intersection of the so-formed supply and demand functions determines the market clearing quantity and gives a range of possible prices from which the market clearing price is chosen according to some arbitrary rule (McAfee and McMillan 1987). One prominent research stream in energy market design was which settlement rule— mostly pay-as-bid vs. uniform price—performs best in terms of efficiency, consumer surplus, profits, welfare, and average prices (Federico and Rahman 2003, Kahn et al. 2001, Son et al. 2004) and came to different results.

In many countries, incumbent market players continued to have high market shares, making them the dominant players in power markets. This left large companies with some potential to act strategically and gave rise to research streams focusing on (the potential for) market power exertion, mainly applying game theoretic approaches (Stoft 1999) or agent-based simulation (Borenstein et al. 1999, Nicolaisen et al. 2001, Weidlich and Veit 2008). In comparison, game theoretic approaches to study power markets started to be conducted earlier and remained a bit more popular than agent-based approaches, if the number of published papers in either field is taken as an indicator (as illustrated in Fig. 2). However,

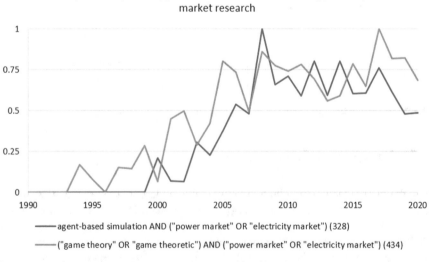

Fig. 2 Relative number of publications in power market research; papers with the given keywords in either title or abstract were set in relation to all publications of the same year; plots show development relative to the year with the highest publication count for the respective keyword; the number in brackets shows the total number of papers; data taken from https://app.dimensions. ai/

while game theoretic models allow for analyzing strategic bidding in very specific market settings, agent-based computational models provide a lot of flexibility in representing the system under study, allowing to tackle both long-term decisions (e.g., Czernohous et al. 2003) and short-term reoccurring trading situations (e.g., Weidlich 2008).

In the early years of the current millennium, many governments started to support power generation from renewable energy sources and, in parts, other forms of decentralized energy resources, such as small-scale combined heat and power generation. Since then, the number of generators has been on the rise globally, and system operations became more challenging. Therefore, decentralized markets as coordination mechanisms moved into the focus of research, addressing a number of both technical and economic questions, e.g., Can decentralized markets solve the coordination problem of increasingly dispersed electricity generation? (How) can information and communication technology help organize decentralized markets? To solve these questions, researchers started to use the analogy of decentralized energy systems to the inherently decentralized organization principles of the Internet, providing interesting insights. These studies can be seen as pioneering work in the newly emerging research field of *energy informatics*. The SESAM ("Self-organization and spontaneity in liberalized and harmonized markets," BMBF, 2003–2007) project was one prominent example for these kinds of research endeavors in the German energy market (Kamper et al. 2005).

2.2   Introduction of Emissions Trading

In Europe, the establishment of the first and largest cross-country greenhouse gas emissions trading scheme (EU-ETS, Directive 2003/87/EC of the European Union (EU)) had a considerable impact on electricity market prices. It introduced a limit on the total amount of greenhouse gases that the industries covered by the EU-ETS were allowed to emit. Other countries also introduced similar mechanisms. Trading emission certificates is supposed to efficiently reduce CO_2 emissions at the lowest overall cost (Dales 1968).

One key market design challenge related to emissions trading was the optimal allowance allocation mechanism for existing power plants. Allowances might either be auctioned among the emitters or they can be allocated free of charge, according to a fixed allocation method. Allocation rules can be based on past emissions in a selected base year or on the output that an emitter would have achieved using the best available technology in a reference period. The method of allowance allocation to existing installations does not basically affect the static efficiency of emissions trading. Investment patterns under an emissions trading system depend mainly on the stringency of the overall emission cap and, thus, on the resulting price of allowances. Practice has shown that the emissions cap in the EU-ETS was set rather laxly, which led to low allowance prices and reduced incentives to reduce emissions.

While the allowance method does not affect the mechanism's static efficiency, it influences the competitive situation of companies. Some companies that would be net sellers under grandfathering could become net buyers under benchmarking. Besides, free allocation leads to windfall profits for power generators (Betz et al. 2010), as they would still reflect the allowance's opportunity cost in their bid prices. Moreover, many researchers (e.g., Jung et al. 1996) argued that auctioned allowances would create greater incentives for technology diffusion and adoption than allowances allocated free of charge, since that reduces allowance prices. The innovator can benefit from this price decrease, since he will not have to pay as much for his remaining emissions. In the case of free allocation, however, the price decrease due to innovation would lower the value of the innovator's allowances, which makes innovation less attractive. The EU-ETS opted for free allocation in the pilot phase and introduced auctioning for the power sector in the second trading period.

2.3   Empowering the Demand Side

Various European policy initiatives are related to demand-side participation, in particular the Electricity Directive 2009/72/EC, the Energy Efficiency Directive 2012/27/EU, and the e-Directive 2019/944/EU. They stipulate that the national energy regulatory authorities must encourage concepts such as demand response and demand-side market participation. Beginning in 2021, electric mobility solutions must also be encouraged by the EU Member States. Similarly, they must ensure that aggregators can offer aggregation contracts to customers and that citizen energy communities to offer energy services to its members or shareholders can be formed. These regulatory underpinnings have seen a prelude of research activities aiming to model and assess the mechanics of demand response in smart distribution networks. While key findings date back to the 1980s, the bulk of publications emerged over in the 2010s. Here, we cluster these contributions along the dimensions modeling, marketing, and aggregation.

In the research community, topics addressing load flexibility in the context of energy markets and smart charging of electric vehicles are notably reflected in a similar manner in the number of publications. Figure 3 shows that these topics started to be covered shortly before 2010, had a first peak in 2013, and are now gaining momentum again. Research related to congestion management has been on the agenda for a longer time. Consequently, publications on this topic increased substantially in the last years and are covered further in Sect. 2.4.

2.3.1   Modeling Flexibility

Keshav and Rosenberg (2011) and Ramchurn et al. (2012) illustrate how smart grid design can leverage on concepts from the domains of Internet communication and

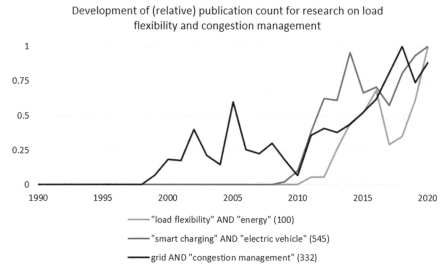

Fig. 3 Relative number of publications on load flexibility and smart charging, following the same approach and data source as in Fig. 2; total number of papers in brackets

artificial intelligence. They stress that smart grids are constituted by a multitude of individual actors which are individually *small* relative to the aggregate system. Therefore, decentralization is a key feature of smart grid systems. It follows that successful coordination of dispersed entities is crucial for enabling effective and efficient systems. Adopting the ideas from experimental and computational economics, these individuals should be interpreted as economic agents (Holland and Miller 1991). By combining appropriate agent models, the emergent aggregate behavior of an agent population can be used to characterize the likely system behavior (Smith 1982). This is of particular interest when new market platforms need to be evaluated before their deployment (Bichler et al. 2010, Weinhardt et al. 2003).

The fundamental building blocks of modeling and managing decentral energy market actors were already identified in the 1980s: In particular, Constantopoulos et al. (1983) and Schweppe et al. (1988) laid out the general idea of modeling customers facing varying electricity prices. Models of particular load types included space heating (O'Rourke and Schweppe 1983), electric vehicle charging (Heydt 1983), and decentral storage (Daryanian et al. 1989).

In the absence of the Internet and ubiquitous computing, it was not until the late 2000s that many of these ideas were re-discovered and put into action in the context of smart grid research. Taking an engineering perspective, Stamminger et al. (2008) rigorously quantified the potentials of smart devices in smart households. In particular, they established demand response potentials of appliances such as refrigerators or washing machines. Building upon these insights, Gottwalt et al. (2011) characterized the system-wide impact of rolling out smart devices at scale.

With significant efforts of decarbonizing the transportation sector, the emerging potentials of electric vehicles were put forward by Kempton and Letendre (1997). As these loads are both large and shiftable, they can also make major contributions to the power system. The established approach to model these loads is to combine a storage optimization logic for the vehicle battery with driving profiles, as well as characterizing the available charging locations (see, e.g., Flath et al. 2012, Schuller et al. 2014; 2015). Combining household, storage, and electric vehicle flexibility models to assess their load shifting potentials, Gottwalt et al. (2016) provide a holistic treatise of flexibility modeling in smart grids.

2.3.2 Marketing Flexibility

Flexibility is the ability to deviate from a plan. In the case of the power system, the plan is the load schedule that needs to be served. Traditionally, this load was not flexible or had no incentive to be so. Nowadays, the power system has become increasingly inverted in this respect, as there is a considerable share of volatile generation from renewable energy. So the plan changes—generation becomes less flexible, and demand must better *fit* the supply.

Demand flexibility shares a main characteristic with most volatile energy sources: it is distributed across the whole system. Therefore, it must be aggregated in order to be marketable in the different power markets, since one source of demand flexibility will usually not meet the capacity limits that still apply for most power markets (Quinn et al. 2010). Flexibility can be offered on different markets, e.g., in ancillary services markets and intraday (regular) markets or in a rather bilateral manner, for instance, for the relief of distribution grids in a regional context. The value of flexibility can thus vary considerably, given the local grid context and the ability of the flexibility resource to be combined with other complementary sources. Studies thus aimed at assessing the relative value of demand flexibility in a given context and at identifying the incentives and market structures needed to harvest the flexibility.

Dauer et al. (2015), for instance, propose an auction-based market for the regional allocation of demand-side flexibility that can help the distribution system operator to locally balance the power grid. This work incorporates the specific requirements for flexibility procurement, while it remains incentive compatible for the bidders. Salah and Flath (2016) and Salah et al. (2016) provide insights into how to create price-based incentives for the provision of demand-side flexibility while mitigating renewable generation uncertainty in a local context. Finally, in Salah et al. (2017), the idea of quality of service differentiation is applied to the energy sector. The general idea is to differentiate demand requirements by the service quality, i.e., the supply security and the demand pattern that need to be fulfilled.

2.3.3   Group Formation for Flexibility Aggregation

In order to gain impact, micro-flexibility must be aggregated for both trading and putting to use. In this, the success and the possibilities of scheduling loads are strongly affected by the composition of a demand flexibility aggregator's customer portfolio and by the corresponding customers' flexibility provision (Gärttner 2016). However, flexibility does not come for free. Domestic customers that offer flexibility must be compensated for their discomfort from demand-side management (Haring and Andersson 2014). Discomfort results from changes in daily environmental and behavioral preconditions, e.g., room temperature, starting times of semi-automatically controlled appliances, or available electric vehicle driving ranges. Therefore, the portfolios must be designed carefully. This is realized via the design of tariffs that incentivize customers to offer flexibility (Gärttner et al. 2018). To enable the aggregator to properly design incentives, knowledge about both customer flexibility and the optimal composition of a customer portfolio is needed. Considering the aggregator's decision dilemma, cost for scheduling flexible supply from conventional power plants or the spot market must be limited. Alike, demand flexibility contracting and dispatching costs must be restrained.

The process of designing flexibility portfolios spans a wide range of time. Hence, energy retailers face a complex multistage decision problem. They can procure demand response capacities from heterogeneous retail customers and also need long-term supply contracts. Procured capacities need to be dispatched in response to fluctuating renewable power generation and stochastic demand (Zugno and Conejo 2015). The attainable scheduling quality (with respect to a given objective) critically hinges on the structural composition and capacities of the portfolio. Electricity retailers also need to manage the composition of the customer portfolio. Customers whose flexibility is contracted for demand-side management may receive more favorable electricity rates. Similarly, the energy retailer has to engage in forward transactions for conventional power supply. These long-term actions need to cope with the uncertainty of possible future realization of scenarios with respect to renewable generation, as the portfolio design decisions have to be taken in advance, i.e., without recourse. With a shorter lead time, supply and flexible demand must be scheduled. The recourse scheduling decisions are obviously taken in the absence of uncertainty, as these are typically taken a day ahead or potentially even in real time. Customer flexibility endowments in the load scheduling problem hence depend on the decisions in the first-stage portfolio composition problem.

Expanding the question of how to optimally design demand response portfolios, flexibility aggregators must focus on the framing of mechanisms to incentivize the flexibility provision by household customers. This may be accomplished through offering tariffs that delineate the contractual conditions for scheduling flexibility as well as its remuneration. The development of demand tariffs builds upon knowledge about household characteristics, i.e., the availability of flexibility and the consumers' willingness to provide this flexibility (Gottwalt et al. 2016). Switching the perspective, consumers face a trade-off between remuneration payments and their perceived discomfort. The latter includes possible load adaptations which induce environmental and behavioral changes as well as risk aversion. In conclusion, the interplay between flexibility aggregators and electricity consumers resembles a never-ending game of acting and reaction. No doubt, however, the provision and utilization of demand flexibility come with a wide and strong set of advantages for all stakeholders. Not least, it allows for efficiently integrating renewable energy sources without taking the reliability of power supply at risk.

2.4 Renewable Energy Integration and Congestion Management

Recently, generation from new renewable sources (i.e., wind and solar) surpassed generation from conventional fossil or nuclear generation in several countries, including Germany. While being an important step in the agenda of the EU to bring clean energy to all citizens, this success didn't go without impact on the grid operation in Europe. The cost for redispatch measures to avoid surpassing grid capacity constraints rose to one billion euro in Germany, and neighboring countries were intervening at the European Union due to cross-order energy flows from northeastern Germany (Staudt et al. 2018c). At the same time, opposition was forming in Germany against transmission grid expansion, and skeptics of the energy transition pointed to curtailments of renewable generation and high redispatch costs (Galvin 2018), which had been discussed as the not-in-my-backyard phenomenon in other countries (Cotton and Devine-Wright 2010). The European Commission threatened to divide Germany into two price zones, as they had done in Sweden to advance the integration of the European electricity market (Bemš et al. 2016).

In parallel, governments began the mobility transition toward more electric mobility. Furthermore, the cost of installing photovoltaic modules was dropping, and self-consumption became a more attractive option than feeding the generated electricity into the grid (Bertsch et al. 2017). With the first installations to drop out of the feed-in tariff support scheme by 2020, households are looking for alternatives to use their renewable generation. In this time, blockchain emerged as a new concept that promised to facilitate (decentralized) peer-to-peer trading between households (Mengelkamp et al. 2018a). These developments fueled the further decentralization of the power sector that was promoted by the European Union. Through citizen energy communities, the EU intended to emphasize the role of citizens in energy systems. Neighborhoods and industry campuses started to use regulation that allowed them to share electricity at reduced rates (Weinhardt et al. 2019). Researchers began to be concerned about capacity constraints in the distribution grid, and grid operators newly had to curtail renewable generation (Schermeyer et al. 2018).

2.4.1 Congestion Management in the Transmission Grid

Developments around renewable energy generation and grid congestion had a large impact on the research community. European scholars began to re-address research that had been performed years before with regard to nodal pricing or redispatch markets (Trepper et al. 2015). Congestion management, which had its peak in research output mainly from a US perspective in the early 2000s—according to Fig. 3—had a small revival caused by the large costs of redispatch in Germany in 2015 and by the European directive demanding market-based approaches for congestion management. This initiative included a change in the transaction object by adding a spatial component, opening new markets for redispatch as an ancillary service (Hirth et al. 2018). The European cost-based redispatch had first been described academically by Nüßler (2012) before it became a large concern in Europe.

As congestion raised more awareness in the European Union, previous research from the USA was re-discovered concerning nodal pricing (Hogan 1999). The graph in Fig. 3 shows that grid congestion as a research topic had its advent in the late 1990s and early 2000s and is now gaining momentum again. When the problem became apparent, researchers quickly published studies on the effects of the division of Germany into two price zones (Egerer et al. 2016, Trepper et al. 2015). Others proposed to use nodal pricing or any other market design with spatial components in the transaction object (Kunz et al. 2016, Richstein et al. 2018). In general, this period can be characterized by the discussion on different ways to address the reduced flexibility in the electricity grid. While some favored market mechanisms to cope with the problem (e.g., Staudt 2019), others made a case for more demand-side integration and flexibility (Huber et al. 2018). The approaches differed in the perspective on the market. While the first group intended to amend a spatial component to the transaction object on the energy-only market, others were in favor of a completely new market design. While market power had long been a concern, it re-surfaced with the discussion on regional redispatch markets because opponents of such markets feared that a regionalization of power markets would further encourage market power exertion (Staudt et al. 2018a). The desired market outcome was clear (a cost-optimal redispatch with regional investment incentives), but the main question was whether the agent behavior would be as desired, given the proposed market design. Finally, the discussion on redispatch markets went hand in hand with the question of transmission grid expansion. While the government emphasized the need for these expansions, some scholars argued that it might be inflated (Kemfert et al. 2016). However, besides one paper by Staudt and Oren (2020), no discussion on market-based solutions emerged, even though alternatives to grid expansion leveraging advances in machine learning exist (Aznarte and Siebert 2016).

2.4.2 Market-Based Congestion Management at the Distribution Level

Decentralized renewable power generation does not only affect the transmission grid but also challenges the distribution system. In Germany, grid operators currently manage congestion at the distribution level by curtailment and demand-side management (EnWG §13.2 and § 14a). As these measures are cost-based and costs are not transparent, the discussion on market-based congestion management in the distribution grid emerged (Ecofys und Fraunhofer IWES 2017). Market-based solutions aim at coordinating flexibility deployment more efficiently and create a market outcome that prevents local congestion. Several examples of this were implemented in the German SINTEG demonstration projects (Huber et al. 2018). As with the market-based redispatch, problems with gaming (inc/dec) and local market power remain an unsolved challenge in these markets.

Another field of discussions are the transaction objects to be traded on these markets. Different mechanisms allow for coordinating the flexibility of decentralized renewable energy sources (Lehmann et al. 2019). While time-varying prices allow for a voluntary reaction, other mechanisms require the generators or consumers to describe and guarantee flexibility before delivery. In this description, more advanced models allow describing all possible future actions of the flexibility units, while simple models are the foundation for comparable products (Villar et al. 2018).

Depending on the desired market outcome, the transaction objects and the market micro-structure have to be adapted. In case the only purpose of the market is congestion management, with the system operator acting as a single buyer, there is no need to describe the flexibility in more complex models, as congestion is likely to occur only occasionally, and load adaption can solve the congestion. Simple products, however, cannot map temporal dependencies (Dauer et al. 2015) and other restrictions (e.g., ramping, must-run) and are not suited to coordinate the full flexibility potential of participants. This reduction in potential would be wasted in case the flexibility is to be used by other participants for other uses, e.g., portfolio management (Gärttner et al. 2018) or system services (Staudt et al. 2018b).

While market-based solutions might suffer from strategic behavior of agents (see redispatch inc/dec; Hirth et al. 2019), it seems likely that market participants at lower grid levels, who are often private households, will not behave in the same way as (more) rational agents on wholesale markets. For instance, households' energy consumption and electric vehicle users' flexibility provision are driven not only by monetary benefits but also by idealism and convenience (Mengelkamp et al. 2019). While former research shows that different consumer types have different flexibility (Schuller et al. 2015) and motivation to use smart charging (Will and Schuller 2016), recent research uses these insights to make individual users more flexible (Salah and Flath 2016) and sustainable in their decisions (Huber et al. 2019).

2.5 Peer-to-Peer Energy Markets

In line with the decentralization of the energy system, local energy markets gained increasing attention in the last two decades as one of the opportunities to harness flexibility on an end customer (consumer, prosumer, and producer) level. Figure 4 shows how the rapidly growing amount of publications in the field of local energy markets represents the increasing significance of the topic in academia.

Right along the increasing share of renewable (mostly) volatile distributed generation, small-scale actors become increasingly involved in the overall energy system (Koirala et al. 2016). Local energy markets (LEMs) often represent a peer-to-peer approach of distributing limited energy or flexibility among the market participants (Weinhardt et al. 2019). In the case of geographically limited LEM, a physical microgrid is likely to be the grid equivalent of the virtual market mechanism (Mengelkamp et al. 2018a). Figure 4 shows that the slope of academic publications starts to exponentially grow around 2010, which is about one decade later than the topic of LEMs. Nevertheless, the total amount of publications is larger than for LEMs. Related to this is the topic of energy communities (mostly between prosumers). While energy communities are nowadays often seen as the first step toward a microgrid of an LEM, their rise of academic attention is delayed by about 5 years compared to the microgrids, as Fig. 4 shows.

Within the last 5 years, the idea of bringing the decentralization of energy communities, LEMs, and microgrids toward the level of information systems has

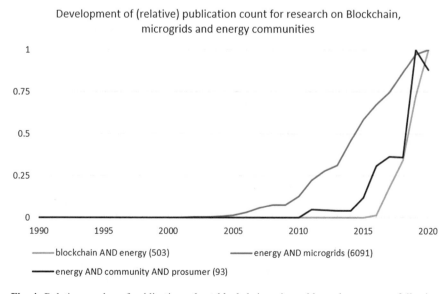

Fig. 4 Relative number of publications about blockchain, microgrids, and prosumers, following the same approach and data source as in Figs. 2 and 3, but limited to the research fields of information systems and electrical and electronic engineering; total number of papers in brackets

reached an enormous scale. Distributed ledger technologies (often simply referred to as blockchain technology) represent the prevalent distributed and decentralized information technology in use. Figure 4 depicts the effect over time. Blockchain technology has since made its way in almost all distributed energy realms, e.g., vehicle-to-grid, smart charging, capacity markets, energy storage.

The first famous blockchain-based LEM project is the Brooklyn Microgrid (reviewed in Mengelkamp et al. 2018a). It began to gain attention when executing the (allegedly) first blockchain-based electricity trade in 2016 and has since expanded from a virtual to a (partly) physical microgrid and a large energy community (Weinhardt et al. 2019). A large number of additional projects in the overlapping domains of microgrids (e.g., Block et al. 2008), LEMs (e.g., the LAMP project; Mengelkamp et al. 2018b), and energy communities (e.g., the Quartierstrom project; Brenzikofer et al. 2019) have since developed. In 2018, more than 120 organizations had started projects regarding LEMs (Metelitsa 2018). So far, however, most projects remain in the pilot or proof-of-concept phase. Their real-world applicability remains to be proven in the long term (Weinhardt et al. 2019).

Increasing consumer interest in renewable and local energy generation (Mengelkamp et al. 2019) gave rise to so-called regional energy markets or energy communities that allow consumers to track energy balances throughout the communities and can ensure on-balance sheet evening up of generation and consumption of the participants. However, these products usually offer a fixed tariff and do not implement an actual market mechanism that incentivizes a change of generation and consumption on a decentralized level.

3 The Next Steps for Decentralized Energy Markets

In 2019, energy transition has picked up pace, partly spurred by the *Fridays for Future* demonstrations and their demand for decisive and fast action against climate change, which is strongly supported by different scientists (Hagedorn et al. 2019). Afterward, the COVID-19 pandemic caused national and international stimulus packages that further promote green initiatives, at least in Europe (Forster et al. 2020). In this process, hydrogen is proposed as one important pillar of a carbon emission-free economy (Dincer 2020). From a market engineering perspective, this development leads to new and interesting questions. Hydrogen is both a storage medium for excess green electricity and can provide value beyond the power system. By fueling air traffic or the energy-intensive industry, a new hydrogen economy could be created (Abe et al. 2019). This hydrogen economy interplays with the electricity market in a still unforeseen manner. Beyond the national markets, it is expected that international hydrogen trade will develop from countries with cheaply available renewable energy resources to countries with higher population densities and less favorable meteorological conditions (Boretti 2020). In regard to electricity market engineering, it will be important to consider system topologies when siting electrolyzers for hydrogen production in markets with single market clearing prices, as in the European Union. Electrolyzers are large consumers that can exacerbate existing mismatch between generation and consumption, if they are not carefully placed (vom Scheidt et al. 2021), which relates well to the already existing research on congestion management. Furthermore, regulatory decisions will be important. Relevant regulations from a market engineering perspective are rules on carbon leakage, which are supposed to protect industries from competitors with less severe regulations (Naegele and Zaklan 2019).

Furthermore, the public importance of the energy transition is recognized by large corporations. Google pursues a strategy of "24/7 carbon-free energy" which means that the company intends to use only green energy in real time (Miller 2020), which sets a new goal beyond the former 100% renewable pledge by many countries and promotes demand-side flexibility options. Also, demand response is increasingly implemented, as seen from the research presented in this chapter. Germany and California, for example, have integrated battery storage capacity aggregators into their electricity markets (Angenendt et al. 2020). In September 2020, FERC passed Order No. 2222, which allows distributed and aggregated resources to participate in the electricity market starting at a capacity of 1 kW. The Texan market operator ERCOT already allows time-of-use tariffs, critical peak pricing, or peak time rebates (Du et al. 2019); the first real-time pricing tariff has recently been launched in Germany by the company aWATTar (Basmadjian 2020).

The trend to deploy flexibility through appropriate regulation and incentives is supported by the ever-decreasing costs of battery storage. Cole and Frazier (2019) project a battery cost decrease of 32–80% from the 380 dollar per kWh in 2018, until 2050, which is mostly driven by the increase in electric vehicle deployment. In September 2020, the Tesla Model 3 was the most registered car in Switzerland, and Tesla's market share was the same as that of Audi. While car sales generally dropped in July and August 2020 in Germany, electric vehicle registrations increased. Additionally, Tesla announced in September 2020 to equip its cars with vehicle-to-grid technology. This comes at a time when researchers start to believe that vehicle-to-grid may be profitable, even when considering battery degradation (Ginigeme and Wang 2020). These developments show that the deployment of demand-side flexibility and local optimization will play an important role in research in the near future. This includes addressing public acceptance and trust and designing attractive schemes for aggregators and consumers.

Aggregators and consumers will continue to move into the spotlight of energy market engineering, with regard to the local coordination of supply and demand. The EU has recently proposed citizen energy communities as a regulatory concept that should allow neighborhoods to locally share and trade generated power (Lowitzsch et al. 2020). This moves peer-to-peer trading from a conceptual idea into deployment. Furthermore, many large utilities are now involved in research projects on citizen energy communities, such as E.ON (in the project IELECTRIX), and the real-world laboratory SmartQuart, funded by the German federal government. In the USA, similar concepts are now tested at large scale. For instance, Portland General Electric since 2018 experiments in the Portland Microgrid Testbed that covers an area of more than 20,000 customers. These concepts are pursued at a time when photovoltaic power generation is increasingly curtailed worldwide, which causes the need for local solutions (O'Shaughnessy et al. 2020). New regulation on mandatory installations of solar panels on newly developed buildings, as discussed in Germany and implemented in California (Senet 2019), might further increase the need for smart energy solutions in densely populated areas. The newly developing local markets are not only intended to supply neighbors with cheap green electricity but will also play an important role in the implementation of local sector coupling, that is, the joint supply of heat, electric, and transportation energy demand (Arabzadeh et al. 2020). The research community has to support energy communities, aggregators, and infrastructure developers to develop tailored solutions for different neighborhoods (Golla et al. 2021), but also to design trusted interfaces that can be used to operate such communities (Golla et al. 2020).

4   Conclusion and Outlook

Since the beginning of energy sector liberalization, markets have become an important and widely applied concept to support a variety of processes in the operation of today's energy systems. The first research questions to which market engineering delivered valuable insights were related to auction designs for whole-sale power trading. Very quickly, a plethora of further market-based instruments was established, facilitating control reserve procurement, carbon emissions restrictions, congestion management, and renewable energy support or involving prosumers in local energy markets, to mention a few. In view of the current goal of the European Union to provide "Clean energy for all Europeans," it can be said that many of the necessary developments to promote this goal can be supported by energy market engineering. The potential contributions of market engineering to a clean and participatory energy system can be concluded on the basis of some perceived ongoing trends, which we summarize in the following:

- Energy markets evolve slowly toward decentralization. On the one hand, millions of small dispersed (renewable) generation units have to be integrated into power systems; on the other hand, smaller stakeholders increasingly participate in markets, and their spatial distribution becomes more relevant. As a consequence, regional markets are emerging, and national markets must better accommodate for the spatial characteristics of generation and demand in the future.
- Energy markets are becoming more dynamic, as trading periods approach the real time. Therefore, markets must enable a high temporal resolution, and dynamic forecasting methods have to be available to facilitate shorter-term trading.
- Diversity of stakeholders is increasing. Aggregators will play an important role in pooling diverse small devices such as batteries and thermal storage units. This has an impact on the modeling requirements of these agents and on their representation in the current market frameworks.

- The urgency of climate protection has catapulted energy and emissions markets to the top of global decision-makers' agenda. Proper integration of greenhouse gas emission reduction schemes into energy markets is crucial. Here, the regulatory framework must be properly designed too, so that the market mechanisms can unfold their potential. A well-designed carbon trading scheme is useless if the emissions cap is set too laxly. Therefore, market mechanisms must always be regarded in the broader context of energy system regulation.
- New technological advancements, for example, in storage technologies and also in smart meter deployment, make flexibility potentials available. Markets can facilitate its efficient use for the benefit of the whole system. Research questions on where flexibility deployment can provide the largest benefit remain open, so more dynamic and highly temporally and spatially resolved models are needed to provide answers to questions about the coordination challenge of flexibility.

The majority of energy research from the last decade is now on the brink of being implemented, as it has been illustrated in this chapter with numerous examples. Increasing focus is currently put on the distribution grid and on congestion management. This underscores the importance of modeling individual actors instead of simply considering the system as a whole, for which this review gives multiple examples. At the same time, it summons up many interesting challenges for researchers in energy system modeling and energy market engineering in the coming years and opens the floor for propositions on how to cope with the most important problems of today's energy systems.

Acknowledgments The authors would like to thank Dr. Carsten Block and Dr. Florian Salah, both alumni, and Sarah Henni, research assistant at the Institute of Information Systems and Marketing, for their valuable and profound comments during the completion of this chapter.

References

Abe JO, Popoola A, Ajenifuja E, Popoola O (2019) Hydrogen energy, economy and storage: review and recommendation. International journal of hydrogen energy 44(29):15072–15086

Angenendt G, Merten M, Zurmühlen S, Sauer DU (2020) Evaluation of the effects of frequency restoration reserves market participation with photovoltaic battery energy storage systems and power-to-heat coupling. Applied Energy 260:114186

Arabzadeh V, Mikkola J, Jasiūnas J, Lund PD (2020) Deep decarbonization of urban energy systems through renewable energy and sector-coupling flexibility strategies. Journal of Environmental Management 260:110090

Aznarte JL, Siebert N (2016) Dynamic line rating using numerical weather predictions and machine learning: A case study. IEEE Transactions on Power Delivery 32(1):335–343

Basmadjian R (2020) Optimized charging of pv-batteries for households using real-time pricing scheme: A model and heuristics-based implementation. Electronics 9(1):113

Bemš J, Králík T, Knapek J, Kradeckaia A (2016) Bidding zones reconfiguration—current issues literature review, criterions and social welfare. In: 2016 2nd International Conference on Intelligent Green Building and Smart Grid (IGBSG), IEEE, pp 1–6

Bertsch V, Geldermann J, Lühn T (2017) What drives the profitability of household pv investments, self-consumption and self-sufficiency? Applied Energy 204:1–15

Betz R, Seifert S, Cramton P, Kerr S (2010) Auctioning greenhouse gas emissions permits in Australia. Australian Journal of Agricultural and Resource Economics 54(2):219–238

Bichler M, Gupta A, Ketter W (2010) Designing smart markets. Information Systems Research 21(4):688–699

Block C, Neumann D, Weinhardt C (2008) A market mechanism for energy allocation in microchip grids. In: Hawaii International Conference on System Sciences, Proceedings of the 41st Annual, IEEE, pp 172–172

Borenstein S, Bushnell J, Knittel CR (1999) Market power in electricity markets: Beyond concentration measures. The Energy Journal 20(4)

Boretti A (2020) Production of hydrogen for export from wind and solar energy, natural gas, and coal in Australia. International Journal of Hydrogen Energy 45(7):3899–3904

Brenzikofer A, Meeuw A, Schopfer S, Wörner A, Dürr C (2019) Quartierstrom: A decentralized local p2p energy market pilot on a self-governed blockchain. In: CIRED 2019

Cole WJ, Frazier A (2019) Cost projections for utility-scale battery storage. Tech. rep., National Renewable Energy Lab.(NREL), Golden, CO (United States)

Constantopoulos P, Larson RC, Schweppe FC (1983) Decision models for electric load management by consumers facing a variable price of electricity. Energy Models and Studies pp 273–291

Cotton M, Devine-Wright P (2010) NIMBYism and community consultation in electricity transmission network planning. Renewable energy and the public: From NIMBY to participation 115

Czernohous C, Fichtner W, Veit D, Weinhardt C (2003) Management decision support using long-term market simulation. Journal of Information Systems and e-Business Management (ISeB) 1(4):405–423

Dales JH (1968) Pollution, Property and Prices: An Essay in Policy Making and Economics. University of Toronto Press, Toronto

Daryanian B, Bohn RE, Tabors RD (1989) Optimal demand-side response to electricity spot prices for storage-type customers. IEEE transactions on Power Systems 4(3):897–903

Dauer D, Karaenke P, Weinhardt C (2015) Load balancing in the smart grid: A package auction and compact bidding language. In: Proceedings of the 36th International Conference on Information Systems (ICIS 2015), December, 13–16, Fort Worth, TX, USA

Dincer I (2020) Covid-19 coronavirus: Closing carbon age, but opening hydrogen age. International Journal of Energy Research 44(8):6093

Du P, Lu N, Zhong H (2019) Demand responses in ERCOT. In: Demand Response in Smart Grids, Springer, pp 85–119

Ecofys und Fraunhofer IWES (2017) Smart-market-design in deutschen verteilnetzen. Tech. rep., Studie im Auftrag von Agora Energiewende

Egerer J, Weibezahn J, Hermann H (2016) Two price zones for the German electricity market— market implications and distributional effects. Energy Economics 59:365–381

Federico G, Rahman D (2003) Bidding in an electricity pay-as-bid auction. Journal of Regulatory Economics 24(2):175–211

Flath C, Ilg J, Weinhardt C (2012) Decision Support for Electric Vehicle Charging. In: Proceedings of the Americas Conference on Information Systems, Seattle, Washington

Forster PM, Forster HI, Evans MJ, Gidden MJ, Jones CD, Keller CA, Lamboll RD, Le Quéré C, Rogelj J, Rosen D, et al. (2020) Current and future global climate impacts resulting from covid-19. Nature Climate Change pp 1–7

Galvin R (2018) Trouble at the end of the line: local activism and social acceptance in low-carbon electricity transmission in lower Franconia, Germany. Energy Research & Social Science 38:114–126

Gärttner J (2016) Group formation in smart grids: Designing demand response portfolios. PhD thesis, Karlsruher Institut für Technologie (KIT)

Gärttner J, Flath CM, Weinhardt C (2018) Portfolio and contract design for demand response resources. European Journal of Operational Research 266(1):340–353

Ginigeme K, Wang Z (2020) Distributed optimal vehicle-to-grid approaches with consideration of battery degradation cost under real-time pricing. IEEE Access 8:5225–5235

Golla A, Henni S, Staudt P (2020) Scaling the concept of citizen energy communities through a platform-based decision support system. European Conference on Information Systems (ECIS)

Golla A, Meinke J, Liu V, Staudt P, Anderson L, Weinhardt C (2021) Direct policy search for multiobjective optimization of the sizing and operation of citizen energy communities. In: HICSS, pp 1–10

Gottwalt S, Ketter W, Block C, Collins J, Weinhardt C (2011) Demand side management—a simulation of household behavior under variable prices. Energy policy 39(12):8163–8174

Gottwalt S, Gärttner J, Schmeck H, Weinhardt C (2016) Modeling and valuation of residential demand flexibility for renewable energy integration. Smart Grid, IEEE Transactions on

Hagedorn G, Loew T, Seneviratne SI, Lucht W, Beck ML, Hesse J, Knutti R, Quaschning V, Schleimer JH, Mattauch L, et al. (2019) The concerns of the young protesters are justified: A statement by scientists for future concerning the protests for more climate protection. GAIA-Ecological Perspectives for Science and Society 28(2):79–87

Haring T, Andersson G (2014) Contract design for demand response. In: IEEE PES Innovative Smart Grid Technologies, Europe, IEEE, pp 1–6

Heydt GT (1983) The impact of electric vehicle deployment on load management strategies. IEEE transactions on power apparatus and systems (5):1253–1259

Hirth L, Glismann S, et al. (2018) Congestion management: From physics to regulatory instruments. Tech. rep., ZBW-Leibniz Information Centre for Economics

Hirth L, Schlecht I, et al. (2019) Redispatch markets in zonal electricity markets: Inc-Dec gaming as a consequence of inconsistent power market design (not market power). Tech. rep.

Hogan WW (1999) Transmission congestion: the nodal-zonal debate revisited. Harvard University, John F Kennedy School of Government, Center for Business and Government Retrieved August 29(4)

Holland J, Miller J (1991) Artificial adaptive agents in economic theory. The American Economic Review 81(2):365–370

Huber J, Köppl S, Klempp N, Schutz M, Heilmann E (2018) Engineering smart market platforms for market based congestion management. In: Proceedings of the 9th International Conference on Future Energy Systems, ACM, pp 544–549

Huber J, Jung D, Schaule E, Weinhardt C (2019) Goal framing in smart charging—increasing bev users' charging flexibility with digital nudges. In: Proceedings of the 27th European Conference on Information Systems (ECIS), Stockholm and Uppsala, Sweden, pp 8–14

Jung C, Krutilla K, Boyd R (1996) Incentives for Advanced Pollution Abatement Technology at the Industry Level: An Evaluation of Policy Alternatives. Journal of Environmental Economics and Management 30(1):95–111

Kahn AE, Cramton PC, Porter RH, Tabors RD (2001) Pricing in the California power exchange electricity market: Should California switch from uniform pricing to pay-as-bid pricing? Blue ribbon panel report

Kamper A, Weinhardt C, Lockemann P, Franke M, Geyer-Schulz A, Rolli D, Dietrich A, Schmeck H (2005) Impacts of distributed generation from virtual power plants. In: Proceedings of the Annual International Sustainable Development Research Conference, ERP Environment, vol 11, pp 1–12

Kemfert C, Kunz F, Rosellón J (2016) A welfare analysis of electricity transmission planning in Germany. Energy Policy 94:446–452

Kempton W, Letendre SE (1997) Electric vehicles as a new power source for electric utilities. Transportation Research Part D: Transport and Environment 2(3):157–175

Keshav S, Rosenberg C (2011) How internet concepts and technologies can help green and smarten the electrical grid. ACM SIGCOMM Computer Communication Review 41(1):109–114

Koirala BP, Koliou E, Friege J, Hakvoort RA, Herder PM (2016) Energetic communities for community energy: A review of key issues and trends shaping integrated community energy systems. Renewable and Sustainable Energy Reviews 56:722–744

Kunz F, Neuhoff K, Rosellón J (2016) Ftr allocations to ease transition to nodal pricing: An application to the German power system. Energy Economics 60:176–185

Lehmann N, Huber J, Kießling A (2019) Flexibility in the context of a cellular system model. In: 2019 16th International Conference on the European Energy Market (EEM), IEEE, pp 1–6

Lowitzsch J, Hoicka C, Van Tulder F (2020) Renewable energy communities under the 2019 European clean energy package–governance model for the energy clusters of the future? Renewable and Sustainable Energy Reviews 122:109489

McAfee RP, McMillan J (1987) Auctions and Bidding. Journal of Economic Literature 25(2):699–738

Mengelkamp E, Gärttner J, Rock K, Kessler S, Orsini L, Weinhardt C (2018a) Designing microgrid energy markets: A case study: The Brooklyn microgrid. Applied Energy 210:870–880

Mengelkamp E, Gärttner J, Weinhardt C (2018b) Decentralizing energy systems through local energy markets: The lamp-project. In: Multikonferenz Wirtschaftsinformatik, pp 924–930

Mengelkamp E, Schönland T, Huber J, Weinhardt C (2019) The value of local electricity-a choice experiment among German residential customers. Energy policy 130:294–303

Metelitsa C (2018) Blockchain for energy 2018: Companies & applications for distributed ledger technologies on the grid. Tech. rep., GreenTechMedia

Miller G (2020) Beyond 100% renewable: Policy and practical pathways to 24/7 renewable energy procurement. The Electricity Journal 33(2):106695

Naegele H, Zaklan A (2019) Does the EU ETS cause carbon leakage in European manufacturing? Journal of Environmental Economics and Management 93:125–147

Nicolaisen J, Petrov V, Tesfatsion L (2001) Market power and efficiency in a computational electricity market with discriminatory double-auction pricing. IEEE Transactions on Evolutionary Computation 5(5):504–523

Nüßler A (2012) Congestion and redispatch in Germany. a model-based analysis of the development of redispatch. PhD thesis, Universität zu Köln

O'Rourke P, Schweppe FC (1983) Space conditioning load under spot or time of day pricing. IEEE Transactions on Power Apparatus and Systems (5):1294–1301

O'Shaughnessy E, Cruce JR, Xu K (2020) Too much of a good thing? global trends in the curtailment of solar pv. Solar Energy 208:1068–1077

Quinn C, Zimmerle D, Bradley TH (2010) The effect of communication architecture on the availability, reliability, and economics of plug-in hybrid electric vehicle-to-grid ancillary services. Journal of Power Sources 195(5):1500–1509

Ramchurn S, Vytelingum P, Rogers A, Jennings N (2012) Putting the "smarts" into the smart grid: A grand challenge for artificial intelligence. Communications of the ACM 55(4):86–97

Richstein JC, Neuhoff K, May N (2018) Europe's power system in transition: How to couple zonal and locational pricing systems? Tech. rep., ZBW-Leibniz Information Centre for Economics

Roth AE (2002) The Economist as Engineer: Game Theory, Experimentation, and Computation as Tools for Design Economics. Econometrica 70:1341–1378

Salah F, Flath CM (2016) Deadline differentiated pricing in practice: marketing EV charging in car parks. Computer Science-Research and Development 31(1–2):33–40

Salah F, Schuller A, Weinhardt C (2016) Mitigating renewable energy generation uncertainty by deadline differentiated pricing. In: 24th European Conference on Information Systems, ECIS 2016

Salah F, Flath C, Schuller A, Will C, Weinhardt C (2017) Morphological analysis of energy services: Paving the way to quality differentiation in the power sector. Energy Policy 106

vom Scheidt F, Qu J, Staudt P, Mallapragada D, Weinhardt C (2021) The effects of electricity tariffs on cost-minimal hydrogen supply chains and their impact on electricity prices and redispatch costs. In: HICSS, pp 1–10

Schermeyer H, Vergara C, Fichtner W (2018) Renewable energy curtailment: A case study on today's and tomorrow's congestion management. Energy Policy 112:427–436

Schuller A, Dietz B, Flath CM, Weinhardt C (2014) Charging strategies for battery electric vehicles: Economic benchmark and v2g potential. IEEE Transactions on Power Systems 29(5)

Schuller A, Flath CM, Gottwalt S (2015) Quantifying load flexibility of electric vehicles for renewable energy integration. Applied Energy 151:335–344

Schweppe FC, Caramanis MC, Tabors RD, Bohn RE (1988) Spot pricing of electricity. Springer, Boston, MA

Senet TL (2019) New solar energy requirements for residential construction and the transition to energy independence. Tech. rep.

Smith VL (1982) Microeconomic systems as an experimental science. The American Economic Review 72(5):923–955

Son YS, Baldick R, Lee KH, Siddiqi S (2004) Short-term electricity market auction game analysis: Uniform and pay-as-bid pricing. IEEE Transactions on Power Systems 19(4):1990–1998

Stamminger R, Broil G, Pakula C, Jungbecker H, Braun M, Rüdenauer I, Wendker C (2008) Synergy potential of smart appliances. Report of the Smart-A project pp 1949–3053

Staudt P (2019) Transmission congestion management in electricity grids-designing markets and mechanisms. PhD thesis, KIT-Bibliothek

Staudt P, Oren SS (2020) A merchant transmission approach for uniform-price electricity markets. In: HICSS, pp 1–10

Staudt P, Gärttner J, Weinhardt C (2018a) Assessment of market power in local electricity markets with regards to competition and tacit collusion. Tagungsband Multikonferenz Wirtschaftsinformatik 2018 pp 912–923

Staudt P, Schmidt M, Gärttner J, Weinhardt C (2018b) A decentralized approach towards resolving transmission grid congestion in Germany using vehicle-to-grid technology. Applied energy 230:1435–1446

Staudt P, Träris Y, Rausch B, Weinhardt C (2018c) Predicting redispatch in the German electricity market using Information Systems based on Machine Learning. Proceedings of the International Conference on Information Systems (ICIS), San Francisco

Stoft S (1999) Using game theory to study market power in simple networks. IEEE Tutorial on Game Theory in Electric Power Markets pp 33–40

Strecker S, Weinhardt C (2001) Wholesale electricity trading in the deregulated German electricity market. In: An energy odyssey? Proceedings. 24th Annual IAEE International Conference, Houston, IAEE, pp 1–6

Trepper K, Bucksteeg M, Weber C (2015) Market splitting in Germany–new evidence from a three-stage numerical model of Europe. Energy Policy 87:199–215

Villar J, Bessa R, Matos M (2018) Flexibility products and markets: Literature review. Electric Power Systems Research 154:329–340

Weidlich A (2008) Engineering interrelated electricity markets: an agent-based computational approach. Springer Science & Business Media

Weidlich A, Veit D (2008) Agent-based simulations for electricity market regulation advice: procedures and an example. Jahrbücher für Nationalökonomie und Statistik 228(2–3):149–172

Weinhardt C, Holtmann C, Neumann D (2003) Market-engineering. Wirtschaftsinformatik 45(6):635–640

Weinhardt C, Mengelkamp E, Cramer W, Hambridge S, Hobert A, Kremers E, Otter W, Pinson P, Tiefenbeck V, Zade M (2019) How far along are local energy markets in the DACH+ region? a comparative market engineering approach. In: Proceedings of the Tenth ACM International Conference on Future Energy Systems, pp 544–549

Will C, Schuller A (2016) Understanding user acceptance factors of electric vehicle smart charging. Transportation Research Part C: Emerging Technologies 71:198–214

Zugno M, Conejo AJ (2015) A robust optimization approach to energy and reserve dispatch in electricity markets. European Journal of Operational Research 247(2):659–671

Can Immersive Systems Help Address Sustainability Goals? Insights from Research in Information Systems

Jella Pfeiffer, Jonas Fegert, Anke Greif-Winzrieth, Greta Hoffmann, and Christian Peukert

Abstract Several developments in recent years have highlighted the urgent need for an increase in sustainable behavior. In an effort to systematically achieve global human well-being and create a more sustainable and equal world by 2030, the United Nations passed the Sustainable Development Goals in 2015. In this chapter, we discuss several different approaches for Information Systems (IS) to contribute to these goals. We present ideas and first results from different research approaches in which we analyze how immersive systems, in particular, are capable of addressing challenges regarding awareness, motivation, information transfer, and educating citizens to act in a sustainable manner. We conclude that the main features of immersive systems are particularly suited to approach challenges related to sustainable behavior and attitude change. With this chapter, we hope to inspire further research efforts on how IS can make a contribution to a more sustainable world.

1 Introduction

In 2015, the United Nations' General Assembly passed the Sustainable Development Goals (SDGs) as an agenda to achieve a more sustainable and equal world by 2030. The 17 goals aim to address all sectors of society and seek to rethink social,

Jella Pfeiffer, Jonas Fegert, Anke Greif-Winzrieth, Greta Hoffmann and Christian Peukert contributed equally with all other contributors.

J. Pfeiffer (✉)
Faculty of Economics and Business Studies, Justus Liebig University Gießen, Gießen, Germany
e-mail: jella.pfeiffer@wirtschaft.uni-giessen.de

J. Fegert · A. Greif-Winzrieth · G. Hoffmann · C. Peukert
Institute of Information Systems and Marketing, Karlsruhe Institute of Technology, Karlsruhe, Germany
e-mail: jonas.fegert@kit.edu; anke.greif-winzrieth@kit.edu; greta.hoffmann@kit.edu; christian.peukert@kit.edu

© The Author(s) 2021
H. Gimpel et al. (eds.), *Market Engineering*,
https://doi.org/10.1007/978-3-030-66661-3_8

economic, and environmental interactions globally. They stretch from "zero hunger" to "climate action" to "peace and justice strong institutions."

Five years prior to the launch of the SDGs, Watson et al. (2010) criticized the hesitancy within the Information Systems (IS) community to address issues of sustainability and pointed toward the "transformative power of IS to create an environmentally sustainable society" (Watson et al. 2010). In 2015 vom Brocke and others took up this call to action by publishing *Grand Societal Challenges in Information Systems Research and Education* (vom Brocke et al. 2015), the results of a student research project on this topic.

In 2020, the societal consequences of not taking action seem very present: The global refugee crisis, the global protests for climate justice around the Fridays for Future movement, and the Covid-19 pandemic have revealed the necessity to implement the SDGs as soon as possible. Gradual processes such as the transformation toward a digital and more sustainable economy as well as the worldwide urbanization of cities highlight the challenges lying ahead and the need for the field of IS to focus on the interests of society.

Building on the research mentioned above and the call for urgent action by Gholami et al. (2016), this chapter addresses several SDGs, in particular: SDG 1 (no poverty), SDG 3 (good health and well-being), SDG 10 (reduced inequalities), SDG 11 (sustainable cities and communities), SDG 12 (responsible consumption and production), SDG 13 (climate action), and SDG 16 (peace, justice, and strong institutions). This chapter presents concrete findings of IS research studies that discuss the possibilities of immersive systems to accomplish their realization.

As we believe in diversifying the efforts to tackle societal challenges, we propose the strategy that IS researchers should first take initiatives in their respective domains. We thus focused on immersive systems, such as virtual reality (VR) and augmented reality (AR), as our expertise lies in this research field, and we found several indicators that such immersive systems can be used as a powerful instrument to address issues of sustainable development.

Achieving the SDGs is challenging for several reasons. We focus on the following four challenges in this chapter: *Awareness*, *Motivation*, *Information Transfer*, and *Learning to Act*. First, in our everyday lives, we are rarely aware of all the different problems and consequences of our actions that actually relate to sustainability issues. The consequences of unsustainable behavior can be far in distance and time for at least part of the population. Unfortunately, this ignorance is often true for that part of the population which is highly responsible for it but does not feel its immediate consequences; for example, climate change still has few noticeable consequences for individuals living in Central European countries or the USA but very noticeable consequences for the population of South Africa. Second, there is little extrinsic motivation to act and participate in order to reach the sustainability goals. Intrinsic motivation as a sole driver may be too weak to compete against other tasks and duties of our everyday lives. Third, in a world of information overload and complex facts, transferring the relevant information at the right time is difficult. The challenge at hand is to provide easy-to-understand information exactly when sustainable actions are needed and can be implemented.

For example, knowing about a phenomenon such as an inferior working situation in the cloth industry particularly helps in reaching the UN goals if this information is available during the purchasing process. Fourth, some of the necessary actions can be trained in order to incorporate them into our everyday lives. For example, continually looking up the right bin for a waste item is tedious, and thus learning how to act by being trained to recycle properly would help with the necessary behavioral change.

In this chapter, we postulate that immersive systems can be used to support the implementation of certain SDGs in addressing the four challenges mentioned above. Immersive systems are characterized to "purposefully change or enhance the user's perception of reality" (Cavusoglu et al. 2019) and comprise AR as well as VR. Immersion describes the degree to which a VR system's output is comparable to physical stimuli (Bowman and McMahan 2007). The key characteristic of immersive systems, in particular VR, is the capability to create telepresence (Steuer 1992), which means feeling present in an environment mediated by any communications technology (Pfeiffer et al. 2020). We argue that high telepresence can help people to be fully present and involved in contexts that are distant in time and space, and thus evoking telepresence could help with processes aimed to increase awareness. Second, immersive systems have been considered among the most notable evolving technologies in the area of Information and Communications Technology (ICT) (Steininger 2019). We therefore further assume that using this technology as a way to participate in sustainable behavior or to provide information about sustainability problems might be very motivating. Third, immersive systems allow for novel forms of information representation which can strongly benefit cognitive load and information transfer. The technology also facilitates the application of smart algorithms that use multi-modal data input for intelligent personal assistants that transfer information at suitable moments. For example, when going shopping in a virtual reality store, nudges about poor manufacturing conditions during the purchasing process can lead to more sustainable purchase decisions. Finally, because of the possibilities to imitate interactions of the real world, immersive systems allow for novel training opportunities that have the potential to aid more efficiently with the transfer of skills and knowledge to reality in comparison to standard e-learning contexts.

The goal of the chapter is to stimulate both researchers and professionals to think about how and whether immersive IS can help with the process of reaching the goals set by the UN. For this, the chapter provides first evidence and ideas from our research.

2 Immersive Systems as a Tool to Increase Awareness

The SDGs were set in 2015 by the members of the United Nations General Assembly, but achieving these ambitious goals doesn't only require support from the political leaders who put their signature on the resolution. It also requires people all over the world to align their everyday decisions and behaviors with these goals.

With several large campaigns, the United Nations attempted to raise awareness, but action to meet the goals in 2030 is not yet advancing at the speed or scale required.

With just under 10 years left to achieve the SDGs, world leaders at the SDG Summit in September 2019 called for a "Decade of Action" on different levels including "people action" in order to generate a strong movement pushing for the required transformations. Raising awareness is a crucial prerequisite for encouraging action, but it is a difficult endeavor when it comes to global challenges such as those addressed by the SDGs. In 450 BC Confucius is reputed to have said: "Tell Me and I Will Forget; Show Me and I May Remember; Involve Me and I Will Understand." This is also reflected in more recent theories of learning or behavior stating that personal experience plays a decisive role when it comes to behavior change. How can we make people all over the world more aware of the most pressing contemporary global challenges such as climate change that will not affect our lives tomorrow but those of the generations to come, or poverty affecting populations living thousands of kilometers away?

Based on first evidence from literature and our own studies, we propose that by allowing people to engage in experiences that reach far beyond their own physical reality independent of time and physical location, immersive systems can change the way people see the world. This is made possible because of the immersive system's feature that allows people to feel present in an artificially created world. This digital world can be a replication of the real one that makes people aware of and experience geographically remote places or lets them experience the future. This digital world can also show completely fictional worlds and allow, for example, behaviors that would be harmful to the self, others, or the environment in the physical world. This might make people experience emotionally difficult or physically harmful situations and increase awareness. With the development of affordable hardware and the emergence of a wide range of content, the concept is already within the reach of the general public.

For example, in most cases taking action against global climate change (SDG 13: climate action) requires the sacrifice of concrete, immediate benefits for the sake of abstract, distant goals. Many theories deal with the psychological background of human behavior associated with future consequences of present behavior, or decisions showing that humans tend to discount the importance of an outcome with greater temporal, social, or geographical distance. Construal level theory, for example, posits that humans have distinct psychological associations with events based on their perceived temporal and personal distance (Liberman and Trope 1998). Abstract representations of consequences in the distant future usually lack the concrete associations connected to near-present events and thus may not be as feared (Gifford et al. 2009). The closer and the more personally relevant potential consequences seem to be, the more people are aware of these problems and take them seriously, and the more likely it is that protective or mitigating action is taken. The use of immersive systems to promote more sustainable environmental behavior has been evaluated since 2008 (Fiore et al. 2009). In particular, the influence of

VR experiences on risk perception regarding wildfires (Fiore et al. 2009) or floods (Bateman et al. 2009; Zaalberg and Midden 2010) is widely addressed. Further attention is given to the consequences of wasteful energy consumption (Bailey et al. 2015), napkin wastage (Ahn et al. 2014), environmental pollution (Fox et al. 2020), and climate change (Nelson et al. 2020). However, more research is needed to examine the long-term effects of virtual experiences and to increase the external validity and generalizability of the findings that are mainly based on hypothetical decisions in artificial lab settings.

Immersive systems are not only capable of overcoming temporal or geographical distance, which may be key to raising awareness of global climate issues. Much hope is also based on the technologies' capability to convey another person's experience or feelings to a viewer by putting him or her either right into the body of that character (embodiment) or close to him or her in the virtual space. Several studies have looked at the effect of embodiment in virtual reality and suggest that when people have an illusion of body ownership over a body different to their own, this can induce perceptual, attitudinal, and behavioral change (Maister et al. 2015; Slater and Sanchez-Vives 2014). Findings show, for example, that virtual embodiment can reduce implicit racial biases toward dark-skinned people (Banakou et al. 2016; Maister et al. 2013; Peck et al. 2013), and embodiment of adults in the bodies of children results in their overestimation of object sizes and a shift in attitudes about the self toward being child-like (Banakou et al. 2013).

Immersive systems are already successfully used to increase empathy with refugees (Gürerk and Kasulke 2017), and as a part of the UN SDG Action Campaign, a series of VR films was published that are intended to provide a deeper understanding for those living with the most complex development challenges. There is some recent work indicating that immersion in VR might enhance empathy (Schutte and Stilinovic 2017; Shin 2018) and increase intentions to voluntarily support charitable purposes (SDG 1: no poverty). However, the best intentions are worthless if they are not put into action. But do immersion effects translate into real action, and what emotional and motivational mechanisms are the driving forces? In a first pilot study (Greif-Winzrieth et al. 2020), we use electroencephalography (EEG) to reveal cognitive processes during VR experiences and examine chances in frontal alpha asymmetry (FAA) scores as a measure of approach/avoidance motivation (Briesemeister et al. 2013) and a potential predictor of monetary donations (Huffmeijer et al. 2012). Our results indicate that donation behavior might be linked to chances in the FAA score. Building on this finding, we plan to further investigate the effects of immersion on cognitive-affective processes, hoping to gain a deeper understanding of how immersive systems can help not only to increase awareness but also to inspire action needed to achieve the SDGs.

3 Immersive Systems as a Tool to Increase Motivation to Participate

We argue that immersive systems can be used as a tool to increase motivation to participate in reaching the UN goals and provide a research example that addresses sustainable urbanization and reduced inequalities (SDGs 10 and 11). Since SDG 16, peace, justice, and strong institutions, points to the importance of the public sector in implementing the SDGs, we aim to show how immersive systems can be used by public institutions.

Urbanization has led to an increase in urban population worldwide (United Nations 2019). In recent years, disputes about the design of urban space have emerged in city planning. Especially when it comes to construction projects, public debates and protests may arise, if construction plans remain unshared with the citizens they may affect. This kind of behavior, shown by various governments and construction project initiators, seems to be short-sighted and is therefore unsustainable as it constructs urban space without the potential users of the space: the city's inhabitants. Involving citizens early on in processes of transformation can secure or even strengthen trust in public institutions and thereby leads to a sustainable relationship with the surrounding urban space. E-Participation, as a subform of Digital Government, tries to elaborate new forms of involvement of citizens created by making use of digital technologies. As those digital forms open up numerous new technological possibilities of involvement, we are researching the potential of immersive systems to increase the citizens' motivation to participate. Although there is a wide use of ICTs in the daily life of individuals all around the world, we have the feeling that classical e-participation lacks wide acceptance also due to the fact that from a user-centered design point of view, many tools are simply not comparable with the often fun and simple user experience of other applications. This might be related to out-of-date implementation of some apps and the challenge of translating complex political decision-making processes into a user-friendly platform design (Toots 2019). As Scholl (2008) already stated early on, Digital Government is an interdisciplinary field of study, where a shared understanding of public administration and IS design might lead to better Digital Government solutions. As we see the possibilities IS research offers mostly for the business context, and the lack of innovation public administration offers, we try to bring the disciplines closer together in an interdisciplinary research project, where we aim to counter the lack of motivation to participate in public services, by adding technological innovations such as immersive systems.

Within the research project "Take Part" (funded by the German Federal Ministry of Education and Research), we have the possibility to experiment with immersive systems as a means to improve digital citizen participation (Fegert et al. 2019). Cooperating with public institutions, we have the opportunity to get direct feedback from citizens and initiators. The application enables the public to participate in construction projects. Moreover, it allows participants to see the respective construction project from different perspectives and eventually see different versions of the construction project both in AR and VR. The users can submit their feedback, comments, and design suggestions within the applications. The application is designed for smartphones, tablets, and head-mounted displays (HMDs) and is controlled by lifting, lowering, and turning the mobile device, or in the case of HMDs is navigated with the help of controllers.

As we have shown within our research, there is an overwhelming interest in using AR and VR for e-participation to better visualize construction planning and to engage with urban planning (Fegert et al. 2020a). Furthermore, the technologies helped the participants imagining the construction project, positively impacting their willingness to engage with and donate to the construction project.

The United Nations (2018) points out that "online tools can enhance access to information and public services, as well as promote better public policy decision-making" (p. 33) and thereby might help lower the digital divide and produce more accountability. Based on our research, we definitely agree with the statement and go one step further, by seeing in the combination of the e-participation and immersive systems one of the (hopefully many) possible ways to achieve SDGs 10 and 11.

For SDG 10, reduced inequalities, we see the potential of immersive systems in the user's fascination with the technology experience and the effect of telepresence. There seems to be a high interest in the use of the technology regardless of gender, age, or educational background (Fegert et al. 2020a, b). Moreover, in our quantitative study, most participants felt virtually transported from the study's environment to the construction project site when using the VR prototype. By this means, we could prove that the technologies offer the possibility to participate more easily in decision-making processes from a distance, thereby making participation more accessible and inclusive for those who could not travel due to financial reasons or because their special needs restrict them to one place.

SDG 11, sustainable cities and communities, responds to the boom of urbanization and suggest the following measures: "investment in public transport, creating green public spaces, and improving urban planning and management in participatory and inclusive ways" (UNDP 2020). This call seems to fit perfectly with the mission of "Take Part" which aims to be an IS tool that improves urban and construction planning by making it more participatory and through its visualization more inclusive. Wolf et al. (2020) go in a similar direction by showing with their literature review the potential in the use of mixed reality for urban planning.

4 Immersive Systems as a Tool for Smart Information Transfer

Even though many people state that they strive to behave in an environmentally conscious manner, they often fail to do so because they receive incorrect, misleading, overly complex, insufficient, or even no information during their decision-making process. Immersive systems could remedy some of the information deficits (i.e., information transfer) and at the same time support the decision-making process in an intelligent (i.e., smart) way to avoid a potential information overload or even nudge people to select a more sustainable option. Numerous examples of decisions that hinder reaching the sustainability goals can be seen in the context of purchase decisions.

Even today, one of the major drawbacks of e-commerce transactions encompasses "the inability of online consumers to feel, touch, and sample products through Web interfaces, as they are able to do in conventional in-store shopping" (Jiang and Benbasat 2004, p. 111), which may still lead to difficult product quality assessments and thus product uncertainties (Suh et al. 2011; Hong and Pavlou 2014; Dimoka et al. 2012). To address this issue, various attempts have already been made to enrich the product presentation in e-commerce settings (e.g., through virtual product experiences) (Jiang and Benbasat 2007a, b), which, however, were mostly implemented in a desktop environment and were not overly effective. Especially from a sustainability point of view, the numerous product returns as a result of a poor product fit and false expectations constitute an ecological disaster that could be avoided through a better a priori presentation of products. Furthermore, false expectations naturally lead to dissatisfied consumers. Consequently, Hong and Pavlou (2014, p. 342) demand that "online marketplaces should allocate more resources to reduce consumers' uncertainty about product fit with the aid of new Internet-enabled systems, such as virtual reality and 3D representations." Indeed, practitioners such as Amazon (Amazon AR), Alibaba (Buy+), or IKEA (IKEA Immerse), but also scholars (e.g., Peukert et al. 2019a, b; Meißner et al. 2020), followed the call by launching immersive shopping environments or studying the effect of immersive systems on consumer behavior in experiments. With the help of VR and AR visualizations, consumers are now able to evaluate products in real-scale and from different perspectives (Peukert et al. 2018). In a fashion-shopping context, Yang and Xiong (2019) revealed that virtual fitting rooms reduce product returns, providing first evidence of the potential effectiveness.

Whereas the previous paragraph focused on the presentation of the product itself via immersive features, additional product information may also be transferred by immersive systems. Thereby, the timing as well as the content plays a crucial role. For instance, Peukert et al. (2020) propose the idea of an "intelligent invocation" by a context-aware user assistance system that takes over the decision of *how* to assist and *when* based on the on-the-fly detection of different decision phases. In the same vein, Pfeiffer et al. (2020) show how machine learning can help to train models based on eye-tracking data in order to detect the consumer's shopping context. This knowledge can then be used for smart information transfer in assistance systems. Such systems may reduce the overall cognitive load and thus release cognitive capacities to also consider aspects related to a product's sustainability. In addition, the assistance system could also transfer targeted information related to sustainability, for example, the listing of unhealthy ingredients in food (SDG 3: good health and well-being) or the CO_2 emissions (SDG 13: climate action). Such information can be conveniently displayed in an additional AR view supporting the consumer in identifying a sustainable product or service. Moreover, the indication of the consequences of consumption or the conditions under which the product was manufactured might be more convincing when transferred in an immersive way than by the mere listing of facts and numbers as described earlier. Think of an application sketching out how you would look (from the outside and inside) when eating 5 kg of candy on a daily basis (post-consumption perspective) or an application letting you perceive how it feels to be locked up in a tiny cage such as experienced by some fattening animals. Yet again, the challenge is to transfer this kind of information to the consumer at the right point in time, so that they can be nudged toward a more environmentally conscious alternative.

However, application areas of immersive systems for the purpose of smart information transfer are by no means restricted to sustainable purchase behavior, but are manifold: For instance, as mentioned in the section above, Fegert et al. (2020a, b) support public participation in construction projects via AR and VR visualizations of a planned construction area. This a priori visualization transfers essential information to involve stakeholders in the project and to foster informed decision-making. Similarly, AR and VR are increasingly used for early prototyping to avoid waste in the form of many different models and modeling materials, which later only end up in the dumpster. In the tourism and real estate sectors, VR is already used to provide potential visitors or buyers a realistic virtual image of the accommodation or the object of interest, which could reduce the number of physical on-site inspection appointments, hence saving time and avoiding CO_2 emissions due to travel.

5   Immersive Systems as a Tool for Learning to Act

One of the ongoing challenges for sustainable living is the battle for waste reduction and increase in recycling quality (SDG 12: responsible consumption and production). The EU, acknowledging this problem ("waste has a negative impact on the environment, climate, human health and the economy" [European Parliament 2018]), responded with a plan to raise EU-wide recycling to 55% and decrease landfill use to 10% by 2025 (European Parliament 2018). However, many recycling and waste sorting facilities are still unable to reach maximum efficiency without pre-sorting measures (Bucciol et al. 2011). In countries like Germany, Austria, and Switzerland, this domestic pre-sorting is made a citizen's responsibility (Buclet and Godard 2000), while municipal waste sorting authorities are tasked with providing the necessary education. However, often the actual conduct of teaching is insufficient, among other reasons because of a lack of offered incentives (intrinsic or extrinsic), as well as due to outdated measures of communication and information (Hoffmann and Pfeiffer 2021).

Due to their intrinsic qualities, games have long been used as tools for entertainment as well as education. However, with the launch of the commercial video game industry in the early 1970s (with the Arcade Game (Atari Inc. 1972) Pong having sold more than 8000 units by the end of 1974 [Kent 2001]), digital gameful systems started to be developed, affording fully immersive experiences of being transported to an elaborately simulated location (Murray 1997). During the same period, the theory of experiential learning was formulated and expanded by David A. Kolb (1984). The rapid developments in both fields laid the foundation for the emergence of a market successfully providing serious games and digital edutainment in domains ranging from health to business trainings to general education. In 2016 the global serious games market was valued at $2731 million with expectations to reach $9167 million by 2023 (Sonawane 2020).[1] Furthermore, research on serious games and gamification measures in the field of Information Systems has shown promising results in regard to raising learning outcomes in unremunerated contexts (Santhanam et al. 2016; Franceschi et al. 2009; Cavusoglu et al. 2015), by intrinsically enhancing the fun and intrigue of interacting with the application while transmitting its content through the experience of the players (Deterding 2015).

However, while according to the theory of experiential learning every interaction and experience contributes to learning, it can be difficult to control what is learned from the experience and how and where the learned content is reproduced. In a study that measured learning outcomes under different constellations of game design configurations in an educational game on correct waste sorting, we found that by playing the game, participants' learning outcomes had been successfully and significantly increased (between 7% and 10% better sorts of waste items) when tested within the game. Yet, the effect could not be reproduced in a measure with real-life waste objects, indicating that the transfer of the trained knowledge to real life was not as successful. Other studies have struggled with a similar translation problem. In a study on gamification in business simulators, Größler et al. (2000) state: "Participants were not capable of accessing the knowledge gained outside the gaming context" (p. 271). Such insights highlight the importance of measuring the reproducibility of trained knowledge across different media—especially if the context medium in which the knowledge should be applied differs from the medium in which the knowledge is trained. As identified by Kolers and Paradis (1980), different tasks nominally tapping the same skill, and different symbols used in the tasks, yield different outcomes depending on attitude and mental state. Studies on context-dependent learning find strong evidence that the informational value of contexts affects the strength of context-dependent learning (Lucke et al. 2013). Such findings make the case for the necessity of implementations of real-life applied learning tasks in VR environments, where a strong fit between the training and real-life application context can be afforded (Hoffmann and Pfeiffer 2021). By combining immersive technology (affording surrounding sensory experiences) with immersive content, prospects are raised of reaching optimal learning outcome for the respective training matter.

---

[1] https://www.alliedmarketresearch.com/serious-games-market. Accessed 22 Feb 2020.

6   Conclusion and Outlook

Many challenges lie ahead for the IS community to help in forwarding efforts to achieve the SDGs. In this publication, we provide insights from research on immersive systems and how different approaches can help to address some of the challenges that we face in reaching these goals, namely, *Awareness*, *Motivation*, *Information Transfer*, and *Learning to Act*.

Our research presents the starting points for addressing different aspects of several SDGs. For example, regarding SDG 1: no poverty, an immersive system can virtually put its user in the shoes of another, thus holding the potential to foster stronger feelings of empathy, which might help to inculcate intentions to volunteer for charitable purposes. By integrating assistance systems for smart information transfer into immersive systems, users can be reached directly with targeted information relating to sustainability. We gave several examples of SDGs that can be supported by this means: Listing of unhealthy ingredients in food on demand can lead to an increase of SDG 3: good health and well-being, while on-the-spot information on CO_2 emissions could drastically help to further SDG 13: climate action. For SDG 10: reduce inequalities, the effect of adjustable telepresence (with regard to a person's digital representation) can serve as a leveling mechanism with the potential to overcome prejudices relating to gender, age, or educational background. Furthermore, by allowing instant "transport" to any digital location, such technologies afford participation independent of distance. This inherent feature further supports SDG 16: peace, justice, and strong institutions, through its enhanced possibilities for participation. For SDG 11: sustainable cities and communities, immersive systems allow for more efficient urban planning processes through accessible and inclusive visualizations. Finally, in SDG 12: responsible consumption and production, educating the public is directly addressed as a subgoal. With their high congruence with real life, immersive systems are particularly suitable for the training of sustainable behavior, and thus we recommend fostering the development of learning and training software for VR in particular.

To some readers the presented research might seem impractical in terms of imme- diate application, as immersive systems have not yet fully penetrated the market. However, current developments relating to the ongoing crisis (Covid-19) have led to a formerly unpredicted increase in teleworking and virtual meetings, as well as a general increase in digitization efforts. Educational and entertainment institutions are forced to migrate to digital formats such as virtual tours in museums or virtual concerts, while the digital entertainment industry, the biggest driver of commercial use of immersive systems, is at an all-time high. With these developments boosting the market, the relevance for research in immersive systems—specifically with its focus on sustainability—is rapidly increasing, especially as certain areas of human welfare are projected to suffer greatly during the pandemic.

Arguably, all of the different facets of the research discussed in this publication have a very optimistic perspective. We did not discuss, for example, the CO_2 footprint of immersive systems, which still seems to be an under-researched field.

This is crucial because the footprint of ICT is growing continuously (Gelenbe and Caseau 2015) and computational effort toward rendering and so on needed for immersive system technology is high. It is already estimated that around 4% of all electricity consumption and over 2% of all CO_2 emissions are the result of ICT use (Fagas et al. 2017). Thus, in future research, benefits and disadvantages must be balanced thoroughly (Dedrick 2010), in order to judge the actual effect of IS, and in our case immersive systems, on SDG. With this in mind, we believe that this publication can give readers an overview of promising approaches in the light of an optimistic outlook.

For the future, we hope to inspire further research efforts into how IS can make a real contribution to a more sustainable world.

References

Ahn S J, Bailenson J N, Park D (2014) Short- and long-term effects of embodied experiences in immersive virtual environments on environmental locus of control and behavior. Computers in Human Behavior 39:235-245

Bailey J O, Bailenson J N, Flora J, Armel K C, Voelker D, Reeves B (2015) The Impact of Vivid Messages on Reducing Energy Consumption Related to Hot Water Use. Environment and Behavior 47(5):570-592

Banakou D, Groten R, Slater M (2013) Illusory ownership of a virtual child body causes overestimation of object sizes and implicit attitude changes. In: Proceedings of the National Academy of Sciences 110(31):12846-12851

Banakou D, Hanumanthu P, Slater M (2016) Virtual Embodiment of White People in a Black Virtual Body Leads to a Sustained Reduction in Their Implicit Racial Bias. Frontiers in Human Neuroscience 10:1-12

Bateman I J, Day B H, Jones A P, Jude S (2009) Reducing gain-loss asymmetry: A virtual reality choice experiment valuing land use change. Journal of Environmental Economics and Management 58(1):106-118

Bowman D, McMahan R (2007) Virtual reality: how much immersion is enough? Computer 40(7):36-43

Briesemeister B, Tamm S, Heine A, Jacobs A M (2013) Approach the Good, Withdraw from the Bad—A Review on Frontal Alpha Asymmetry Measures in Applied Psychological Research. Psychology 4:261-267

Bucciol A, Montinari N, Piovesan M (2011) Do not trash the incentive! Monetary incentives and waste sorting. Scandinavian Journal of Economics 117(4):1204-1229

Buclet N, Godard O (2000) Municipal Waste Management in Europe. Netherlands: Springer Science and Business Media.

Cavusoglu H, Li Z, Huang K-W (2015) Can Gamification Motivate Voluntary Contributions? The Case of StackOverflow Q&A Community. In: Proceedings of the 18th ACM Conference Companion on Computer Supported Cooperative Work & Social Computing, Association for Computing Machinery, New York, USA, pp 171-174

Cavusoglu H, Dennis A, Parsons J (2019) Immersive Systems. Journal of Management Information Systems 36(3):680-682

Dedrick J (2010) Green IS: concepts and issues for information systems research. Communications of the Association for Information Systems 27(1):11

Deterding S (2015) The Lens of Intrinsic Skill Atoms: A Method for Gameful Design. Human–Computer Interaction 30(3-4):294-335

Dimoka A, Hong Y, Pavlou P (2012) On product uncertainty in online markets: Theory and evidence. MIS Quarterly 36(2):395-426

European Parliament. (2018). The circular economy package: new EU targets for recycling. http://www.europarl.europa.eu/news/en/headlines/priorities/circular-economy/20170120STO59356/the-circular-economy-package-new-eu-targets-for-recycling. Accessed 20 Feb 2019

Fagas G, Gallagher J, Gammaitoni L, Paul D J (2017) Energy challenges for ICT. ICT—Energy Concepts for Energy Efficiency and Sustainability, IntechOpen, London, UK, 2017

Fegert J, Pfeiffer J, Golubyeva A, Pfeiffer-Leßmann N, Hariharan A, Renner P, Pfeiffer T, Hefke M, Straub T, Weinhardt C (2019) Take Part Prototype: Creating New Ways of Participation Through Augmented and Virtual Reality. In: Proceedings of 29th Workshop on Information Technologies and Systems (WITS), Munich, Germany

Fegert J, Pfeiffer J, Peukert C, Golubyeva A, Weinhardt C (2020a) Combining e-Participation with Augmented and Virtual Reality: Insights from a Design Science Research Project, Proceedings of the International Conference on Information Systems (ICIS 2020), India, 2020

Fegert J, Pfeiffer J, Peukert C, Weinhardt C (2020b) Enriching E-Participation through Augmented Reality: First Results of a Qualitative Study. In: Proceedings der 15. Internationalen Tagung Wirtschaftsinformatik 2020, Posdam, 2020

Fiore S M, Harrison G W, Hughes, C E, Rutström E E (2009) Virtual experiments and environmental policy. Journal of Environmental Economics and Management 57(1):65-86

Fox J, McKnight J, Sun Y, Maung D, Crawfis R (2020) Using a serious game to communicate risk and minimize psychological distance regarding environmental pollution. Telematics and Informatics 46:101320

Franceschi K, Lee R, Zanakis S, Hinds D (2009) Engaging group e-learning in virtual worlds. Journal of Management Information Systems 26(1):73-100

Gelenbe E, Caseau Y (2015) The impact of information technology on energy consumption and carbon emissions. Ubiquity:1-15

Gholami R, Watson R, Hasan H, Molla A, Bjorn-Andersen N (2016) Information Systems Solutions for Environmental Sustainability: How Can We Do More?. Journal of the Association for Information Systems 17(8):521-536

Gifford R, Scannell L, Kormos C, Smolova L, Biel A, Boncu S (2009) Temporal pessimism and spatial optimism in environmental assessments: An 18-nation study. Journal of Environmental Psychology 29(1):1-12

Greif-Winzrieth A, Knierim M, Peukert C, Weinhardt C (2020) Feeling the Pain of others in Need: Studying the Effect of VR on Donation Behavior Using EEG. In: Proceedings of NeuroIS Retreat 2020, Springer, pp 172-180

Größler A, Maier F, Milling P (2000) Enhancing learning capabilities by providing transparency in business simulators. Simulation & Gaming 31(2):257-278

Gürerk Ö, Kasulke A (2017) Does Virtual Reality Increase Charitable Giving? An Experimental Study. SSRN Electronic Journal

Hoffmann G, Pfeiffer J (2021) Correct Waste Sorting through Gameful Learning: Measuring the Effect of Design Elements on Long-Term Learning Outcome. Working Paper

Hong Y, Pavlou P (2014) Product fit uncertainty in online markets: Nature, effects, and antecedents. Information Systems Research 25(2):328-344

Huffmeijer R, Alink L, Tops M, Bakermans-Kranenburg M, Van IJzendoorn M (2012) Asymmetric frontal brain activity and parental rejection predict altruistic behavior: Moderation of oxytocin effects. Cogn. Affect. Behav. Neurosci. 12(2):382-392

Jiang Z, Benbasat I (2004) Virtual product experience: Effects of visual and functional control of products on perceived diagnosticity and flow in electronic shopping. Journal of Management Information Systems 21(3):111-147

Jiang Z, Benbasat I (2007a) Research note—investigating the influence of the functional mechanisms of online product presentations. Information Systems Research 18(4):454-470

Jiang Z, Benbasat I (2007b) The effects of presentation formats and task complexity on online consumers' product understanding. MIS Quarterly 31(3):475-500

Kent S (2001) The King and Court. Ultimate History of Video Games. Three Rivers Press, 2001

Kolb D (1984) Experiential Learning. Experience as the source of learning and development. Englewood Cliffs: Prentice-Hall

Kolers P, Paradis M (1980) Psychological and linguistic studies of bilingualism. Canadian Journal of Psychology, Canadian Journal of Psychology 34(4):287-303

Liberman N, Trope Y (1998) The role of feasibility and desirability considerations in near and distant future decisions: A test of temporal construal theory. Journal of Personality and Social Psychology 75(1):5-18

Lucke S, Lachnit H, Koenig S et al (2013) The informational value of contexts affects context-dependent learning. Learn Behav 41(3):285-297

Maister L, Sebanz N, Knoblich G, Tsakiris M (2013) Experiencing ownership over a dark-skinned body reduces implicit racial bias. Cognition 128(2):170-178

Maister L, Slater M, Sanchez-Vives M, Tsakiris M (2015) Changing bodies changes minds: owning another body affects social cognition. Trends in Cognitive Sciences 19(1):6-12

Meißner M, Pfeiffer J, Peukert C, Dietrich H, Pfeiffer T (2020) How virtual reality affects consumer choice. Journal of Business Research 117:219-231

Murray J (1997) Hamlet on the Holodeck: The Future of Narrative in Cyberspace. Simon & Schuster, New York

Nelson K, Anggraini E, Schlüter A (2020) Virtual reality as a tool for environmental conservation and fundraising. PloS one 15(4):e0223631

Peck T, Seinfeld S, Aglioti S, Slater M (2013) Putting yourself in the skin of a black avatar reduces implicit racial bias. Consciousness and Cognition 22(3):779-787

Peukert C, Brossok F, Pfeiffer J, Meißner M, Weinhardt C (2018) Towards designing virtual reality shopping environments. In: Conference Booklet of the 13th International Conference on Design Science Research in Information Systems and Technology (DESRIST), Chennai, India, 2018

Peukert C, Pfeiffer J, Meißner M, Pfeiffer T, Weinhardt C (2019a). Acceptance of Imagined Versus Experienced Virtual Reality Shopping Environments: Insights from Two Experiments. In: Proceedings of the 27th European Conference on Information Systems (ECIS), Stockholm & Uppsala, Sweden.

Peukert C, Pfeiffer J, Meißner M, Pfeiffer T, Weinhardt C (2019b) Shopping in virtual reality stores: The influence of immersion on system adoption. Journal of Management Information Systems 36(3):755-788

Peukert C, Lechner J, Pfeiffer J, Weinhardt C (2020). Intelligent Invocation: Towards Designing Context-Aware User Assistance Systems Based on Real-Time Eye Tracking Data Analysis. In: Davis F, Riedl R, vom Brocke J, Léger PM, Randolph A, Fischer T (eds) Information Systems and Neuroscience. Lecture Notes in Information Systems and Organisation, vol 32. Springer, Cham.

Pfeiffer J, Pfeiffer T, Meißner M, Weiß E (2020) Eye-Tracking-Based Classification of Information Search Behavior using Machine Learning: Evidence from Experiments in Physical Shops and Virtual Reality Shopping Environments. Information Systems Research (ISR) 31(3):675-691

Santhanam R, Liu D, Shen W (2016) Gamification of technology-mediated training: Not all competitions are the same. Information Systems Research 27(2): 453-465

Scholl H (2008) Discipline or Interdisciplinary Study Domain? Challenges and Promises in Electronic Government Research. In: Chen H, Brandt L, Gregg V, Traunmüller R, Dawes S, Hovy E, Macintosh A, Larson C, Digital Government: E-Government Research, Case Studies, and Implementation, Springer US, Boston, pp 21-41

Schutte N, Stilinovic E (2017) Facilitating empathy through virtual reality. Motivation and Emotion 41(1):708–712

Shin D (2018) Empathy and embodied experience in virtual environment: To what extent can virtual reality stimulate empathy and embodied experience? Comput. Human Behav. 78:64-73

Slater M, Sanchez-Vives M (2014) Transcending the Self in Immersive Virtual Reality. Computer 47(7):24-30

Steininger D M (2019) Linking information systems and entrepreneurship: A review and agenda for IT-associated and digital entrepreneurship research. Information Systems Journal 29(2):363–407

Steuer J (1992) Defining virtual reality: Dimensions determining telepresence. Journal of communication 42(4):73-93

Suh K, Kim H, Suh E (2011) What if your avatar looks like you? Dual-congruity perspectives for avatar use. MIS Quarterly 35(3):711-729

Toots M (2019) Why E-Participation Systems Fail: The Case of Estonia's Osale. In: Government Information Quarterly 36(3):546-559

UNDP (2020) Goal 11: Sustainable cities and communities. URL: https://www.undp.org/content/undp/en/home/sustainable-development-goals/goal-11-sustainable-cities-and-communities.html. Accessed 10 Oct 2020

United Nations (2018) UNITED NATIONS E-Government Survey 2018. https://publicadministration.un.org/egovkb/Portals/egovkb/Documents/un/2018-Survey/EGovernment%20Survey%202018_FINAL%20for%20web.pdf. Accessed 10 Jul 2019

United Nations (2019) World Urbanization Prospects: The 2018 Revision. United Nations, Department of Economic and Social Affairs. (2019). URL: https://population.un.org/wup/Publications/Files/WUP2018-Report.pdf. Accessed 10 Jul 2019

vom Brocke J, Stein A, Hofmann S, Tumbas S (2015) Grand Societal Challenges in Information Systems Research and Education. Springer International Publishing

Watson R T, Boudreau M-C, Chen A J (2010) Information Systems and Environmentally Sustainable Development: Energy Informatics and New Directions for the IS Community. MIS Quarterly 34(1):23-38

Wolf M, Söbke H, Wehking F (2020) Mixed Reality Media-Enabled Public Participation in Urban Planning. In: Jung T, Dieck T, Rauschnabel C, Philipp A, Augmented Reality and Virtual Reality: Changing Realities in a Dynamic World, Springer International Publishing, pp 125-138

Yang S, Xiong G (2019) Try It On! Contingency Effects of Virtual Fitting Rooms. Journal of Management Information Systems 36(3):789-822

Zaalberg R, Midden C (2010) Enhancing Human Responses to Climate Change Risks through Simulated Flooding Experiences. In: Ploug T, Hasle P F V, Oinas-Kukkonen H (Eds) Persuasive technology, ser. Lecture Notes in Computer Science, 6137 Springer, Berlin, pp 205-210

Jella Pfeiffer is a professor of Digitalization, E-Business, and Operations Management at the Department of Economics and Business Studies, Giessen University. Previously, she worked as a postdoc at the Karlsruhe Institute of Technology and was the manager of the Karlsruhe Decision & Design Lab (KD^{2}Lab). Her research on decision support systems in e-commerce and VR-commerce and her works on experimental research have been published in *Information Systems Research*, the *Journal of Management Information Systems*, the *Journal of the Association for Information Systems*, the *Journal of Behavioural Decision Making*, and the *European Journal of Operational Research*, among others.

Jonas Fegert is a research associate at FZI Research Center for Information Technology in Berlin. He studies subjects around digital government, e-democracy, and e-participation—a field on which he is doing his PhD at the Karlsruhe Institute of Technology with Christof Weinhardt as his supervisor. He studied political science, governance, and public policy at the Free University of Berlin, Zeppelin University, and the Federal University of Rio Grande do Sul.

Anke Greif-Winzrieth is a PhD student at the Institute of Information Systems and Marketing at the Karlsruhe Institute of Technology supervised by Christof Weinhardt. She is also the manager of the Karlsruhe Decision & Design Lab (KD^{2}Lab). She received her bachelor's and master's degree in Industrial Engineering and Management from the Karlsruhe Institute of Technology. Her research interests include virtual reality, citizen science, and experimental economics.

Greta Hoffmann is guest researcher at the Institute of Information Systems and Marketing at the Karlsruhe Institute of Technology under the supervision of Christof Weinhardt and holds a diploma in Product Design and Media Art. She conducts research on game design elements that are directed toward the improvement of knowledge and motivation in social and ecological public contexts. Her projects have won several awards, including the IDEENSTARK 2020 Award and best game in the family category of the GIGA Maus Award of Eltern magazine.

Christian Peukert is a postdoc at the Institute of Information Systems and Marketing at the Karlsruhe Institute of Technology, Germany, leading the research group for Digital Experience and Participation. In 2020, he received his PhD in Information Systems from the Karlsruhe Institute of Technology, supervised by Christof Weinhardt. His research interests center on investigating consumer behavior within immersive systems as well as on experimental economics. His work has been published in the *Journal of Management Information Systems*, in the *Journal of Business Research*, and in the Proceedings of the International Conference on Information Systems and the European Conference on Information Systems, among others.

How at the Institute of Information Systems and Marketing One Thing Leads to Another and Eventually Results in a Low-Trade Theorem

Stefan Seifert

Abstract This chapter portrays how research topics arise and develop in the creative environment of the research group Information & Market Engineering of the Institute of Information Systems and Marketing at the Karlsruhe Institute of Technology. It is somewhat long-winded in the beginning but identifies then a clear goal. In the following, it strays around several lines of research; touches on the question of why something like forecasting markets, the actual research topic, works at all – without answering it; and finally reaches a result that has little to do with the original objective. Along the way, the chapter provides some insights into the economic theory of double auctions.

1 Requirements

A good research paper features a clear question and a stringent methodological approach which leads to non-ambiguous results that answer the question. Particularly students and young scientists are reminded ad nauseam about the importance of a carefully formulated and precise research question. This question should be phrased *before* the details of the methodological approach are planned in order to, first, choose a method that is appropriate for the question and, second, avoid erroneous conclusions. Otherwise, there is the risk that random effects which are contained in the data may be interpreted as an own artefact or result. Likewise, a statistical hypothesis should be stated *before* the data of a study are analysed.

Under the direction of Christof Weinhardt, I conducted and supervised several experiments. At the research group Information & Market Engineering (IME), it was common that the experimenter had to specify the most relevant hypotheses relating to her or his research question. Moreover, she or he had to write down how relevant measures were to be operationalized and which tests used for assessing the

S. Seifert (✉)
Lehrstuhl für Technologie- und Innovationsmanagement, University of Bayreuth, Bayreuth, Germany
e-mail: stefan.seifert@uni-bayreuth.de

© The Author(s) 2021
H. Gimpel et al. (eds.), *Market Engineering*,
https://doi.org/10.1007/978-3-030-66661-3_9

hypotheses. The statistical necessity of this procedure becomes apparent in a simple thought experiment in which dice are thrown n times. Specific outcomes, such as particularly frequent observations of the number '6', may suggest that the dice are not fair.

In order to actually assess whether the dice are fair or not, introductory statistics textbooks suggest, for example, Pearson's chi-square test based on the relative frequencies of all numbers (e.g. Freedman et al. 2007, ch. 28). This test checks whether the frequencies of all numbers are equal. Dice that yield the numbers '1', '2', '3', '4', '5', '6', '1', '2', ... in this fix order are certainly not ideal dice. Pearson's chi-square test, though, would not reveal any irregularity. Accordingly, there are many possibilities in which dice may deviate from perfectly independent and uniform randomness: A number of the pair '1' and '2' may be thrown more often than '3' or '4', odd numbers may be observed more often than even numbers or a low number may be followed more often by an even than an odd number and so forth. Given a respective data set, the hypothesis that all numbers occur independently and with equal probability could be rejected for some significance level α based on any of the above observations.

The significance level α describes the probability of error, that is, the possibility that a null hypothesis is rejected even though it is true. If one considers a sufficiently large number m of independent or orthogonal test statistics, then one will find up to $m \times \alpha$ reasons to reject the hypothesis of ideal dice even though it actually holds true. This means that if a researcher searches long enough, she or he may identify results that point in the wrong direction. A prior determination of hypotheses (in an appropriate number), a specification of their operationalization and the respective test procedure minimize the risk of this fatal error.

While in some projects it is at least possible to state the research question as well as the relevant hypotheses in advance, actual research often follows a different path. Some results are simply coincidental. An example is the famous apple that supposedly fell on Isaac Newton's head, an event that allegedly led him to formulate the laws of gravitation (Stukeley 1752, p. 43). Whereas the historical content of Newton's apple is at least contested,[1] it is considered certain that, for example, the discovery of penicillin is based on petri dishes of Alexander Fleming contaminated with fungal spores (Geo 2017). Similarly, the invention of Teflon or polytetrafluoroethylene traces back to unexpected polymerization in a pressure tank used by Roy Plunkett at DuPont for experiments while searching for a refrigerant (Deutschlandradio 2016), and cornflakes have their roots in dried wheat dough of the brothers John Harvey and Will Keith Kellogg (Geo 2019).

In the above examples, coincidences and mishaps led to new findings. While there is no need for adversities, it is important to seize accidental observations and develop them further. Innovation management investigates, among other things, how research environments can be designed and tailored to foster development. Tidd and

---

[1]*Der Standard* (online issue of January 18, 2010, section "Zeit") quotes Keith Moore, archivist of the Royal Society, as saying that Newton himself is likely to have polished this tale.

Bessant (2014, p. 62) mention, for example, *shared vision*, *key individuals*, *efficient working teams* and a *creative climate* as relevant components of an innovation organization.

A paradigm for such an organization is the IME, a research group of the Institute of Information Systems and Marketing (IISM) under the direction of Christof Weinhardt at the Karlsruhe Institute of Technology (KIT). Similar to a case study, this chapter depicts an example of a fruitful research project that continuously adapted to new stimuli it collected along its path. It first presents a rather clear question; strays then around several lines of research; touches on the question of why something like forecasting markets, the actual research topic, works at all (unfortunately without answering it); and finally reaches a result that has little to do with the original objective. Thus, the chapter provides some insights into the economic theory of double auctions. Apart from this, it does not fulfil the basic requirements of a good research report. The main reason is that it is incomplete. At the IME, the preliminary results would have been challenged and discussed in several research seminars. With much valuable and constructive feedback, they finally would have been sent back to the right path of academic virtue and the quality standards of the research group. Judged in retrospective, apparently, I left the IME too early to achieve this success.

2 Setting

Christof Weinhardt's research group IME at the IISM has been dealing with 'Market Engineering', the design of markets, for many years. Against this background, in the *STOCCER* project a prediction market was operated in the run-up to the 2006 Soccer World Cup in Germany, in the course of which, among other things, various market models and order types were examined (Luckner et al. 2005). The idea of such a prediction market is that virtual shares promise a payout that depends on future events. From a theoretical point of view, according to the so-called efficient market hypothesis (Fama 1970), the market price should reflect the aggregated assessment of the participants regarding the probability of occurrence of future events. Empirical evidence for the efficiency of prediction markets is given by Berg et al. (2001) referring to the *Iowa Electronic Market*.

When designing *STOCCER*, the IME discussed various incentive schemes, for example, the question of whether participants should be given monetary payments or non-monetary prices for their participation and whether, in the case of monetary payments, they should be based on absolute performance (prediction accuracy), relative performance (ranking compared to other participants) or activity (e.g. based on transactions). In addition, the number of participants needed for such a market and the budget required for this market were also considered.

Unfortunately, these questions are not easy to answer. The auction theoretical literature provides comprehensive and far-reaching results on one-sided auctions of individual goods for which the bidders have private valuations. However, if these criteria are relaxed, the results become much thinner. If the focus on one-sided auctions is abandoned and double auctions are addressed, a literature strand around Myerson and Satterthwaite (1983) deals with the question of whether and, if so under which conditions, efficient, incentive-compatible and budget-balanced mechanisms exist. For relatively general assumptions, the budget balance of a mechanism results in inefficiency. Thus, if the prices paid by the buyers equal in sum the revenues of the sellers, the mechanism does not reconcile all profitable transactions. Some possible gains from trade are left on the table. These results contrast with studies such as those of Wilson (1985) and Rustichini et al. (1994), which show that inefficiency falls quickly as the number of traders increases. If one takes into account the possibility that in a prediction market bidders can buy or sell not only one but several units of a good, the incentive to reduce quantity, a phenomenon called *strategic demand* or *supply reduction*, increases inefficiency (Ausubel et al. 2014). The analysis is further complicated by the fact that the shares traded on prediction markets are not goods for which the bidders have private valuations. After the end of the soccer world championship, the events to be forecasted are known and the shares have the same value for all players. Taking a common value component into account increases the complexity of the analysis, but, on the other hand, efficiency considerations become less important, since any allocation of common value goods is Pareto efficient.

With the exemplary questions 'How does a performance-oriented payment scheme differ from rank- or transaction-based incentives with regard to the prediction accuracy of a forecast market?' and 'What influence does the size of the group have on the result of a forecasting market?', the *STOCCER* project, with which the investigation of market models and order types actually pursued a completely different research agenda, generated further research challenges which were only waiting to be taken up. In the creative environment of the IME, they did not have to wait long. As a sort of *case study*, the present chapter reports how they were addressed and developed further.

3   Model

To assess the result of a market, a stock exchange is considered as a strategic game. The analysis aims to identify bidding equilibria and describe their characteristics. For simplification, a model with only two risk-neutral market participants, a buyer B and a seller S, is considered. The seller S owns a share that promises a payout depending on a future event. This payment is the same for both players (*common value* item, cf. Milgrom and Weber 1982). Other goods are not traded. With regard to the future event, both players possess a private signal or piece of information each, which is denoted by x (buyer) and y (seller). Both x and y are real numbers from an interval $[\underline{x}; \overline{x}]$ and $[\underline{y}; \overline{y}]$, respectively. The expected value of the share, given the two pieces of information x and y, is given by $v(x, y)$. The value function

$v(\cdot, \cdot)$ is monotonically increasing in both arguments. However, both the buyer and seller only know their own signal. They consider the signal of the other player as a realization of a random variable X and Y, respectively. The (conditional) densities $g(x|Y=y)$ and $h(y|X=x)$, in the following shorter $g(x|y)$ and $h(y|x)$, of these random variables X and Y are commonly known. The market mechanism is assumed to be a k-double auction with $k = \frac{1}{2}$ (Satterthwaite and Williams 1989): The two players B and S each submit a bid $b = b(x)$ and $s = s(y)$, respectively. If $b(x) > s(y)$, B acquires the item from S and pays a price of $\frac{b(x)+s(y)}{2}$.[2] Otherwise, no trading occurs: S keeps the item and B makes no payment. The two functions $b(\cdot)$ and $s(\cdot)$ are assumed to be monotonically increasing and, thus, in particular to be invertible.

From applying the inverse $s^{-1}(\cdot)$ of the seller's bidding function on the inequality $b > s(y)$, it follows that the buyer acquires the good with a bid b, if for the signal y of the seller $y < s^{-1}(b)$ holds. In this case, the expected payment of B is

$$v(x, y) - \frac{b + s(y)}{2}.$$

The expected payment of the buyer is therefore calculated as

$$u_B(b, x) = \int_{\underline{y}}^{s^{-1}(b)} \left(v(x, y) - \frac{b + s(y)}{2} \right) h(y|x)\, dy.$$

The Leibniz rule for the derivative of parameter integrals provides the necessary condition for an optimal purchase bid:

$$\frac{du_B(b, x)}{db} = \left(v\left(x, s^{-1}(b)\right) - \frac{b + s\left(s^{-1}(b)\right)}{2} \right) h\left(s^{-1}(b)|x\right) s^{-1'}(b)$$

$$- \int_{\underline{y}}^{s^{-1}(b)} \frac{1}{2} h(y|x)\, dy$$

$$= \left(v\left(x, s^{-1}(b)\right) - b \right) h\left(s^{-1}(b)|x\right) s^{-1'}(b)$$

$$- \frac{1}{2} H\left(s^{-1}(b)|x\right) \overset{!}{=} 0. \tag{1}$$

---

[2]Whether or not trading takes place in case $b(x) = s(y)$ is not relevant for the following considerations. However, the result can be formulated more strikingly if no trading occurs in this case. Thus, strictly speaking, the result determines—somewhat unscientifically—the design of the model. For defense, the author argues that in the case of strictly monotonically increasing bidding functions and continuous signals, the probability that bids are equal (independent of the special properties of the result) is zero.

Regarding the seller, two cases are to be distinguished: If $s \geq b(x) \Leftrightarrow x \leq b^{-1}(s)$, the seller keeps the good with the value $v(x, y)$. If $s < b(x) \Leftrightarrow x > b^{-1}(s)$, S sells the item and receives a payment from buyer B of $\frac{b(x)+s}{2}$. The seller's expected payment is

$$u_S(s, y) = \int_{\underline{x}}^{b^{-1}(s)} v(x, y)\, g(x|y)\, dx + \int_{b^{-1}(s)}^{\overline{x}} \frac{b(x) + s}{2}\, g(x|y)\, dx$$

and we obtain the following first-order condition for equilibrium:

$$\frac{du_S(s, y)}{ds} = v\left(b^{-1}(s), y\right) g\left(b^{-1}(s)|y\right) b^{-1'}(s)$$

$$- \frac{b(b^{-1}(s)) + s}{2}\, g\left(b^{-1}(s)|y\right) b^{-1'}(s)\, dx + \int_{b^{-1}(s)}^{\overline{x}} \frac{1}{2}\, g(x|y)\, dx$$

$$= \left(v(b^{-1}(s), y) - s\right) g\left(b^{-1}(s)|y\right) b^{-1'}(s) + \frac{1}{2}\left(1 - G\left(b^{-1}(s)|y\right)\right) \overset{!}{=} 0.$$

$$(2)$$

For illustration, consider an example where the signals of the players are independent of each other and uniformly distributed over the interval $[0; 1]$. The densities and distribution functions are then given by $g(x|y) \equiv h(y|x) \equiv 1$, $G(x|y) \equiv x$ and $H(y|x) \equiv y$. For the example, it is further assumed that the expected value of the traded share under the presence of the signals x and y be given by $v(x, y) = \frac{x+y}{2}$. Then the necessary equilibrium conditions (1) and (2) simplify to

$$\left(\frac{x + s^{-1}(b)}{2} - b\right) s^{-1'}(b) - \frac{1}{2} s^{-1}(b) \overset{!}{=} 0$$

and

$$\left(\frac{b^{-1}(s) + y}{2} - s\right) b^{-1'}(s) + \frac{1}{2}\left(1 - b^{-1}(s)\right) \overset{!}{=} 0.$$

A solution[3] to the above functional equation system are the two bid functions

$$b(x) = \frac{1}{2}x \quad \text{and}$$

$$s(y) = y + \frac{1}{2}.$$

---

[3] There is a variety of solutions, including at least the family of linear solutions $b(x) = tx - t + \frac{1}{2}$; $s(y) = \frac{t}{3t-1}y + \frac{1}{2}$ with $t > \frac{1}{3}$.

Remarkably, given this solution, the item is never traded. The bids of the buyer are never larger than ½, and the bids of the seller are never lower than ½. Thus, the bid of the buyer is never sufficiently high to meet the seller's ask price.

Interestingly, this observation is not a peculiarity of the example. Consider the first-order condition from the buyer's point of view at the point $\hat{x}$ with $\underline{z} := b(\hat{x}) = s(y)$, that is, the signal at which the buyer's bid is just as high as the minimum seller's bid. From (1) follows

$$\left(v\left(\hat{x}, s^{-1}(\underline{z})\right) - \underline{z}\right) h\left(s^{-1}(\underline{z})|\hat{x}\right) s^{-1\prime}(\underline{z}) - \frac{1}{2} H\left(\underbrace{\overbrace{s^{-1}(\underline{z})}^{=y}|\hat{x}}_{=0}\right) \overset{!}{=} 0$$

$$\Longleftrightarrow \left(v(\hat{x}, y) - \underline{z}\right) h(y|\hat{x}) s^{-1\prime}(\underline{z}) \overset{!}{=} 0.$$

Since $s(\cdot)$ is strictly monotonously increasing, $s^{-1\prime}(\cdot) > 0$; this also holds for the density $h(\cdot|\cdot) > 0$. Thus, the minimum amount that the seller asks for is

$$s(y) = b(\hat{x}) = \underline{z} = v(\hat{x}, y).$$

This means that the lowest bid of the seller is just $v(\hat{x}, y)$. Assume for the moment $\hat{x} < \bar{x}$. Then one obtains from (2) at the same point

$$\left(v\left(b^{-1}(s(y)), y\right) - s(y)\right) \underbrace{g\left(b^{-1}(s(y))|y\right)}_{>0} \underbrace{b^{-1\prime}(s(y))}_{>0}$$

$$+ \frac{1}{2}\underbrace{\left(1 - G\left(\overbrace{b^{-1}(s(y))}^{=\hat{x}<\bar{x}}|y\right)\right)}_{>0} \overset{!}{=} 0$$

the condition $s(y) > v(b^{-1}(s(y)), y) = v(\hat{x}, y)$. This means that the lowest bid of the seller is higher than $v(\hat{x}, y)$, which contradicts the above observation $s(y) = v(\hat{x}, y)$. This contradiction can only be resolved if $\hat{x} = \bar{x}$ and, thus, $1 - G(\hat{x}|y) = 0$. Consequently, the maximum bid that the buyer submits at signal $\bar{x}$ is just as high as the minimum bid of the seller that the latter submits at signal y. Thus, the result already observed in the above example holds independently of the value function $v(\cdot, \cdot)$ and the distributions $g(x|y)$ and $h(y|x)$ of the signals x and y of B and S, respectively. And if the first-order conditions allow for several equilibrium candidates, all these candidates will share this property.

First of all, the result is surprising: It suggests that on a prediction market where shares can be traded that promise uncertain but equal payments for all participants, from a theoretical point of view, no trading should occur. This means that no market price would be generated and the market would be of no use as a forecasting tool. But not only that: Actual shares also have an unknown value that is identical for all participants. For these markets, too, the above model implies that – regardless of the information that individual traders might have regarding the value of the stock – there should be no trade.

The above result is quite radical, so it is reasonable to assume that it is possibly not correct or already known. Intuitively, however, it is easy to comprehend: An allocation of common value goods is always efficient. Consequently, transactions among participants do not promote welfare. Thus, there is no efficiency gain that can be shared. Rather, what one participant would gain, another participant would lose. There are no incentives that could tempt buyers and sellers alike to engage in a transaction.[4] Thus, the possibility that the result is correct gains plausibility. Consequently, the question remains whether perhaps it is already known.

Solitary thinking about the critical but constructive culture of scientific discussions at the IME led the author to take another look at the literature before presenting the above result in the research group's colloquium. And indeed, with the knowledge of what to look for, namely, the lack of trade in markets, that which was searched for was quickly found: As early as 1982, Milgrom and Stokey established a general *No-trade* theorem. They show that based on a Pareto-efficient initial allocation of goods, additional private information about the value of the goods does not induce trade. Similarly, in the present model the initial endowment according to which S owns a good is efficient regardless of the signals of the traders. According to the *No-trade* theorem, private information (an individual signal) does not induce trade. In comparison with the above calculations, Milgrom and Stokey relax the assumption of risk-neutral to (weakly) risk-averse market participants and thus arrive at more general insights than those presented in this chapter.

Today, Milgrom and Stokey's *No-trade* theorem is applied in a somewhat more far-reaching interpretation primarily in the context of prohibiting insider trading. Regarding the existence of trading in stock markets, there are various approaches to mitigate the *No-trade* theorem. Grossman and Stiglitz (1980) consider a model in which traders can acquire information and thereby gain an information advantage. Uninformed and informed traders then meet in the market. In contrast to the present chapter (or the model by Milgrom and Stokey), in which traders receive their signals for free, Grossman and Stiglitz assume that the acquisition of information is costly. Moreover, Grossman and Stiglitz' traders do not act strategically with respect to price formation, but rather accept as price-taker the price that results from mapping aggregated supply with aggregated demand. Grossman and Stiglitz also emphasize the importance of *noise* as a fuzziness of the pricing system with regard to the

---

[4]It is no secret at the IME that the author became aware of this simple, intuitive explanation only after he had finally come to the presented result after long calculations.

disclosure of information. Kyle (1985), Black (1986) and De Long et al. (1990) as well as the literature based on these articles also refer to *noise traders* to explain trading.

Another strand of literature is based on excessive reliance on one's own information. According to Odean (1998, 1999), *overconfidence*, that is, too much emphasis on one's own information, is an essential reason for motivating an actor to trade. Odean claims that '[t]rading volume increases when price takers, insiders, or marketmakers are overconfident' (1998, p. 1888). In a broader interpretation, actual private motives for trading may exist as well. The latter could be based on the fact that an institutional investor must invest liquid funds according to certain parameters, or a private investor sells securities not because the assets are considered overvalued but because other financial needs must be covered. The core idea of these considerations is to abandon the assumption of a common value. The next section considers a corresponding variation of the model, in which private information – in game theory modeling the type of an actor – is weighted more heavily.

4 Excursus

If we replace the assumption of a common value in favour of private valuations for the traded good, the value function depends only on a market participant's own respective signal. For the buyer it simplifies to $v_B(x)$ and for the seller to $v_S(y)$. Without loss of generality, we equate the private signal of a player with his valuation and substitute $v_B(x) = x$ and $v_S(y) = y$. Apart from this, nothing else changes in the model. The equilibrium conditions (1) and (2) are now given by

$$(x - b) \ h\big(s^{-1}(b)|x\big) \ s^{-1'}(b) - \frac{1}{2} \ H\Big(s^{-1}(b)|x\Big) \overset{!}{=} 0$$

and

$$(y - s) \ g\big(b^{-1}(s)|y\big) \ b^{-1'}(s) + \frac{1}{2} \ \Big(1 - G\big(b^{-1}(s)|y\big)\Big) \overset{!}{=} 0.$$

For simplification it shall be assumed that the signals x and y are independently uniformly distributed over the interval [0; 1] as in the example above. Thus, the equilibrium conditions shorten to

$$(x - b) \ s^{-1'}(b) - \frac{1}{2} \ s^{-1}(b) \overset{!}{=} 0$$

and

$$(y - s) \ b^{-1'}(s) + \frac{1}{2} \ \Big(1 - b^{-1}(s)\Big) \overset{!}{=} 0.$$

Harmonizing the running variable to z instead of b and s, substituting $z = b(x)$ $= s(y)$ and accordingly $x = b^{-1}(z)$ and $y = s^{-1}(z)$ and using the abbreviations $u(z) = b^{-1}(z)$ and $v(z) = s^{-1}(z)$ yields the following system of ordinary differential equations (ODE) with respect to the inverse functions $u(\cdot)$ and $v(\cdot)$ of $b(\cdot)$ and $s(\cdot)$, respectively:

$$v'(z) = \frac{v(z)}{2\,(u(z) - z)}$$

$$u'(z) = \frac{1 - u(z)}{2\,(z - v(z))}.$$

The above ODE has, among other solutions, the (linear) solution

$$v(z) = \frac{3}{2}z - \frac{3}{8} \quad \text{and}$$

$$u(z) = \frac{3}{2}z - \frac{1}{8},$$

the reversal of which yields the searched bidding functions in equilibrium

$$b(x) = \frac{2}{3}x + \frac{1}{12} \quad \text{and}$$

$$s(y) = \frac{2}{3}y + \frac{1}{4}.$$

The experience with Milgrom and Stokey's *No-trade* theorem reminds us to re-examine the literature before claiming a new finding. In fact, this result is not new either. Already Chatterjee and Samuelson (1983) have derived these bidding functions for the considered double auction with two bidders. Based on Chatterjee and Samuelson's result, Satterthwaite and Williams (1989) examine the double auction with private values that are uniformly distributed in the interval [0; 1] and find that the necessary equilibrium conditions describe in the interior of the tetrahedron $0 \le y \le z \le x \le 1$ a vector field, so that *any* arbitrary point $0 < y < z$ $< x < 1$ represents an initial value condition for a trace $(s^{-1}(z), z, b^{-1}(z))$ that relates to a pair of functions $b(z)$ and $s(z)$ which constitute equilibrium bidding strategies of the double auction. All these traces or the respective bidding functions leave the tetrahedron in one direction through the edge $(0, z, z)$ and in the other direction through the edge $(z, z, 1)$. This means that any possible bid z with $0 < z < 1$ and any x and y with $x > z > y$ may represent an equilibrium, so that $x = b^{-1}(z)$ and $y = s^{-1}(z)$.

Let's try not to completely lose the central train of thought: With the assumption of a *common value* good, we obtain the result that in equilibrium no trade occurs. On the other hand, anything can happen if a *private value* good is traded, in the sense that every point $0 < y < z < x < 1$ relates to some bidding equilibrium. It also follows that in the case of a double auction with a private value good, there is a positive probability of trading in each equilibrium. However, Satterthwaite and Williams also show that not only the linear equilibrium mentioned above but all equilibria are inefficient, that is, there are always cases in which $y < x$, but trading does not occur. In fact, the linear solution given above and known from Chatterjee and Samuelson maximizes among all solutions the expected trading volume and efficiency.[5] In this equilibrium, trading takes place if $b(x) > s(y) \iff \frac{2}{3}x + \frac{1}{12} > \frac{2}{3}y + \frac{1}{4} \iff x > y + \frac{1}{4}$. The probability of trade is

$$\int_0^{\frac{3}{4}} \int_{y+\frac{1}{4}}^1 1 \, dx \, dy = \frac{9}{32} \approx 28,1\%.$$

If the equilibrium were efficient, trade, however, would occur in 50% of all cases.

5 Digression

The excursus above shows one way in which the model can be changed so that trade occurs in a market even among purely rational actors. However, the approach is not very helpful with regard to trading in securities whose payoffs are the same for all actors. In this respect, this section examines a hybrid model that combines *common* and *private value* aspects. For this purpose, the value function is adjusted again without changing the other elements of the model. In order to allow a numerical comparison with the example of the private values, the assumption of the independently and uniformly distributed signals over the interval [0; 1] is maintained.

To model the value of the traded good, the pair of functions

$$v_B(x, y) = ax + (1 - a) y \text{ for the buyer and}$$

$$v_S(y, x) = ay + (1 - a) x \text{ for the seller}$$

with $a \in [\frac{1}{2}; 1]$ are being used. These functions describe, on the one hand, a common value component in the amount of $(1 - a)(x + y)$; on the other hand, they also feature a private value component with a value of $(2a - 1)x$ (buyer) and $(2a - 1)y$ (seller).

---

[5]For a proof, see Satterthwaite and Williams (1989).

For $a = \frac{1}{2}$, the model is identical to the above common value approach; the larger a is, the stronger the influence of the private value component, and for $a = 1$, the private value case is modeled.

The equilibrium conditions of the hybrid approach stem again from (1) and (2). We obtain:

$$\left(ax + (1 - a) s^{-1}(b) - b \right) s^{-1'}(b) - \frac{1}{2} s^{-1}(b) \overset{!}{=} 0$$

$$\left(ay + (1 - a) b^{-1}(s) - s \right) b^{-1'}(s) + \frac{1}{2} \left(1 - b^{-1}(s) \right) \overset{!}{=} 0.$$

Again, there is a continuum of solutions for the inverse $b^{-1}(s)$ and $s^{-1}(b)$ of the bidding functions of B and S, including for each a a pair of linear functions. From their reversal, we get the linear equilibrium

$$b(x) = \frac{2}{3}x + \frac{3a - 2}{6(3a - 1)}$$

$$s(y) = \frac{2}{3}y + \frac{a}{2(3a - 1)}.$$

The correctness of the above solution can be easily checked by inserting it into the equilibrium conditions (1) and (2).

Besides the given linear equilibrium, there is usually a continuum of further solutions for all a. For the pure common value case with $a = \frac{1}{2}$, an alternative equilibrium has already been presented above (see also footnote 3). Numerical calculations, which will not be discussed in detail here, show that for all a the given linear equilibrium maximizes the trading probability and efficiency among all solution candidates. This observation is consistent with the results of Satterthwaite and Williams (1989), who had already established this for the private value case. Using the efficiency argument as a dominance criterion, we focus on linear equilibria. In these equilibria, trade occurs if

$$b(x) > s(y)$$

$$\Longleftrightarrow \frac{2}{3}x + \frac{3a - 2}{6(3a - 1)} > \frac{2}{3}y + \frac{a}{2(3a - 1)}$$

$$\Longleftrightarrow x > y + \frac{1}{2(3a - 1)}.$$

The probability of trading thus calculates to

$$\int_0^{1-\frac{1}{2(3a-1)}} \int_{y+\frac{1}{2(3a-1)}}^1 1 dx \, dy$$

$$= \frac{9\,(2a-1)^2}{8\,(3a-1)^2}$$

For $a=1$ and $a=\frac{1}{2}$, we obtain the already known values $\frac{9}{32}$ and 0, respectively.

The above expression also shows a beautiful regularity: The larger a is, that is, the higher the private value component, the higher the probability of trade. An efficient market result, however, is never reached. For all $a > \frac{1}{2}$, efficiency would require that in exactly 50% of the cases trade occurs. In contrast, the inefficiency of the double auction, which is well known for the case of private values, increases with an increasing common value component of the traded good. This means that with an increasing common value component, not only the size of the cake, which buyers and sellers may share, but also the portion of the cake that is actually realized decreases. The author is inclined to assume a more general 'low-trade' theorem behind this phenomenon, which is shown in the above example of the model under consideration.

6   Assessment

The research question which was raised in this chapter and which targeted the prediction accuracy of a forecasting market under different incentive schemes and different numbers of traders could not be answered. The foregoing only examined the case of a utility function, which depends linearly on the payment of the traded good. The characteristics of rank- or transaction-based payments were not addressed. Neither was the impact of the group size explored, as only a game with two players was considered. Furthermore, the model did not take into account that in a typical prediction market several goods are traded in larger numbers.

In the considered model of a market with two participants, one potential buyer and one potential seller, who can trade a single good, it was found, though, that trade among rational actors occurs only with a relatively low probability. Furthermore, this probability of trade depends on the weight of the private component with respect to the total value of the good. Thus, only a small portion of the possible welfare gain is realized.

With regard to the actual object of investigation, prediction markets on which common value goods are traded, the obtained result is somewhat irrelevant. On the contrary, the design of a prediction market should ensure that private value components do not play a role. Rather, market prices of the traded shares should reflect some objective and unbiased value relating to the forecasted future event, which is the same for all traders.

If, however, one frees oneself from the compulsion to answer a previously posed research question, the chapter, which somewhat cheekily has also been dubbed a 'case study', shows how in a cooperative environment, such as the IME, different research projects can cross-fertilize each other and how questions posed in one project can provide food for thought for further projects. Good research management features breeding ground for developing these questions and leveraging synergies.

The connection between the share of private and common value components of a good in relation to the probability that this good will be traded has – in contrast to other results presented in this chapter – not been known to me from the literature. Nevertheless, I consider this an interesting observation and have enjoyed the freedom at the IME to devote myself to this but also to other questions that, so to speak, suddenly fell from the sky, and to be able to discuss them in a great team with great colleagues and an outstanding supervisor. The openness to take up questions, develop them further and thereby open up new areas of research and activity has shaped and helped me greatly in my subsequent work. A special feature of the IME, however, is to actually answer these questions and complete projects without getting bogged down. Unfortunately, 10 years after I left the IME, I have not been able to do this with this chapter.

I learned a lot from Christof Weinhardt during my time at the IME. But in many ways he remains unrivaled. This chapter, which has also been described as a case study, does not go far enough to learn from it. A case study should actually identify and work out relevant aspects. So, what is the secret of the atmosphere that Christof has created at his institute? Certainly, the joy of work, the good relationship among colleagues and the inspiration and stimulation of a creative and inspiring director. But how one can replicate such a productive environment remains a mystery (at least to me). I am thankful for the experience I was able to gain and for the many things I learned at the IME and from Christof. And concerning the remainder that I did not learn, my respect remains. Chapeau!

References

Ausubel, L. M.; Cramton, P.; Pycia, M.; Rostek, M.; Weretka, M. (2014): "Demand Reduction and Inefficiency in Multi-unit Auctions", *Review of Economic Studies* 81, 1366–1400.

Berg, J. E.; Forsythe, R.; Nelson, F.; Rietz, T.A. (2001): "Results from a Dozen Years of Election Futures Markets Research", in: Plott, C.; Smith, V. L. (eds.) *Handbook of Experimental Economic Results*, 742–751.

Black, F. (1986): "Noise", *Journal of Finance* 41, 529–543.

Chatterjee, K; Samuelson, W. (1983): "Bargaining under Incomplete Information", *Operations Research* 31, 835–851.

De Long, J. B.; Shleifer, A.; Summers, L. H.; Waldmann, R. J. (1990): "Noise Trader Risk in Financial Markets", *Journal of Political Economy* 98, 703–738.

Deutschlandradio (2016): "75 Jahre Teflon – Siegeszug einer zufälligen Entdeckung", *Deutschlandfunk Kultur* 04.02.2016, www.deutschlandfunkkultur.de/75-jahre-teflon-siegeszug-einer-zufaelligen-entdeckung.932.de.html?dram:article_id=344524 (accessed Nov 04, 2020).

Fama, E. F. (1970): "Efficient Capital Markets, A Review of Theory and Empirical Work", *Journal of Finance* 25, 383–417.

Freedman, D.; Pisani, R.; Purves, R. (2007): *Statistics*, W. W. Norton & Company, New York.

Geo (2017): "Wie Alexander Fleming durch eine Schlamperei das Penicillin entdeckte", *Geo Chronik* 1, www.geo.de/magazine/geo-chronik/19648-rtkl-antibiotika-wie-alexander-fleming-durch-eine-schlamperei-das (accessed Nov 04, 2020).

Geo (2019): "Wie die Kelloggs-Brüder durch Zufall die Cornflakes erfanden", *Geolino* Nr. 5, www.geo.de/geolino/mensch/21389-rtkl-geschichte-der-cornflakes-wie-die-kelloggs-brueder-durch-zufall-die (accessed Nov 04, 2020).

Grossman, S. J.; Stiglitz, J. E. (1980): "On the Impossibility of Informationally Efficient Markets", *American Economic Review* 70, 393–408.

Kyle, A. S. (1985): "Continuous Auctions and Insider Trading", *Econometrica* 53, 1315–1335.

Luckner, S.; Kratzer, F.; Weinhardt, C. (2005): "STOCCER – A Forecasting Market for the FIFA World Cup 2006", *Proceedings of the 4th Workshop on e-Business (WEB 2005)*, Las Vegas, 399–405.

Milgrom, P. R.; Stokey, N. (1982): "Information, Trade and Common Knowledge", *Journal of Economic Theory* 26, 17-27.

Milgrom, P. R.; Weber, R. J. (1982): "A Theory of Auctions and Competitive Bidding", *Econometrica* 50, 1089-1122.

Myerson, R. B.; Satterthwaite, M. A. (1983): "Efficient Mechanisms for Bilateral Trading", *Journal of Economic Theory* 29, 265–281.

Odean, T. (1998): "Volume, Volatility, Price, and Profit When All Traders Are above Average", *Journal of Finance* 53, 1887–1934.

Odean, T. (1999): "Do Investors Trade Too Much?", *American Economic Review* 89, 1279–1298.

Rustichini, A.; Satterthwaite, M. A.; Williams, S. R. (1994): "Convergence to Efficiency in a Simple Market with Incomplete Information", *Econometrica* 62, 1041–1063.

Satterthwaite, M. A.; Williams, S. R. (1989): "Bilateral Trade with the Sealed Bid k-Double Auction: Existence and Efficiency", *Journal of Economic Theory* 48, 107–133.

Standard (2010): "Die ganze Wahrheit über Newtons Apfel", Standard, 18. Januar, Wien, www.derstandard.at/story/1263705369432/die-ganze-wahrheit-ueber-newtons-apfel (accessed Nov 04, 2020).

Stukeley, W. (1752): *Memoirs of Sir Isaac Newton's Life*, MS/142, Royal Society Library, London, ttp.royalsociety.org/accessible/SpreadDetails.aspx?BookID=1807da00-909a-4abf-b9c1-0279a08e4bf2 (accessed Nov 04, 2020).

Tidd, J.; Bessant, J. (2014): *Strategic Innovation Management*, Wiley, Chichester.

Wilson, R. (1985): "Incentive Efficiency of Double Auctions", *Econometrica* 53, 1101–1115.

On the Potency of Online User Representation: Insights from the Sharing Economy

Timm Teubner, Marc T. P. Adam, and Florian Hawlitschek

Abstract Online user representation (UR) is a cornerstone of platform-mediated interactions within the sharing economy. While the general usefulness of UR artifacts for facilitating online and offline interactions is widely acknowledged and understood, the underlying mechanisms and operating principles often require a more detailed analysis. In this chapter, we thus introduce a systematic framework grounded in signaling and social presence theory for analyzing UR artifacts for online platforms in general—and the sharing economy in particular. We apply our framework as a structural lens in a case study on user profiles on Airbnb, unveiling structural similarities and differences between the opposing market sides. We discuss our findings against the backdrop of emerging information systems research directions and suggest paths for future work on the sharing economy.

1 Introduction

An ever-increasing number of businesses in today's e-commerce landscape facilitate the renting, sharing, lending, and selling of resources. In this platform or sharing economy, platforms from A(irbnb) to Z(imride) connect providers (e.g., hosts, sellers) and consumers (e.g., guests, buyers) to co-create value. Importantly, even though many of these multisided markets facilitate interactions that take place in the physical world (e.g., accommodation or ride sharing), the initiation, trust-building, and booking processes are entirely mediated by platforms. To do so, platform companies make use of a variety of *user representation* (UR) artifacts to establish trust between users (Hesse et al. 2020a). In fact, platforms vary greatly with regard

T. Teubner (✉) · F. Hawlitschek
Einstein Center Digital Future, Technische Universität Berlin, Berlin, Germany
e-mail: teubner@tu-berlin.de; florian.hawlitschek@fes-frankfurt.de

M. T. P. Adam
College of Engineering, Science and Environment, The University of Newcastle, Callaghan, Australia
e-mail: marc.adam@newcastle.edu.au

© The Author(s) 2021
H. Gimpel et al. (eds.), *Market Engineering*,
https://doi.org/10.1007/978-3-030-66661-3_10

to how and what kind of value is created (e.g., social and/or economic; Dann et al. 2020). Since this also affects the respective need for trust and how users engage, it is not surprising that platforms also differ with regard to the array of the UR artifacts they employ. Consequently, research on the role, use, and effects of UR artifacts is also diverse in terms of domains, platforms, dependent variables, theory, methods, and publication outlets (Dann et al. 2019).

Notwithstanding the multifaceted platform landscape, we observe a range of commonalities and "best practices" in how platforms employ UR artifacts and how this, in turn, affects user perceptions and behavior. For instance, a great majority of platforms uses rating systems to keep track of their users' behavior and reputation. Star ratings and text reviews are commonly considered the "hardest" currency when it comes to substantiating one's credibility for online transactions (Teubner et al. 2017). These cues (1) are provided by others, (2) aggregate the experience of prior transaction partners, and (3) can only be issued by these partners (e.g., guests or passengers). In particular this seclusion makes such cues reliable (very much in contrast to "open" product review platforms, on which anyone can rate anything— be it products, hotels, restaurants, or medical doctors). While rating systems do not come without shortcomings and side effects (e.g., fake reviews, rating inflation; Filippas et al. 2017; Teubner and Glaser 2018), they have become a central pillar of many platforms' operations and—from the individual user perspective—an essential tool to present oneself, evaluate others, and successfully engage in online markets (Teubner et al. 2017). In view of the importance and prominence of rating systems, other—"softer"—UR artifacts are sometimes overlooked. More specifically, there exists a wide range of other important ways of engendering trust, including the provision of profile photos, self-descriptions, and platform-issued labels.

In this chapter, we propose a conceptual framework for the diverse landscape of UR artifacts and link their cause-and-effect relationships to theory (Sect. 2). We then survey empirical findings on the pathways captured in the framework (Sect. 3), present data from a case study on Airbnb hosts and guests (Sect. 4), discuss ongoing discourse and developments (Sect. 5), and provide concluding thoughts (Sect. 6).

2 Theoretical Background

2.1 Signaling and Social Presence Theory

The way UR artifacts engender trust can roughly be described by two, partially overlapping routes. First, UR artifacts can serve to *signal* a user's trustworthiness (Spence 1973). This acknowledges that, like many other markets, transactions on sharing platforms feature information asymmetry between providers and consumers. Through the signal, a user demonstrates a track record of trustworthy behavior. In most cases, it is the provider who sends the signal. In some cases, however, consumers also have to market themselves and demonstrate their trustworthiness in order to be given permission to book (Karlsson et al. 2017). Since self-references cannot work through this route ("talk is cheap"), the involvement of a third party is required. This is reflected in the omnipresence of numerical and textual rating and review systems. In most cases, platforms use *mutual* rating systems, through which providers and consumers evaluate each other once a transaction has been completed. Thereby, they build up a reputation over time, reflecting the cumulative and aggregated experiences of *prior* transaction partners, which serves as a leap of faith for *future* ones. Moreover, ratings are usually provided *simultaneously*, avoiding (or at least mitigating) the detrimental effects of collusion and fear of retaliation.

The second route is described by *social presence theory* (Cyr et al. 2009; Gefen and Straub 2003; Short et al. 1976). Since the entire pre-purchase phase is carried out online (platform-, online-, and screen-mediated), the evolutionary processes and channels through which people conventionally establish trust are not available (e.g., physical closeness, body language, subtle gestures and countenance, biological messengers). At the same time, however, trust is even more essential in this setup due to information asymmetry and low (perceived) accountability and accessibility in case of problems. To bridge this trust gap, platform operators attempt to convey social cues through the platform's web interface. The resulting *social presence* can be understood as "the degree of salience of the other person in the interaction and the consequent salience of the interpersonal relationships" (Short et al. 1976, p. 65), as enabled by the communication medium. As any pre-transactional communication is mediated through the platform, perceived social presence reflects how different UR artifacts convey a sense of the other person being psychologically present. It is through this social presence that UR artifacts engender trust—even without "proof." Prime examples of cues to achieve this are profile photos, self-descriptions, and the provision of other personal data.

2.2   *Framework of User Representation Artifacts*

As outlined above, many (sharing) platform operators make use of a variety of mechanisms, systems, and UR artifacts that enable the display of personal as well as transactional information. Importantly, trust is a multidimensional construct and involves different actors and relations on sharing platforms (Hawlitschek et al. 2016d). It is hence important to differentiate between the main actors involved. With regard to the "source" of UR artifacts, it can be distinguished between the *users themselves* (who, e.g., upload a photo or write a self-description), *other users* (who, e.g., write text reviews or issue star ratings), and *the platform* (which, e.g., collects, aggregates, and displays corroboratory or transactional information about users, infers data (Custers 2018), awards badges, and verifies identities).

Additionally, artifacts can be distinguished by the type of information they convey (e.g., personal/non-personal) and their visual display (e.g., pictorial, numerical, textual). Last, there are the resulting user perceptions, behaviors, and market out-

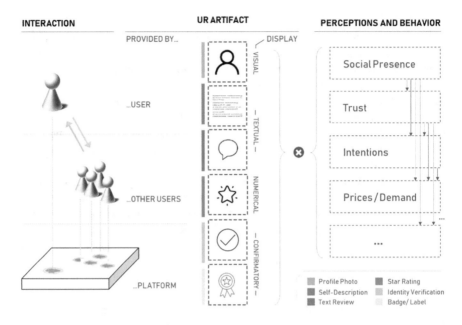

Fig. 1 Sharing economy UR artifact framework

comes caused by the artifacts' presence and specific properties (e.g., social presence, trust, purchase intentions, prices, demand, etc.), which are usually interdependent. Figure 1 summarizes this platform-user interaction, UR artifacts, and outcome variables.

3 User Representation Artifacts

In the following, we explore some of the empirical evidence among the UR artifacts as provided in Fig. 1. There is ample research on the use and effects of UR artifacts in the sharing economy—especially on Airbnb (Dann et al. 2019)—which serves both as a prime example *and* a testbed for platform-related research. Thereby, it is important to note that the UR artifacts employed by Airbnb are widely used across many other platforms.

Profile Photos Faces create trust (Teubner and Hawlitschek 2018). This basic human principle has been widely leveraged by the designers of social media and two-sided market platforms. Several ride-sharing platforms, for instance, prompted their users to complete their profiles, upload pictures, and even provide a filter to search for rides by drivers with a profile photo only. The beneficial effects of profile photos have been demonstrated for various contexts and applications, including accommodation sharing (Abramova 2020; Ert et al. 2016; Ert and Fleischer 2017;

Jaeger et al. 2019), gift-giving networks (Teubner et al. 2013), trust experiments (Bente et al. 2012, 2014), corporate ideation processes (Wagenknecht et al. 2018), and equity crowdfunding (Klement and Teubner 2019). Importantly, *avatars* also engender social presence and trust in a similar way to actual photographs (Al Jaroodi et al. 2019; Teubner et al. 2013, 2014).

Self-Descriptions By deciding which information they disclose, users can determine how they are perceived by others (Tussyadiah and Park 2018). Self-descriptions hence help to create a vivid picture of a particular person and hence allow them to be perceived as a real and multifaceted human being. By making use of self-descriptions, users can trigger expectations of economic and social value (Dann et al. 2020); induce feelings of connectedness, sociability, and intimacy; and hence increase liking and understanding (Altman and Taylor 1973; Janssen et al. 2014). While there exists a range of information that people frequently disclose, information on occupation, personal background, and personal interests is considered particularly beneficial (Ma et al. 2017; Tussyadiah 2016; Zhang et al. 2018).

Rating Scores The trust-building capacity of star ratings as well as the financial premium of a good reputation has been demonstrated repeatedly and for various contexts (Abramova et al. 2017; Teubner et al. 2017). Consequently, recent research has started to shift on the pitfalls and issues of rating systems, such as rating skewness (Teubner and Glaser 2018), rating inflation over time (Filippas et al. 2017), fake reviews (Moon et al. 2020; Wu et al. 2020), as well as rating response mechanisms and strategies (Abramova et al. 2015; Greiner et al. 2020).

Text Reviews The effects of text reviews on user trust and behavior are more complex than numerical scores as they differ in various dimensions such as length, language, valence, and context. Importantly, text reviews combine two important aspects of other trust cues as they are issued by third parties (i.e., credibility such as star ratings) and pertain to personal information (i.e., sociability such as self-descriptions) (Dann et al. 2020). In contrast to most other UR artifacts, text reviews have received little research attention when it comes to assessing their effect through rigorous experimentation.

Identity Verification One means to counter uncertainty, especially against malicious actors on platforms, is identity verification. To do so, the user's face can be screened during a short webcam session, showing their ID card next to their face, possibly having a brief chat with a platform employee passing a basic sanity check. To indicate profile veracity, the platform then shows a small icon that signifies that the user's identity has been certified. While the general idea of verification is widespread across the sharing economy (Hawlitschek et al. 2016c; Mazzella et al. 2016), empirical evidence is still rather scarce. Verification was found to positively influence transaction intentions by increasing trust in the prospective transaction partners (Siegfried et al. 2020). In contrast to other true cues, verified IDs do not, however, necessarily reflect in price markups (Teubner et al. 2017; Xie and Mao

2017). Yet, identity verification represents a popular tool for platform operators as it is inexpensive and can establish a very basic level of trust.

Badges Badges can be regarded as a means for platform operators to address existing weaknesses of reputation systems by introducing additional signals of stellar quality, allowing complementors to stand out even when five-star rating scores are omnipresent. In this regard, Airbnb's *Superhost* badge is one of the most prominent examples for such platform-generated cues (Liang et al. 2017). However, the origin of badges in the gamification literature suggests that their influence exceeds their add-on role in reputation systems. In fact, badges as a simple element of game design have the potential to increase user activity on (sharing) platforms in terms of transactions and comments (Hamari 2017).

Beyond such artifacts, there exist other relevant levers that platform operators employ to promote trust building, including the design (and size) of text input areas (Gebbia 2016) and even the choice of colors (Hawlitschek et al. 2016a). Note that truthful platform design and marketing claims are of particular importance to avoid perceptions of "sharewashing," which may backfire and undermine the platform's trustworthiness in the eyes of current and future consumers (Hawlitschek et al. 2018b). Moreover, beyond strategies to create and increase trust, some measures aim at lowering the necessary levels of trust for users to engage (i.e., the trust thresholds), for instance by providing insurance (Chica et al. 2019).

4   Case Study: User Representation on Airbnb

In this section, we report results from a data-based case study on how hosts and guests present themselves on the accommodation-sharing platform Airbnb through various UR artifacts. To do so, we draw on the online repository InsideAirbnb.com on listing data and user reviews and, based on this, run proprietary web crawlers to extract the relevant information from Airbnb.

Using InsideAirbnb's listing data (*listings.csv*), we identified a random sample of 5000 hosts based in Berlin, Germany, yielding information on name, profile image (URL), rating score, self-description, verifications, etc. Moreover, based on all reviews received by hosts in Berlin (*reviews.csv*) in 2019 (i.e., before the global emergence of COVID-19), we extracted a random sample of 5000 guests. Note that not every transaction is actually reflected in a review and estimates on this fraction vary. Hence this data will be somewhat biased toward "review-writing" guests. While, to the best of our knowledge, data on guests is not provided by any data repository, guests also have profile pages similar to hosts (i.e., a user ID) linked to a unique online profile. By analyzing these profiles, we investigated how guests represent themselves, including their profile image and self-description. For all $2 \times 5000 = 10{,}000$ user profiles (hosts and guests), we manually inspected and categorized the profile photos (portrait-like, multiple persons, etc.). This data allowed us to compare how hosts and guests differ in terms of presenting themselves

Table 1 Summary statistics of hosts and guests

UR artifact	Hosts	Guests	Dif. sig.[a]
Has profile image	99.4%	97.0%	Yes
Portrait-like photo	72.6%	73.3%	No
Multiple persons	11.4%	15.0%	Yes
Person/s visible but no face/s identifiable	8.2%	5.8%	Yes
Objects, landscapes, or buildings	6.2%	2.1%	Yes
Avatar	1.0%	0.8%	No
Has self-description	47.0%	47.2%	No
Explicit statement of occupation	24.3%	19.4%	Yes
Has identity verification	36.0%	73.2%	Yes
Average number of ratings/reviews	19.7	10.7	Yes
Average rating score	94.9	—	—
Also active on the opposite market side	66.7%	8.0%	Yes
Has superhost badge[b]	14.4%	—	—
Fraction of females[(based on name)]	52.4%	49.2%	Yes

Note: [a]Significance of difference based on two-sample proportion test ($p < .05$)
[b]Airbnb issues its superhost badge to "experienced hosts who provide a shining example for other hosts, and extraordinary experiences for their guests" based on transaction volume (≥ 10 stays), rating score (≥ 4.8 stars), response rate ($\geq 90\%$), and cancellation rate ($\leq 1\%$) (Airbnb 2020)

to the respective other market side. Table 1 provides summary statistics for the usage of UR artifacts by hosts and guests in the sample.

It is worth noting that hosts and guests are very similar in terms of how they present themselves on the platform. Specifically, both groups provide a profile photo almost all of the time, with very similar distributions on what these photos actually show. Moreover, both groups provide a self-description (47%) as well as an explicit statement of their occupation with very similar frequency.

The only stark difference occurs with regard to identity verification, where only 36% of all hosts but 73.2% of all guests make use of this feature. Similarly, both market sides exhibit similar shares of male/female users. Overall, one could expect that this high similarity is rooted in a degree of "side-switching" on the platform (Stummer et al. 2018), that is, users who are active both as hosts and guests. However, while 66.7% of hosts also use the platform to travel themselves, only 8% of all guests are also active as hosts. One possible explanation for this symmetry is the fact that the trust requirements are also mutual due to the high degree of economic and social exposure both for hosts and guests. In consequence, there appears to have emerged a common platform etiquette agreed upon by both market sides.

5   Discussion

We shape our tools, and thereafter our tools shape us. (John Culkin)

In the sense of Culkin's *bon mot*, the selection, design, and use of UR tools have tremendous importance for how our (social and economic) online lives are organized (i.e., who gets what). Such tools must hence not be underestimated. Specifically, as UR artifacts depict actual people, they are likely to reproduce many of the problems inherent to social interactions (e.g., discrimination). Take the most common reputation systems as an example. While objectively designed to be equal for everyone, people's online reputation will, not least, depend on whether they manage to conduct their first transactions successfully. However, based on stereotypes and other factors, not everyone is "equally likely to obtain a first review" at all (Kas 2020, p. 13). Reputation systems may hence even exacerbate gender-, age-, or ethnicity-based inequality. This holds particularly true for sharing platforms, considering that platforms and platform paradigms play an ever-increasing role in our professional and private lives—and their strong dependence on personal characteristics. This also concerns a broad variety of domains, be it for booking accommodation (e.g., Airbnb, Booking.com), finding real estate (e.g., ImmoScout24), ride sharing (e.g., BlaBlaCar, Zimride), selling and buying used goods (e.g., eBay, Gumtree), crowdwork platforms for cleaning (e.g., Helpling), or other tasks (e.g., TaskRabbit, MyHammer), to name just a few.

Given this variety of contexts and perspectives, as we have demonstrated in the previous sections, UR needs to be understood in view of factors such as platform commerciality (e.g., Airbnb vs. Couchsurfing), user professionalism (e.g., eBay vs. Etsy), and user role (e.g., provider vs. consumer). Moreover, requirements will be different for different resource types (i.e., products/services; Hawlitschek et al. 2018c) and the implied degree of social interaction (Hesse et al. 2020a). Last, how and by whom matches are made (e.g., by the users or by the platform) is decisive (Hawlitschek et al. 2016b). Hence, different platforms will leverage different trust cues and combinations thereof to their users but, ultimately, to their own benefit. Much of the information systems literature tends to understand UR as a means to an end, for example, for trust building. In this sense, the main stance is often positive. Yet, despite the undisputed beneficial effects of UR, conveying personal information via these artifacts is not necessarily a straightforward decision, and there are a range of caveats that need to be taken into account. We will briefly touch on four views on the use of UR that have typically either received less attention or are still in emerging states.

1. **Privacy and Discrimination**—Users, platform operators, and regulators have to balance competing interests such as trust building versus protecting user privacy (Teubner and Flath 2019) and mitigating discrimination (Airbnb 2016; Cui et al. 2020; Edelman et al. 2017). Especially profile photos and user names are likely to lead to ethnicity-based discrimination. One response to this (as indicated by the case study above) seems to be that hosts, who are typically much more

Fig. 2 Avatar examples

accessible to the general public than guests, use semi- or fully anonymous photos. In fact, hosts employ objects, buildings, and landscapes three times more often and obscured faces 40% more often than guests (see Table 1). Another avenue to address the issue of discrimination may be found in the way the different artifacts and other trust cues interact. For instance, while Edelman et al. (2017) found evidence of discrimination against users with distinctively African American (vs. distinctively white) names, Cui et al. (2020) found that this effect disappears once online reputation is available.

It is hence not surprising that some users have reservations about providing personal data online but—at the same time—the need for building trust (in other people, organizations, and digital services) is only increasing. One means to address this dilemma could be trusted agencies that provide certified UR without publishing the underlying data. Similar to the identity verification process described above, profile photos could be verified and replaced by avatars that credibly portray some of the actual facial features (see Fig. 2). Such images are capable of conveying trust levels comparable to the actual photos (Teubner et al. 2013, 2014), without giving away one's actual photo (and the associated biometric information).

2. **Cross-platform Use**—As of today, platforms operate in mostly unconnected silos where each platform maintains its own set of UR artifacts and typically its own reputation system. Given the personal and social importance of UR for trust building and the fact that people use an increasing number of platforms, it should be asked how trust building may also be achieved across platform boundaries. Profiles may, for instance, refer back to information centrally stored elsewhere, for example, to social media accounts or digital identity aggregation services. Recent research has explored the notion of cross-platform signaling based on numerical rating scores (Hesse et al. 2020b; Hesse and Teubner 2019, 2020; Otto et al. 2018; Teubner et al. 2019, 2020). In fact, several e-commerce platforms already offer functions that allow ratings to be imported from other platforms

(e.g., Bonanza.com and Truegether.com, allowing rating imports from eBay and Amazon).

3. **Fake Reviews**—As outlined above, a particularly potent form of UR is ratings and reviews. Unsurprisingly, there has emerged a secondary (and largely illegal) market for this form of reputation. Meanwhile, there is also a rich body of literature on the prevalence and detection of fake reviews for e-commerce platforms (e.g., Amazon), travel platforms (e.g., Yelp, Tripadvisor, Booking.com), app stores, and many more (Wu et al. 2020). Such platforms are particularly prone to fake reviews as they mostly represent open environments in which almost anyone can rate a product, app, hotel, restaurant, employer, medical doctor, or accommodation at little to no cost. However, hardly any research has considered the role of fake reviews within the more secluded environments of sharing economy platforms (such as Airbnb or BlaBlaCar) where the privilege to submit a rating is directly linked to having actually concluded a transaction (including payment). This is by no means to say that there are no fake reviews in such environments, only that the hurdles to (a) commissioning and (b) detecting such reviews are higher. In fact, companies that offer reviews (e.g., fivestar-marketing.net) list a wide range of target markets including Amazon, app stores, Google, Facebook, Tripadvisor, and Jameda, but none of the popular sharing economy platforms (Ge and Voß 2020). Future work may hence want to take a closer look at the prevalence, causes, and effects of fake reviews on sharing economy platforms.

4. **Other Forms of UR**—In times of increasing numbers of online video conferences, it is highly conceivable that video formats will also find their way into the sharing economy. It is noteworthy that placement services such as *Talentcube* use videos to let job seekers present themselves to employers. Depending on context, other forms such as comp cards, git repositories, StackOverflow accounts, or even physiological data may be used (Peukert et al. 2018). Furthermore, it will be interesting to see how developments in IT and platform infrastructure affect user representation. While the use of distributed ledger technology is repeatedly being proposed for sharing economy applications, it is doubtful whether any application that involves physical interactions lends itself well to this technology (Hawlitschek et al. 2018a, 2020).

6   Concluding Note

You never get a second chance to make a first impression. (Andrew Grant)

Given that almost all sharing economy transactions are facilitated between strangers, UR artifacts replace face-to-face encounters in conveying first impressions. In this chapter, we have proposed a conceptual framework that captures the provision and display of widely used UR artifacts and briefly depicted the rich body of empirical evidence on their impact on user perception and behavior. Our analysis shows that UR artifacts play a critical role in the formation of transactions in the sharing economy, and we observe a range of commonalties in how platforms employ them. We conclude that the role of UR artifacts on sharing economy platforms goes well beyond that of enriching the look and feel of the platform's user interface, even for artifacts that convey features which are not independently verified (e.g., profile photos, self-descriptions). Each individual element has important implications for the way users perceive the level of sociality on the platform, the degree to which they trust one another, and, ultimately, their willingness to engage in actual transactions. Further, our case study on Airbnb demonstrated the strong uptake of UR artifacts by both hosts and guests. We hope that this work provides a useful frame of reference for researchers and practitioners interested in facilitating trust and transactions in the sharing economy.

Acknowledgment This publication was supported by the Open Access fund of Technische Universität Berlin. Support is gratefully acknowledged.

References

Abramova, O. 2020. "Does a smile open all doors? Understanding the impact of appearance disclosure on accommodation sharing platforms," in *HICSS 2020 Proceedings*, pp. 831–840.

Abramova, O., Shavanova, T., Fuhrer, A., Krasnova, H., and Buxmann, P. 2015. "Understanding the sharing economy: The role of response to negative reviews in the peer-to-peer accommodation sharing network," in *ECIS 2015 Proceedings*, pp. 1–16.

Abramova, O., Krasnova, H., and Tan, C.-W. 2017. "How much will you pay? Understanding the value of information cues in the sharing economy," in *ECIS 2017 Proceedings*, pp. 1–18.

Airbnb. 2016. "Airbnb's nondiscrimination policy: Our commitment to inclusion and respect," (available at https://www.airbnb.com/help/article/1405/airbnb-s-nondiscrimination-policy%2D%2Dour-commitment-to-inclusion-and-respect; retrieved September 14, 2017).

Airbnb. 2020. "How do I become a Superhost?," (available at https://www.airbnb.com/help/article/829/how-do-i-become-a-superhost; retrieved October 23, 2020).

Al Jaroodi, H., Chiong, R., Adam, M. T. P., and Teubner, T. 2019. "Avatars and embodied agents in information systems research: A systematic review and conceptual framework," *Australasian Journal of Information Systems*, (23), pp. 1–37.

Altman, I., and Taylor, D. A. 1973. *Social Penetration: The Development of Interpersonal Relationships*, Holt, Rinehart & Winston.

Bente, G., Baptist, O., and Leuschner, H. 2012. "To buy or not to buy: Influence of seller photos and reputation on buyer trust and purchase behavior," *International Journal of Human Computer Studies*, (70:1), pp. 1–13.

Bente, G., Dratsch, T., Kaspar, K., Häßler, T., Bungard, O., and Al-Issa, A. 2014. "Cultures of trust: Effects of avatar faces and reputation scores on German and Arab players in an online trust-game," *PLOS ONE*, (9:6), pp. 1–7.

Chica, M., Chiong, R., Adam, M. T. P., and Teubner, T. 2019. "An evolutionary game model with punishment and protection to promote trust in the sharing economy," *Nature Scientific Reports*, (9), p. 19789.

Cui, R., Li, J., and Zhang, D. 2020. "Reducing discrimination with reviews in the sharing economy: Evidence from field experiments on Airbnb," *Management Science*, (66:3), pp. 1071–1094.

Custers, B. 2018. "Profiling as inferred data. Amplifier effects and positive feedback loops," in *Being Profiled: Cogitas Ergo Sum. 10 Years of "Profiling the European Citizen,"* E. Bayamlıoğlu, I. Baraliuc, and L. Janssens (eds.), Amsterdam University Press.

Cyr, D., Head, M., Larios, H., and Pan, B. 2009. "Exploring human images in website design: A multi-method approach," *MIS Quarterly*, (33:3), pp. 539–566.

Dann, D., Teubner, T., and Weinhardt, C. 2019. "Poster child and guinea pig—Insights from a structured literature review on Airbnb," *International Journal of Contemporary Hospitality Management*, (31:1), pp. 427–473.

Dann, D., Teubner, T., Adam, M. T. P., and Weinhardt, C. 2020. "Where the host is part of the deal: Social and economic value in the platform economy," *Electronic Commerce Research and Applications*, (40), p. 100923.

Edelman, B. G., Luca, M., and Svirsky, D. 2017. "Racial discrimination in the sharing economy: Evidence from a field experiment," *American Economic Journal: Applied Economics*, (9:2), pp. 1–22.

Ert, E., and Fleischer, A. 2017. "What in a photo makes you trust a person online? A structural equation modeling approach," *Working Paper*, pp. 1–17.

Ert, E., Fleischer, A., and Magen, N. 2016. "Trust and reputation in the sharing economy: The role of personal photos in Airbnb," *Tourism Management*, (55:1), pp. 62–73.

Filippas, A., Horton, J. J., and Golden, J. 2017. "Reputation in the long-run," *Working Paper*.

Ge, L., and Voß, S. 2020. "Managing information in the case of opinion spamming," in *Design, User Experience, and Usability: Interaction Design*, A. Marcus and E. Rosenzweig (eds.), Springer, pp. 370–384.

Gebbia, J. 2016. "How Airbnb designs for trust," (available at https://bit.ly/2SOa4PH; retrieved December 12, 2019).

Gefen, D., and Straub, D. W. 2003. "Managing user trust in B2C e-services," *e-Service Journal*, (2:2), pp. 7–24.

Greiner, B., Teubner, T., and Weinhardt, C. 2020. "How to design trust on market platforms?," *Schmalenbachs Zeitschrift für betriebswirtschaftliche Forschung*, (in press).

Hamari, J. 2017. "Do badges increase user activity? A field experiment on the effects of gamification," *Computers in Human Behavior*, (71), pp. 469–478.

Hawlitschek, F., Jansen, L. E., Lux, E., Teubner, T., and Weinhardt, C. 2016a. "Colors and trust: The influence of user interface design on trust and reciprocity," in *HICSS 2016 Proceedings*, pp. 590–599.

Hawlitschek, F., Teubner, T., Adam, M. T. P., Borchers, N., Möhlmann, M., and Weinhardt, C. 2016b. "Trust in the sharing economy: An experimental framework," in *ICIS 2016 Proceedings*, pp. 1–14.

Hawlitschek, F., Teubner, T., and Gimpel, H. 2016c. "Understanding the sharing economy— Drivers and impediments for participation in peer-to-peer rental," in *HICSS 2016 Proceedings*, pp. 4782–4791.

Hawlitschek, F., Teubner, T., and Weinhardt, C. 2016d. "Trust in the sharing economy," *Swiss Journal of Business Research and Practice*, (70:1), pp. 26–44.

Hawlitschek, F., Notheisen, B., and Teubner, T. 2018a. "The limits of trust-free systems: A literature review on blockchain technology and trust in the sharing economy," *Electronic Commerce Research and Applications*, (29), pp. 50–63.

Hawlitschek, F., Stofberg, N. O., Teubner, T., Tu, P., and Weinhardt, C. 2018b. "How corporate sharewashing practices undermine consumer trust," *Sustainability*, (10:8), pp. 1–18.

Hawlitschek, F., Teubner, T., and Gimpel, H. 2018c. "Consumer motives for peer-to-peer sharing," *Journal of Cleaner Production*, (204), pp. 144–157.

Hawlitschek, F., Notheisen, B., and Teubner, T. 2020. "A 2020 perspective on The limits of trust-free systems: A literature review on blockchain technology and trust in the sharing economy," *Electronic Commerce Research and Applications*, (40), p. 100935.

Hesse, M., and Teubner, T. 2019. "Reputation portability – quo vadis?," *Electronic Markets*, (29:5), pp. 1083–1119.

Hesse, M., and Teubner, T. 2020. "Takeaway trust: A market data perspective on reputation portability in electronic commerce," in *HICSS 2020 Proceedings*, pp. 5119–5128.

Hesse, M., Dann, D., Braesemann, F., and Teubner, T. 2020a. "Understanding the platform economy: Signals, trust, and social interaction," in *HICSS 2020 Proceedings*, pp. 5139–5148.

Hesse, M., Teubner, T., and Adam, M. T. P. 2020b. "Bring your own stars—The economics of reputation portability," in *ECIS 2020 Proceedings*, pp. 1–11.

Jaeger, B., Sleegers, W. W. A., Evans, A. M., Stel, M., and van Beest, I. 2019. "The effects of facial attractiveness and trustworthiness in online peer-to-peer markets," *Journal of Economic Psychology*, (75:102125).

Janssen, J. H., IJsselsteijn, W. A., and Westerink, J. H. D. M. 2014. "How affective technologies can influence intimate interactions and improve social connectedness," *International Journal of Human-Computer Studies*, (72:1), pp. 33–43.

Karlsson, L., Kemperman, A., and Dolnicar, S. 2017. "May I sleep in your bed? Getting permission to book," *Annals of Tourism Research*, (62:1), pp. 1–12.

Kas, J. 2020. "Trust and reputation in the peer-to-peer platform economy," *Dissertation, Utrecht University*.

Klement, F., and Teubner, T. 2019. "Trust isn't blind: Exploring visual investor cues in equity crowdfunding," in *ICIS 2019 Proceedings*, pp. 1–9.

Liang, S., Schuckert, M., Law, R., and Chen, C.-C. 2017. "Be a 'Superhost': The importance of badge systems for peer-to-peer rental accommodations," *Tourism Management*, (60), pp. 454–465.

Ma, X., Hancock, J. T., Mingjie, K. L., and Naaman, M. 2017. "Self-disclosure and perceived trustworthiness of Airbnb host profiles," in *CSCW 2017 Proceedings*, pp. 1–13.

Mazzella, F., Sundararajan, A., Butt d'Espous, V., and Möhlmann, M. 2016. "How digital trust powers the sharing economy: The digitization of trust," *IESE Insight*, (30:3), pp. 24–31.

Moon, S., Kim, M. Y., and Iacobucci, D. 2020. "Content analysis of fake consumer reviews by survey-based text categorization," *International Journal of Research in Marketing*, p. in press.

Otto, L., Angerer, P., and Zimmermann, S. 2018. "Incorporating external trust signals on service sharing platforms," in *ECIS 2018 Proceedings*, pp. 1–17.

Peukert, C., Adam, M. T. P., Hawlitschek, F., Helming, S., Lux, E., and Teubner, T. 2018. "Knowing me, knowing you: Biosignals and trust in the surveillance economy," in *ICIS 2018 Proceedings*, pp. 1–11.

Short, J., Williams, E., and Christie, B. 1976. *The Social Psychology of Telecommunications*, John Wiley & Sons Ltd, London.

Siegfried, N., Löbbers, J., and Benlian, A. 2020. "The trust-building nature of identity verification in the sharing economy: An online experiment," in *WI 2020 Proceedings*, pp. 1–16.

Spence, M. 1973. "Job market signaling," *Quarterly Journal of Economics*, (87:3), pp. 355–374.

Stummer, C., Kundisch, D., and Decker, R. 2018. "Platform launch strategies," *Business & Information Systems Engineering*, (60:2), pp. 167–173.

Teubner, T., and Flath, C. M. 2019. "Privacy in the sharing economy," *Journal of the Association for Information Systems*, (20:3), pp. 213–242.

Teubner, T., and Glaser, F. 2018. "Up or out—The dynamics of star rating scores on Airbnb," in *ECIS 2018 Proceedings*, pp. 1–13.

Teubner, T., and Hawlitschek, F. 2018. "The economics of peer-to-peer online sharing," in *The Rise of the Sharing Economy: Exploring the Challenges and Opportunities of Collaborative Consumption*, P. Albinsson and Y. Perera (eds.), Praeger Publishing, pp. 129–156.

Teubner, T., Hawlitschek, F., Adam, M. T. P., and Weinhardt, C. 2013. "Social identity and reciprocity in online gift giving networks," in *HICSS 2013 Proceedings*, pp. 708–717.

Teubner, T., Adam, M. T. P., Camacho, S., and Hassanein, K. 2014. "Understanding resource sharing in C2C platforms: The role of picture humanization," in *ACIS 2014 Proceedings*, pp. 1–10.

Teubner, T., Hawlitschek, F., and Dann, D. 2017. "Price determinants on Airbnb: How reputation pays off in the sharing economy," *Journal of Self-Governance and Management Economics*, (5:4), pp. 53–80.

Teubner, T., Hawlitschek, F., and Adam, M. T. P. 2019. "Reputation transfer," *Business & Information Systems Engineering*, (61:2), pp. 229–235.

Teubner, T., Adam, M. T. P., Hawlitschek, F. 2020. "Unlocking online reputation: On the effectiveness of cross-platform signaling in the sharing economy," *Business & Information Systems Engineering*, (62:6), pp. 501–513.

Tussyadiah, I. P. 2016. "Strategic self-presentation in the sharing economy: Implications for host branding," in *Information and Communication Technologies in Tourism*, pp. 695–708.

Tussyadiah, I. P., and Park, S. 2018. "When guests trust hosts for their words: Host description and trust in sharing economy," *Tourism Management*, (67), pp. 261–272.

Wagenknecht, T., Teubner, T., and Weinhardt, C. 2018. "A Janus-faced matter—The role of user anonymity for communication persuasiveness in online discussions," *Information & Management*, (55), pp. 1024–1037.

Wu, Y., Ngai, E. W., Wu, P., and Wu, C. 2020. "Fake online reviews: Literature review, synthesis, and directions for future research," *Decision Support Systems*, (132), p. 113280.

Xie, K., and Mao, Z. 2017. "The impacts of quality and quantity attributes of Airbnb hosts on listing performance," *International Journal of Contemporary Hospitality Management*, (29:9), pp. 2240–2260.

Zhang, K. Z. K., Barnes, S. J., Zhao, S. J., and Zhang, H. 2018. "Can consumers be persuaded on brand microblogs? An empirical study," *Information & Management*, (55:1), pp. 1–15.

Timm Teubner is an assistant professor of Trust in Digital Services at the Einstein Center Digital Future (ECDF) and TU Berlin. The main focuses of his work are digital platforms, including trust and reputation systems, human-computer interaction, and crowdsourcing. He approaches these subjects from a socio-technical perspective, including the investigation of user behavior and psychology, and technical, legal, as well as strategic aspects. In 2010, he received a diploma in Industrial Engineering and Management from the Karlsruhe Institute of Technology (KIT). In 2013, he received his doctoral degree in Information Systems from KIT, supervised by Christof Weinhardt. His research has been published in international outlets such as the *Journal of the Association for Information Systems, Business & Information Systems Engineering, Electronic Markets, Information & Management*, and the *Journal of Cleaner Production*.

Marc T. P. Adam is an associate professor of Computing and Information Technology at the University of Newcastle, Australia. In his research, he investigates the interplay of users' cognition and affect in human–computer interaction. In 2006, he received an undergraduate degree in Computer Science from the University of Applied Sciences Würzburg, Germany. In 2010, he received a PhD in Information Systems from the Karlsruhe Institute of Technology, Germany, supervised by Christof Weinhardt. He is a founding member of the Society for NeuroIS. His research has been published in top international outlets such as *Business & Information Systems Engineering, Computers in Human Behavior, IEEE Journal on Biomedical and Health Informatics, IEEE Transactions on Affective Computing*, the *Journal of the Association for Information Systems*, the *Journal of Management Information Systems*, and the *Journal of Retailing*.

Florian Hawlitschek is an affiliated researcher to the Chair of Trust in Digital Services in the Faculty of Economics and Management at TU Berlin. He works as an innovation manager for sustainability and digitization at the FES Frankfurter Entsorgungs- und Service GmbH (a German waste management company). In his prior academic work at the Karlsruhe Institute of Technology (Germany), he was supervised by Christof Weinhardt. His research has been published in outlets such as *Business & Information Systems Engineering, Die Unternehmung: Swiss Journal of Business Research and Practice, Electronic Commerce Research and Applications*, the *Journal of Cleaner Production*, and *Sustainability*.

Legal Tech and Lawtech: Towards a Framework for Technological Trends in the Legal Services Industry

Ciaran M. Harper and S. Sarah Zhang

Abstract The use of legal technology (legal tech) and the lawtech ecosystem of legal start-ups has experienced tremendous growth in recent years. To provide a structured approach of analysing IT innovations in the legal sector, we propose a framework for lawtech applications, classifying them into three groups: internal, B2C and B2B applications. In the context of this framework, we examine technological trends in lawtech and their potential to support and transform processes in specific areas of business or personal law. We acknowledge that within lawtech there is a gap between the areas of interest of legal practitioners, IT professionals and academic researchers, and that some areas have received considerable attention by these groups, while other areas have been left relatively unexplored by one or more of these groups. However, the growing interest by legal practitioners in advanced technology such as artificial intelligence (AI) and natural language processing (NLP) is further closing the gap between academic research, IT professionals and legal practice.

1 Introduction

Digital innovations have become ubiquitous in sectors such as finance, insurance and more recently the legal sector. While the use of technology in legal contexts has increased over the last decades, the more recent growth of the ecosystem of legal start-ups has garnered significant attention and interest in IT applications in the legal

---

The views expressed here are solely our own.

C. M. Harper
Fletchers Solicitors, Southport, Merseyside, UK
e-mail: ciaranharper@fs.co.uk

S. S. Zhang (✉)
Alliance Manchester Business School, University of Manchester, Manchester, UK
e-mail: sarah.zhang@manchester.ac.uk

© The Author(s) 2021
H. Gimpel et al. (eds.), *Market Engineering*,
https://doi.org/10.1007/978-3-030-66661-3_11

sector by investors and clients. The increase in investment in legal technology (FT 2019) and an increase in demand by clients (Law Society 2019b) have led to the 'lawtech' and 'legal tech' developments gaining further traction.

Lawtech is broadly defined as 'technologies which aim to support, supplement or replace traditional methods for delivering legal services, or transactions; or which improve the operation of the justice system' (Law Society 2019a). Some sources note that there are differences between the terms legal tech and lawtech (see, e.g., Legal Geek 2018): the former focusses on technological applications which support traditional legal processes, while the latter is used to describe the more recent developments in the legal start-up industry. The expanding lawtech ecosystem includes applications that support legal processes using more advanced technology such as machine learning (ML) and artificial intelligence (AI), as well as applications which seek to provide alternatives to traditional legal processes, such as marketplaces for legal services. We follow this distinction and use the term legal tech for applications which provide technological support for legal practitioners, whereas we use lawtech more broadly for legal tech applications using more advanced technology, as well as legal start-ups which seek to disrupt and replace some legal processes.

The aim of this chapter is to outline recent trends in lawtech and legal tech in a structured framework and provide an overview of recent academic literature in the area. In particular, we propose a lawtech framework which classifies applications into three groups: internal, Business-to-Business (B2B) and Business-to-Consumer (B2C) applications. Furthermore, we highlight that the context of the specific area of law is vital for the application of different types of technologies to different areas of law. We specifically distinguish between personal and business law and identify major technology drivers for lawtech. In the context of our framework for lawtech applications we discuss the suitability of different technological solutions in different areas of law. Based on the academic discussions on lawtech and legal tech, we discuss certain gaps between the academic discussions in computer science and law, as well as differences from the practice-founded discourse, and point out areas for future research.

2 Background/Foundations

In this section, we set out the different areas of law, their potential for automation and the use of lawtech applications. We further discuss recent trends of lawtech in practice and the lawtech research topics in various areas of the academic literature.

2.1   The Role of Technology in Different Areas of Law

The areas of law can be broadly categorised into personal law (legal disputes concerning individuals) and business law (legal issues concerning businesses). In personal law, some of the main areas include: property and housing; wills, trusts and probate; personal injury; consumer and civil rights; crime; employment; family; immigration; banking and debt; and social welfare. Business law includes some of the following areas: commercial law, energy and utilities, regulation and compliance, IT and intellectual property, and litigation and dispute resolution (see University of Law 2020). We note that some areas of law fall into both personal and business law.[1] The areas of practice for lawyers can be further characterised as 'contentious' (involving courts and/or tribunals) or 'non-contentious' (not involving courts and/or tribunals, and which are typically more transactional).

Examples of (mostly) non-contentious areas may include:

- Wills and probate
- Conveyancing and property law
- Corporate finance and corporate commercial
- Energy
- Transportation

Examples of (mostly) contentious areas of legal practice may include:

- Criminal law
- Family law
- Civil litigation
- Immigration
- Personal injury
- Employment law

It is important to appreciate that these areas do frequently overlap in practice, and there is no hard boundary between contentious and non-contentious work. While some lawyers will mostly do contentious work (e.g. personal injury lawyers) and others do mostly non-contentious work (e.g. conveyancers), others will carry out a mixture of work (e.g. a specialist in employment law will handle both contentious matters, such as a claim for unfair dismissal, and non-contentious matters, such as standard employment contracts). Furthermore, some areas of law can focus on the non-contentious aspects (e.g. dry shipping law, the non-contentious aspect of shipping law) and others on the contentious aspects of one overarching practice area (e.g. wet shipping law, the contentious part of shipping law). As there is a very wide range of legal practice, lawtech solutions therefore need to cater to the specific needs of each area of law.

---

[1]The various areas of law are further subject to various rules regimes as well, for example the Civil Procedure Rules or the Criminal Procedure Rules, which set out assorted protocol requirements for the formatting of evidence, service and submission of documents, applications to Court, etc.

We argue that non-contentious law is easier to automate as it involves fewer disagreements on facts or legal interpretations. A good example of a non-contentious area would be conveyancing (the process of transferring real estate from one party to another, typically as a sale of property such as buying a house). This is typically a formulaic process which in most cases contains the same steps in the same order. It is therefore an area which might be more prone to automation with the assistance of legal tech.

However, recent lawtech applications also offer solutions for the contentious areas of law for both individuals and businesses. An example of a contentious area of law which has been transformed by technology would be personal injury. Due to the introduction of a government portal for the issuance of claims regarding personal injury (the first of which was in the sub-field of road traffic accidents), the process of this mostly contentious area of law has been significantly standardised, which has streamlined the claims process and thus increased the efficiency of the handling of personal injury claims.

2.2   Recent Trends in Legal Technology

To provide an overview of recent trends in lawtech, we summarise different areas of lawtech applications in Table 1, based on areas of applications identified by the Law Society (2019b), Cunningham et al. (2018) and Susskind (2017). Some areas of lawtech applications focus on supporting traditional legal processes in established law firms, including practice management, risk and compliance, legal research, contract analysis and intellectual property. Commonly used technologies and methods in this area include cloud-based services, data analytics and process automation.

In recent years, the lawtech start-up sector has gained significant momentum, with some potential for disruptive effects on the traditional legal sector. Areas of applications for lawtech start-ups include legal-docs-as-a service, e-billing, DIY law and marketplaces for legal services.

In terms of specific technologies, AI/ML and blockchain have been commonly mentioned as gamechangers for the legal sector. As noted by the Law Society (2019b), the specific use cases for some of these technologies in a legal context are still relatively sparse. Mik (2017) and Rivas et al. (2018) further comment on the technical and legal limitations of using blockchain technology for contractual transactions, as they are 'incapable of enforcement in a legal sense' (Rivas et al. 2018, p.2). However, there might be potential for the use of blockchain in commercial and business law, for example in the conveyancing and property market.

Table 1 Areas of application for lawtech

Area of application	Area description (cf. Law Society 2019b; Susskind 2017)
Practice management	Solutions for case management, accounting and legal processes, which are frequently cloud-based
Risk and compliance	Process automation (PA) to streamline compliance activities and reduce risk to businesses, such as tech solutions to reduce onboarding time for new clients, or to prevent data breaches such as incorrectly addressed emails
Legal research/analytics	Legal spend and legal trend analysis using predictive analytics/data analytics and the use of technology to understand aspects of service delivery to clients and associated commercial models
Contract analysis/management	Automation of standard contracts or using natural language processing (NLP) and predictive analytics to consider documents so as to, for example, consider when best to settle a claim, or decide how long a matter is likely to take
Intellectual property	Technology supporting the research and protection of trademarks, cost/benefit analysis for licensing and trademark data validation
E-discovery	Technology to facilitate easy search and retrieval of electronically stored information, information transfer to other parties and analysis of information from other parties
DIY law	Apps or chatbots which are used by clients as a first port of call to seek legal advice or engage with legal processes
Legal-docs-as-a-service	Providers of access to a library of standardised legal documents and/or access to a solicitor
Marketplaces	Online platforms which provide transparency in terms of both pricing and process for clients. Examples include a 'GoCompare'-type comparison site or a platform similar to Upwork, where clients can post a legal job/service they require, and firms can then compete for the business
E-billing	E-billing solutions are moving towards a real-time transparency of billing which would provide a better view of work-in-progress and reduce dependency on traditional costs draftsmen
Online dispute resolution	Online platforms to exchange message and documentary evidence between claimants and defendants to support their points in the dispute, with potential to be further enhanced by AI technology.

2.3   Lawtech Research

Lawtech-related research involves multiple disciplines, centred around areas of law and computer science. Research topics on the use of technology in the legal sector have attracted attention from the academic community in both law and computer science in recent decades (since at least the 1980s).

On one side, there are several conferences and journals in computer science dedicated to topics around the intersection of law and technology. Evidently, topics involving AI are a major focus of the computer science community. Research articles in this area cover a wide range of topics, including studies on judicial decision support (Leith 1998), e-discovery (Hogan et al. 2010), the use of machine learning to predict court decisions (Medvedeva et al. 2020), analyses of online terms of service agreements (Lippi et al. 2019; Braun et al. 2019), legal expert systems (Ashley 1992; Visser and Bench-Capon 1998; Dimyadi et al. 2019), online negotiation systems (Barnett and Treleaven 2018) and legal knowledge systems and ontologies (Kurematsu and Yamaguchi 1997; Leone et al. 2020), amongst a variety of other topics. However, Oskamp and Lauritsen noted in 2002 that '[they] are frustrated not to be able to cite any fully unqualified examples of "true AI" that have been successfully deployed in the "real world" of law practice' (Oskamp and Lauritsen 2002, p. 227), indicating a significant gap between academic research on technological solutions and its adoption by legal practice.

On the other side, the interest of research communities in other areas has increased in recent years. Rather than focussing on the specific technological solutions, research in the area of law and innovation studies examines legal technology and lawtech as a driver of innovation and its impact on the legal profession. For example, Webley et al. (2019) provide an overview of different narratives of the engagement of legal practitioners with lawtech and focus on the long-term effects of technology on the legal sector. On one side, they present the hypothesis of a replacement of lawyers by technology and AI as suggested by Susskind (1998, 2017). On the other extreme, they describe a defensive stance of the legal sector towards technological innovations as 'status professionalism'. More moderate narratives include Christensen (1997)'s concept of a technological disruptor, where the legal sector will be significantly transformed by the technological innovations. Finally, Webley et al. (2019) propose the narrative of 'adaptive professionalism', which accepts that the legal field needs to adopt and develop new technology-related skills and competences, but also accounts for the diversity and complexity of the legal sector (cf. Webley et al. 2019, p.17). However, with the increase in interest from the practitioner community in AI/ML and NLP applications more recently, the studies related to these topics have received more attention and have been developed further (cf. Dale 2019; Sun et al. 2020). Other academic studies which focus on the potential for innovation and on the ecosystem of legal start-ups apply theories and methodologies from innovation studies and entrepreneurship (cf. Cunningham et al. 2018; Hongdao et al. 2019; Sako et al. 2019).

Finally, there are increasing calls for the training of legal professionals to include technological aspects, from the use of digital legal resources (Jackson 2016) to the transformation of the legal curricula to include legal tech topics (Ryan 2020). More specifically, Ireland and Hockley (2020) survey legal tech programmes at undergraduate (the Access to Justice module offered by the University of Manchester and the Lawtech module offered by the University of York) and postgraduate (LLM in the Legaltech programme offered by Swansea University and the Future of Legal Practice module offered by University College London) levels. Initiatives involving the academic community and legal practice, such as the Manchester Law and Technology Initiative (Law Society Gazette 2018), further provide a platform to shape law programmes in higher education, but also encourage the discourse between academic researchers and legal practitioners.

3   A Framework for Lawtech Applications

Based on our discussion in the previous section, we propose a structured lawtech framework which combines different areas of law with a wide range of technologies and classifies lawtech applications into three areas. The framework for lawtech applications is presented in Fig. 1.

The first layer of the framework broadly classifies the areas of law into personal law and business law. Both of these areas of law include more and less contentious areas. We further include a second layer which presents technologies that have been commonly applied in recent lawtech applications, such as AI/ML, NLP, process automation, cloud-based services and blockchain technology. We note that the second layer in Fig. 1 highlights recent trends, but is not an exhaustive list of technologies applied in lawtech. Finally, our lawtech framework categorises legal

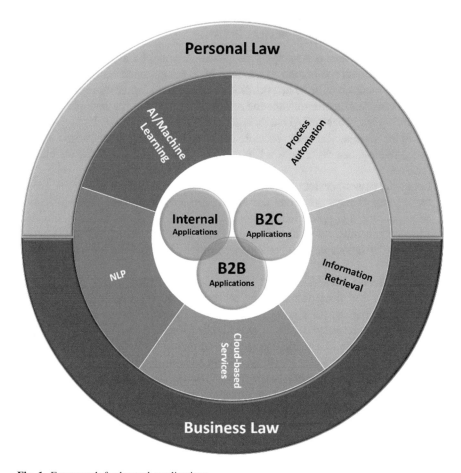

Fig. 1 Framework for lawtech applications

tech into three broad areas, each supporting the legal practice in a different way: (1) Business-to-Consumer (B2C) applications, (2) Business-to-Business (B2B) applications and (3) internal applications. Our classification is broadly in line with previous classifications of lawtech applications (cf. Law Society 2019b; Pourshafie 2020), although in our classification, we focus on the stakeholders involved in a specific lawtech application.

3.1 B2C Applications

Business-to-Consumer (B2C) applications comprise those which are more 'front-end' and client-facing, enabling greater interaction between the lawyer and their client. This is useful for both personal and business clients, albeit for slightly different reasons according to their specific needs. These technologies would therefore facilitate and strengthen the rule of law and access to justice.

Examples of B2C technologies may include:

- **DIY law:** This area covers applications which would be a front line for client engagement with the law so that if they have a legal question, they can either answer it themselves or be in a position to describe the issues more cogently to a lawyer and thus receive quicker and more relevant advice. An example would be e-learning resources and AI chatbots which could answer simple legal questions, and if the issue turned out to be more complex, could refer the client to a lawyer and provide that lawyer with a summarised version of the prospective client's issues.
- **Legal-docs-as-a-service:** In this area, a basic service would simply be access to a library of legal precedent documents, but a more sophisticated application could include a program which asks clients questions about their requirements and then generates a document (e.g. a lease or a will) based on their stated needs. This type of service could be either subscription-based or paid for with a one-off fee.
- **Marketplaces:** This covers any type of online platform which increases the availability and price transparency of legal work. At a basic level it would include the type of price comparison website which is already in wide use for insurance and household utilities (e.g. GoCompare) and review websites such as Trustpilot, but could also include services similar to Upwork, a website which is a marketplace for freelance writing, editing and translation.
- **Alternative/online dispute resolution (ADR/ODR):** This area relates to platforms where parties involved in a dispute can exchange message and documentary evidence to support their points in the dispute. This type of service is already in use in a few places: eBay provides for online dispute resolution between traders and customers, and the European Commission has an online dispute resolution platform. In the future, a more advanced application of ODR could use AI to resolve disputes between parties without having to go through

a formal litigation process. All these methods include a third party (i.e. not one of the parties involved in the dispute) providing assistance either to give a view on which party is correct or to bridge the gap between them so the parties in the dispute can reach an accommodation themselves. It is therefore easy to envisage a situation where AI replicates this functionality to a greater or lesser degree and is incorporated into current ODR platforms.

Computer science research from the 1980s up until the 2000s has focussed on issues surrounding the digitalisation of legal information and its interpretation. More recently, research has emerged which is more applications-focussed, with papers analysing the potential of ODR (Barnett and Treleaven 2018), online platforms for legal information (Ostendorff et al. 2020) or terms of services (Lippi et al. 2019; Braun et al. 2019), among others. Similar to the practitioner community, the attention of the academic community has also shifted slightly from legal technology which supports existing legal processes, to also analysing and proposing alternatives to the same legal processes.

3.2 B2B Applications

Business-to-Business (B2B) applications in the legal arena include, as in other sectors, applications which facilitate communication between businesses, but also, given the specific legal context, large organisations which are business-like, such as courts and tribunals, barristers' chambers, hospital trusts and mediation services.
Examples of B2B technologies may include:

- **Cloud-based services and secure document transfer:** Applications of this sort would be the 'bread and butter' for B2B applications in the legal sector. Law firms need to transfer documents to other law firms, courts and tribunals, barristers, enquiry agents and so on many times every working day. Having a quick and secure method for doing this which integrates well with a law firm's other systems is therefore extremely desirable.
- **Data streams:** The provision of legal services is frequently assisted by businesses, which in turn provide services to law firms. There is accordingly significant scope for these services to be streamlined and integrated into the day-to-day operation of legal service providers via technical means. Examples may include:

  - Trust account monitoring/auditing by an accredited auditing provider
  - Trusted information exchange/blockchain—for example with regard to the ownership of intellectual property
  - Partnering with complementary firms: not every law firm provides every conceivable legal service, but many do operate referral agreements between themselves for those circumstances where they are approached by a potential client with a legal need they cannot meet.

- **E-discovery:** In common law jurisdictions such as England and Wales, litigation is carried out on a 'cards on the table' basis—parties must disclose all documents in their possession which either support or weaken their own case as well as support or weaken the other side's case. For this purpose, 'document' is an extremely broad term and can include information stored electronically. E-discovery applications therefore include applications which facilitate easy search and retrieval of electronically stored information, as well as the transfer of the same to other parties and analysis of documents received from other parties.
- **E-billing:** Legal costs are a good example of an industry which runs in parallel to law firms. For less contentious matters, law firms will be able to produce their own bills; and effective software solutions to do this quickly and easily, as well as to monitor the efficiency of individual lawyers, are desirable for obvious reasons. In more contentious matters, law firms will frequently engage the services of an external costs draftsman to prepare their bills and, if necessary, argue in court that the size of the bill is reasonable and proportionate. Therefore, an e-billing application would ideally be able to carry out the monitoring noted above, and also integrate easily and securely with an external provider such as a costs draftsman and the court.

Some of the areas of B2B applications overlap with the area of B2C applications, for example ODR for contentious business-law-related cases, or subscription-based models for legal services within the context of DIY law. However, most B2B applications are more specialised in the specific area of law and the legal process which needs to be followed.

E-discovery has received much attention from both a legal and a technological perspective (Baron 2011; Hogan et al. 2010), with the latter focussing more on aspects of information and text retrieval (Oard et al. 2008). There has also been an increase in interest and research around the support and automation of court processes (cf. Leith 1998; Susskind 2019). Blockchain technology features among the widely mentioned technologies in this area in the context of smart contracts, although there are certain limitations of the technology and its applications in a legal context (as mentioned above). Despite a significant amount of research in certain areas of applications, we note that some B2B applications, such as cloud-based legal services, have not attracted as much attention as other areas.

3.3   Internal Applications

Internal applications comprise those applications which support the functioning of a legal practice but which a client will not directly interact with. Therefore, this may include not only applications which are concerned solely with the practice itself, such as those which will track KPIs, the business's accounts and other management information, but also applications which support lawyers in doing work for clients.

Examples of these applications may include:

- **Practice management**: As indicated in Table 1, this includes applications for invoice tracking, accounting and case management (which incorporates both filing and task management), but also the substantive processes of being a lawyer in practice, such as time recording and dictation software. Examples here would include Proclaim, which is widely used in the Personal Injury sector and is a 'one-stop' platform which incorporates filing, task management and accounting processes, or Dragon dictation software.
- **Risk and compliance**: These applications exist to minimise the liabilities to any legal practice by ensuring that processes which minimise risk are 'baked in' to day-to-day tasks. This could be mandatory workflows to check a new client's identity for money-laundering (law firms being particularly at risk of attempted money laundering) and conflict purposes, or email software with safeguards to prevent phishing attempts or data breaches due to misaddressed emails.
- **Contract analysis/management**: These applications currently appear to be in their infancy, but could eventually include automation of standard contracts (potentially using blockchain) or NLP to analyse documents and consider the level of legal risk in any given situation.
- **Legal research/analytics**: These applications include straightforward database applications which collate up-to-date legal resources (examples include LexisNexis and Westlaw) and also applications which can help to formulate advice to a client. An example of this would be piCalculator, an online application which helps to derive the value of a client's legal claim based on a number of factors including their age, education level, income and stated losses to date.
- **Intellectual property:** Intellectual property applications comprise, to a large extent, automated search and analysis tools. When registering a trademark or a patent, it is critical to establish that the phrase, image, process or other intellectual property element has not already been registered. A simple application would be the sort of word search function which is common to many applications already, but more sophisticated applications would include elements of NLP and AI to weed out non-relevant matches and provide analysis of the new trademark and existing ones, perhaps with commentary on possible litigation risk.

Some of the applications presented here, such as case management applications and IT support to minimise compliance risk, have been widely adopted by law firms, resulting in large cost savings and high efficiencies. The research in the area of AI and law has supported the development of management applications. As more advanced AI and ML applications could be able to provide a deeper level of analysis of legal information, they might provide further potential for automation in these areas.

4 Discussion and Conclusion

We propose a structured framework for the classification of lawtech applications. Specifically, we distinguish between internal, B2B and B2C applications, which are further embedded into different areas of law and recent technological trends. We postulate that the specific area of law is vital for understanding the effectiveness and impact of a specific lawtech application. In particular, the level of contentiousness in an area of law is one determinant for suitable lawtech applications in this particular area of law.

In considering the different areas of focus for academic research and practitioner discussions, we find gaps between the academic research and IT community and the adoption in legal practice. Within computer science, there is a large body of research on the use of AI in a legal context. Researchers in other areas mostly apply theoretical approaches and methodologies borrowed from innovation studies and entrepreneurship to analyse the ecosystem of lawtech start-ups or to provide predictions regarding the effects of technology on the legal sector as a whole. In contrast, practitioners are mainly focussed on legal technology supporting traditional legal processes, an area which is only partially covered in the context of recent work on AI and law.

Some of the gaps between legal practice and academia provide potential for future research. More research is necessary to support the current developments of lawtech applications and to provide the relevant background from areas of management and business studies. The gap between the research and applications in IT and the needs of the legal practice has to be further closed for a more fruitful discourse between academia, the IT community and legal practitioners.

Finally, we note that our study uses sources from the UK, such as the Law Society of England and Wales, and examples of academic institutions in the UK. We claim that the general classification into areas of law and their potential for technological innovation also applies to other jurisdictions, though the application in practice would certainly depend on the law of the specific country/jurisdiction. However, international studies on lawtech developments in different countries would further the understanding of country-specific (and law-system-specific) factors which influence the lawtech and legal tech sectors.

Going forward, we believe that a sustained interest in lawtech and legal tech applications will further close any gaps between academic research and legal practice and provide further insights into the role of technological innovation in law and legal practice.

References

Ashley KD (1992) Case-based reasoning and its implications for legal expert systems. Artificial Intelligence and Law 1:113–208. https://doi.org/10.1007/BF00114920

Barnett J, Treleaven P (2018) Algorithmic Dispute Resolution—The Automation of Professional Dispute Resolution Using AI and Blockchain Technologies. The Computer Journal 61:399–408. https://doi.org/10.1093/comjnl/bxx103

Baron JR (2011) Law in the Age of Exabytes: Some further Thoughts on 'Information Inflation' and Current Issues in E-Discovery Search. Richmond Journal of Law & Technology 17:1–33

Braun D, Scepankova E, Holl P, Matthes F (2019) The Potential of Customer-Centered LegalTech. Datenschutz und Datensicherheit - DuD 43:760–766. https://doi.org/10.1007/s11623-019-1202-7

Christensen C (1997) The Innovator's Dilemma. Harvard Business Review Press

Cunningham A, James AD, Taylor P, Tether B (2018) Disruptive Technologies and Legal Service Provision in the UK: A Preliminary Study

Dale R (2019) Industry Watch Law and Word Order: NLP in Legal Tech. Natural Language Engineering 25:211–217. https://doi.org/10.1017/S1351324918000475

Dimyadi J, Bookman S, Harvey D, Amor R (2019) Maintainable process model driven online legal expert systems. Artificial Intelligence and Law 27:93–111. https://doi.org/10.1007/s10506-018-9231-3

Financial Times, Croft J (2019) UK lawtech sector gets kick-start from increased investment. In: Dec 5. https://www.ft.com/content/ec995c7e-16bf-11ea-9ee4-11f260415385. Accessed 22 Oct 2020

Hogan C, Bauer RS, Brassil D (2010) Automation of legal sensemaking in e-discovery. Artificial Intelligence and Law 18:431–457. https://doi.org/10.1007/s10506-010-9100-1

Hongdao Q, Bibi S, Khan A, et al (2019) Legal technologies in action: The future of the legal market in light of disruptive innovations. Sustainability 11:1–19. https://doi.org/10.3390/su11041015

Ireland C, Hockley R (2020) A call for introducing LegalTech in the classroom. Computer Law & Security Review 36:105399. https://doi.org/10.1016/J.CLSR.2020.105399

Jackson D (2016) Human-centered legal tech: integrating design in legal education. The Law Teacher 50:82–97. https://doi.org/10.1080/03069400.2016.1146468

Kurematsu M, Yamaguchi T (1997) A Legal Ontology Refinement Support Environment Using a Machine-Readable Dictionary. Artificial Intelligence and Law 5:119–137. https://doi.org/10.1023/A:1008220029904

Law Society (2019a) Introduction to LawTech - A practical guide to legal technology

Law Society (2019b) Lawtech Adoption Research

Law Society Gazette (2018) Firms join university's legal tech initiative. In: Law Society Gazette 28 September 2018. https://www.lawgazette.co.uk/practice/firms-join-universitys-legal-tech-initiative/5067716.article. Accessed 23 Oct 2020

Legal Geek (2018) #LegalTech v #LawTech – WTF? In: Legal Geek. https://www.legalgeek.co/learn/lawtech-legaltech-wtf/. Accessed 23 Oct 2020

Leith P (1998) The Judge and the Computer: How Best "Decision Support"? Artificial Intelligence and Law 6:289–309. https://doi.org/10.1023/A:1008226325874

Leone V, Di Caro L, Villata S (2020) Taking stock of legal ontologies: a feature-based comparative analysis. Artificial Intelligence and Law 28:207–235. https://doi.org/10.1007/s10506-019-09252-1

Lippi M, Pałka P, Contissa G, et al (2019) CLAUDETTE: an automated detector of potentially unfair clauses in online terms of service. Artificial Intelligence and Law 27:117–139. https://doi.org/10.1007/s10506-019-09243-2

Medvedeva M, Vols M, Wieling M (2020) Using machine learning to predict decisions of the European Court of Human Rights. Artificial Intelligence and Law 28:237–266. https://doi.org/10.1007/s10506-019-09255-y

Mik E (2017) Smart contracts: terminology, technical limitations and real world complexity. Law, Innovation and Technology 9:269–300. https://doi.org/10.1080/17579961.2017.1378468

Oard DW, Hedin B, Tomlinson S, Baron JR (2008) Overview of the TREC 2008 Legal Track. In: Proceedings of the seventeenth text retrieval conference proceedings (TREC 2008)

Oskamp A, Lauritsen M (2002) AI in Law Practice? So far, not much. Artificial Intelligence and Law 10:227–236. https://doi.org/10.1023/A:1025402013007

Ostendorff M, Blume T, Ostendorff S (2020) Towards an Open Platform for Legal Information. In: Proceedings of the ACM/IEEE Joint Conference on Digital Libraries in 2020. ACM, New York, NY, USA, pp 385–388

Pourshafie Q (2020) Introducing the Future Framework for Legal Practice (Part 1) – Legal Tech Weekly. In: Legal Tech Weekly. https://contractbook.com/legaltechweekly/introducing-the-future-framework-for-legal-practice-part-1. Accessed 19 Oct 2020

Rivas AG, Tsyganova M, Mik E (2018) Smart Contracts and their Identity Crisis. In: ICIS 2018 Proceedings

Ryan F (2020) Rage against the machine? Incorporating legal tech into legal education. The Law Teacher 1–13. https://doi.org/10.1080/03069400.2020.1805927

Sako M, Qian M, Verhagen M, Parnham R (2019) Scaling Up Firms in Entrepreneurial Ecosystems: FinTech and LawTech Ecosystems Compared. 1–48

Sun C, Zhang Y, Liu X, Wu F (2020) Legal Intelligence: Algorithmic, Data, and Social Challenges. In: Proceedings of the 43rd International ACM SIGIR Conference on Research and Development in Information Retrieval. ACM, New York, NY, USA, pp 2464–2467

Susskind RE (1998) The Future of Law: Facing the Challenges of Information Technology. Clarendon Press

Susskind RE (2017) Tomorrow's lawyers: An introduction to your future. Oxford University Press, Oxford

Susskind RE (2019) Online Courts and the Future of Justice. Oxford University Press

University of Law (2020) Legal Practice Areas. https://www.law.ac.uk/employability/legal-practice-areas/

Visser PRS, Bench-Capon TJM (1998) A Comparison of Four Ontologies for the Design of Legal Knowledge Systems. Artificial Intelligence and Law 6:27–57. https://doi.org/10.1023/A:1008251913710

Webley L, Flood J, Webb J, et al (2019) The Profession(s)' Engagements with LawTech: Narratives and Archetypes of Future Law. Law, Technology and Humans 1:6–26. https://doi.org/10.5204/lthj.v1i0.1314

Ciaran M. Harper is a solicitor and senior litigation executive at Fletchers Solicitors of Southport and Manchester, United Kingdom. He completed his LLB at the College (now University) of Law, Chester, and completed his training contract at BTMK Solicitors of Southend-on-Sea, Essex, United Kingdom, and was admitted as a solicitor in 2012. His main area of practice is clinical negligence, acting for claimants in a range of matters, including, but not limited to, dental, cancer and ophthalmology cases.

S. Sarah Zhang is an assistant professor of finance at Alliance Manchester Business School of the University of Manchester, United Kingdom. She received her PhD in Economics from Karlsruhe Institute of Technology, supervised by Professor Dr. Christof Weinhardt. Her research focusses on market microstructure, technological innovations in financial markets and law, and experimental finance. Her work has been published in the *Journal of Banking and Finance*, the *Journal of Futures Markets* and the *Financial Review*, amongst others.

The Socialoid: A Computational Model of a City

Margeret Hall, Christian Haas, Johanna Schacht, and Steven O. Kimbrough

Abstract A *socialoid* (our term) is an integrated collection of data and models about a society. As such, and accepting that it can never be complete, it is a computational model of a society. We are in the early stages of building a socialoid for Philadelphia, PA. We call it the Philadelphioid. The Philadelphioid is a diachronic (temporal), mashed, geographic information system (GIS) with an extensive integrated library of integrated analytics tools. The purpose of this chapter is to articulate our design rationale for the Philadelphioid and to illustrate its underlying concepts and premises. Central among these concepts is the principle of *solution pluralism,* which enjoins us to use analytics and visualization to create and explore multiple solutions to decision problems. We illustrate an application of this philosophy by discussing analysis pertaining to food deserts carried out with the Philadelphioid.

1 Introduction

Data on and about the lives of cities are abundant, although how best to harness and support data-driven insights for urban environments remains an open question. Put another way, modeling with urban data is not only or is not just an information problem, it is also a design problem. In the context of attempting to solve or address socioeconomic problems through modeling, we focus on designing an information

M. Hall (✉) · C. Haas
College of Information Science and Technology, University of Nebraska at Omaha, Omaha, NE, USA
e-mail: mahall@unomaha.edu; christianhaas@unomaha.edu

J. Schacht
Head of AI @ Orbisk, Utrecht, The Netherlands
e-mail: johanna@orbisk.com

S. O. Kimbrough
The Wharton School, University of Pennsylvania, Philadelphia, PA, USA
e-mail: kimbrough@wharton.upenn.edu

© The Author(s) 2021
H. Gimpel et al. (eds.), *Market Engineering*,
https://doi.org/10.1007/978-3-030-66661-3_12

system oriented toward optimization problems, which is to say problems of how best to allocate existing but limited resources.

In this chapter, we focus on a common urban design use case in which resources are available for improving services and data are available for assessing proposed configurations, yet, inevitably, resources are insufficient and data are incomplete, and so the task is to make the best of the situation. Essential to that goal, in our view, are two requirements for supporting public deliberation, which we conceive of as being broadly interactive, affording open and accessible support of multifaceted exploration of possibilities. The first of these requirements is that relevant data be curated, validated, and made available in an open system. The second requirement is that the open system affords discovery and comparison of multiple options by a broad public. Our aim here is to describe progress we have made to date in the specific context of food deserts in Philadelphia, with emphasis on the second requirement.

Our principled response to the first requirement is to build a socialoid for Philadelphia. A *socialoid* (our term) is an integrated collection of data and models that reflect the complex societal fabric constituting everyday social life. Accepting that no socialoid can ever be complete, we may think of them as computational models of their target societies. Such models can assist with large-scale planning, can computationally address problems that are otherwise off-limits, and can deliver data-driven insights to stakeholders, among other possibilities (Bankes 1993). This chapter discusses a work-in-progress socialoid for Philadelphia, PA. We call it the Philadelphioid, conceived as a *d*iachronic, *m*ashed GIS with an extensive integrated library of integrated *a*nalytics tools (beyond those commonly found in GIS). As such it is an example of what we can call a diachronic, mashed, with analytics GIS (DMA-GIS).[1] Our purpose in this chapter is to introduce the project and its goals, as well as to present and discuss certain innovative (and we hope widely useful) contributions arising from the project. In addition to contributing to HCI and IS research on urban data, we have a specific interest in presenting the Philadelphioid as an example of designing information systems in response to significant social problems.

Our principled response to the second requirement (to support discovery and comparison of multiple design options) is to adopt the stance of what we call *generalized optimization*. Conventionally, when an optimization problem is posed, a single, best optimal solution (aka decision) is sought, usually by either the exact or heuristic method. As such, conventional optimization ignores our second requirement, which is to support discovery and comparison of multiple good solutions, recognizing that data are always incomplete and models inexact. In generalized optimization, we begin with an optimization problem, specify a set of *decisions of interest* (DoIs), and then use computational means to discover elements of the set of DoIs.

---

[1] The Philadelphioid in its current state—including shape files, associated data, heuristic optimization code in Python, data generated by this code, and MAD modeling in Python with the generated data—is freely available from the authors.

To illustrate, our focus problem in this chapter is the optimal placement of a number of grocery stores for the sake of relieving the food desert problem in Philadelphia. We define our DoIs as placements of five grocery stores so as to do well at minimizing the number of people in a food desert. We develop a heuristic search technique that generates a plurality—hundreds, even thousands—of good-quality placement designs. We then develop a multiattribute decision (MAD) model that compares the designs in the discovered DoIs *using an expanded data set that brings to bear information about the designs that were too complex to consider in the heuristic search for DoIs.* Although our data are limited (as is always the case) and we are focused only on Philadelphia, the methods we use are general and intended to be transferable to other urban environments and problems.

Philadelphia flourishes in informative online GIS applications, including Policy Map,[2] Open Data Philly,[3] Plan Philly,[4] Culture Blocks,[5] Community Commons,[6] Community Health Explorer,[7] Community Health Database,[8] Next City,[9] and FixList.[10] Many of these examples include temporally conditioned data, thereby supporting diachronic analysis. In addition, these initiatives typically present results using analytics tools, although these are largely limited to data visualization. Our project goes beyond the functionality of these kinds of systems, which might be characterized as rich, state-of-the-art online GIS applications, to develop next-generation applications that meet the following goals:

1. In general, we want to support research and to "house scholarship." That is, we want the Philadelphioid to serve as (1) a repository of data, procedures, reports of research results, and other intellectual work products, (2) a primary tool for conducting research, and (3) a primary tool for supporting social deliberation. We see its development as open-ended, and we proceed inspired by, and very much in the spirit of, the Wisconsin Idea.[11]
2. Support for diachronic (time-based, longitudinal) data and analysis. In terms of standard GIS, this implies that the system delivers multiple maps with layers conditioned by a time frame. The key to this delivery is that the results are easy to use and interpret for human readers.
3. Support for mashing, that is, for pulling together and integrating data from multiple disparate sources. Not only must the data be obtained and combined,

---

[2] http://hdl.library.upenn.edu/1017/76970.

[3] https://www.opendataphilly.org/.

[4] http://planphilly.com/.

[5] http://www.cultureblocks.com/.

[6] http://www.communitycommons.org/maps-data/.

[7] http://cityofphiladelphia.github.io/community-health-explorer/.

[8] http://hdl.library.upenn.edu/1017/88388.

[9] https://nextcity.org/.

[10] http://thephiladelphiacitizen.org/stacey-mosley-fixlist/.

[11] See, e.g., http://www.wisc.edu/wisconsin-idea/ and https://en.wikipedia.org/wiki/Wisconsin_Idea.

but it must be managed, archived, and subject to provenance control and documentation. This includes support for linked data (e.g., linked open data,[12] and Hafford 2014).

4. Assume (and support) GIS capabilities as well as other forms of visualization such that the delivered analysis eases comprehension of results for its readers.
5. Support for a broad range of social modeling and analytics. Data- and model-driven decision support for urban stakeholders is a main focus of the project.

This chapter describes our efforts to meet these objectives through the Philadelphioid, drawing inspiration from existing scholarship on urban data and decision modeling.

2 Background: Smart Cities and Urban Data Modeling

Our work is connected to an interdisciplinary body of scholarship that considers the intersection of urban environments and data, sometimes gathered under the label smart cities, or cities where digital technologies are embedded into infrastructure (Smyth and Helgason 2010). These initiatives emphasize using novel technologies to gather data about everyday life in ways that can lead to increased efficiency and automation of urban systems management (Klauers et al. 2014, Zheng et al. 2014). As a paradigm of urban design, smart cities have been critiqued as problematic for ethical surveillance and the corporatization of urban life (Kitchin 2013). In particular, the flows of data comprising smart cities tend to be one-directional, with data being gathered from but not accessible to individual city residents (Klauers et al. 2014, Odom 2010), even as the stories told with this data tend to benefit commercial interests (Söderström et al. 2014), or to support narrow political views of urban participation (Halpern et al. 2013, Vanolo 2014). A core thread that emerges across these critiques is an insistence on acknowledging that while smart city initiatives are intended to benefit urban residents, the distribution of those benefits is often uneven, with disparities that reflect existing inequalities of race, class, and privilege.

Researchers have noted the opportunities of smart cities as media-rich design environments for provoking new relationships to technology (Di Mascio et al. 2016, Messeter and Johansson 2008). Previously, a variety of outcomes have been produced from urban data, including location-based social media data to detect events (Schwartz et al. 2013, Xia et al. 2014) and activity patterns (Cranshaw et al. 2012, Gallacher et al. 2015), using crowdsourced data to manage hyper-local city services (De Melo Borges et al. 2016) and to encourage learning about neighborhood information and resources (Claes and Moere 2013). In the context of

---

[12]See, e.g., http://labs.europeana.eu/api/linked-open-data-introduction, http://doi.org/doi:10.4018/jswis.2009081901, https://www.w3.org/DesignIssues/LinkedData.html, and http://www.linkeddatatools.com/semantic-web-basics.

research that pertains to food deserts, Choudhury et al. (2016) used a mass analysis of Instagram posts to develop models for detecting food deserts, with a fairly high accuracy. Similarly interested in detection, Yu and Nahapetian (2013) developed a food consumption app to gain a grounded account of the kinds of food available for purchase within a given neighborhood or city, with the goal of producing maps that can be used for advocacy purposes.

These projects tend to rely on social media data, smartphones, and mobile apps and more specifically on the locative functionality of mobile phones, meaning the ability to tag social media content with geographic coordinates. In contrast to this emphasis on events and activity, our work on modeling is intended to provide an example of how to develop sophisticated models for understanding city space using accessible data analysis tools. These modeling projects have implications for both scientific and policy applications.

3   Modeling for Scientific Applications and Policy Purposes

Whether as individuals or as institutional actors, people can rarely make use of all of the disparate data sources available to them for making decisions. Reasons are many and are well covered in such works as Georges et al. (2016), Laurel et al. (1990), Sweller (1994), Todd and Benbasat (1994). Here, we address the use of computational models for informing stakeholders of consideration sets for decisions that are driven by actual data. Models, broadly construed, are both tools for and primary work products of applied and theoretical research. Although boundaries are inevitably fuzzy, it is useful for present purposes to think in terms of four kinds of models.

1. *Presentation and visualization.* Standard GIS, such as those referred to above, are largely visual presentations of data. They, along with other forms of data visualization, are prototypical examples of this kind of modeling.
2. *Description.* Regression and classification models are prototypical approaches for describing relationships in data. They are able to condense and summarize large amounts of data and afford our seeing of significant patterns in the data. This is true of supervised learning and unsupervised learning algorithms.
3. *Prediction or forecasting.* These models take an explicitly diachronic perspective, allowing us to predict what has not yet been observed (or not used in constructing the model). Valuable as they are, these kinds of models are challenging in our context because so much of available data is synchronic (cross-sectional), not diachronic (longitudinal). Even so, forecasting models constitute an important class of models for socialoids and DMA-GIS in general.
4. *Prescription.* Prescriptive models aim to support decision-making. They introduce the concept of an objective function to be optimized. We solve them in order to find decisions (actions to be taken) that do well with regard to a given objective. Prescriptive models are very common in engineering, policy-making,

and business (operations research (OR), management science, etc.). Constrained optimization models are a prime example, whether expressed as mathematical programs or not.

Multiattribute decision (MAD) models are another important class of prescriptive modeling. We discuss them in the next section.

Prescriptive modeling with spatial data and problems is comparatively underdeveloped. The "urban OR" field, for example, had impressive successes in the 1970s but has since withered from lack of support by financially challenged urban interests. This said, there is certainly ample high-quality work to draw upon and with contemporary informatics resources (GIS, cloud computing, advances in metaheuristics, the open-source culture, etc.). We believe that prescriptive modeling for socialoids, and urban OR problems generally speaking, is primed for great advances. In cases where stakeholders have not yet defined the totality of the problem (i.e., wicked urban problems), models with inclusive data can estimate many scenarios in a less emotionally charged environment (Davies and Nutley 2000). For these reasons, prescriptive modeling is an important, but hardly exclusive, focus of our project. With that in mind, we now discuss some of our efforts and results in this regard.

4 Modeling Example

4.1 Generalized Optimization

So far, we have defined the Philadelphioid as an integrated information system of complex and multifaceted urban data, and we argued that modeling with this data can point to solutions for addressing significant socioeconomic problems. We illustrate these latter claims by focusing on the problem of food deserts (Cannuscio et al. 2014, Mayer et al. 2014), at present a serious and persistent issue in Philadelphia. Food deserts present a serious urban problem, with dramatic health consequences that can include increased rates of obesity and poor nutrition (Ploeg et al. 2009). These consequences may be especially acute for vulnerable and immobile populations—the elderly and the young. Given the pressing nature of the issue and the broad availability of grocery store locations, food deserts were chosen as a modeling example to outline usability of the Philadelphioid and thus socialoids.

While definitions of food deserts can vary, in general, the term refers to neighborhoods where residents experience severe shortages in local access to grocery stores (Bernstein and Shierholz 2014). The 0.5-mile criterion is the lowest of three suggested distances by Ploeg et al. (2009) and the Philadelphia health department. They introduce three distance markers: for rural areas, a distance of up to 10 miles is feasible for not being considered living in a food desert; for urban areas (such as Philadelphia), a 0.5–1.0 mile walking distance is considered feasible. Of course, the cutoff of 0.5 mile is simply a parameter in our modeling and can be changed at will, which is a major advantage of computational modeling. By this criterion,

Fig. 1 The current situation
in Philadelphia. Black dots
represent supermarkets; gray
lines represent streets

about two-thirds (968,081 of 1,526,006 people) of Philadelphia's population live in
a food desert (Fig. 1). A question then is "given additional resources for placing n
new grocery outlets, where should they be placed?" This is the design question we
address with the Philadelphioid as an information system.

Complicating any approach to answering this question is the fact that models
are inaccurate and inevitably fail to include important data for the problem. This
may happen because the data are not available, because including the data would
make the model prohibitively expensive computationally, and for many other
reasons (Bankes 1993). Attempting to determine solutions for placing grocery stores
immediately raises a host of continent questions: Who should receive priority for
being served? The old? The young? Ethnic minorities and if so, which ones? What
about communities of common interest? How, if at all, can distance be mitigated
by public transportation? By proximity to places of employment? It is a challenging
task even listing the relevant criteria and/or to have agreement between stakeholders,
let alone finding relevant and usable data to incorporate into a tractable model.

For these reasons, we adopted the philosophy of *solution pluralism* and *generalized optimization* (Chou et al. 2014, Hall et al. 2013, Kimbrough and Lau 2016) in
which we seek multiple good solutions to the question at hand, rather than a single
"best" (optimal) solution.[13] The plurality of solutions—the discovered DoIs—are
then to be used for collective deliberation, which we demonstrate next.

Before describing our model in depth, we offer a final caveat: while we focus
in this chapter on supermarket placement, there are a number of other means of
mitigating the social and health consequences of food deserts, including education,
transportation, affordable housing, and access to medical care and expertise. These

---

[13]What counts as a good solution will of course be problem specific. In Kimbrough and Lau
(2016), four types of good solutions are identified for constrained optimization problems generally:
(A) feasible, with near-optimal objective values; (B) feasible, with objective values better than a
given threshold and having large amounts of slack on the constraints; (C) infeasible, but having
small amounts of constraint violations; and (D) infeasible, with amounts of constraint violation
below a given threshold and having objective values superior to the optimal. In the case of food
deserts, good solutions are feasible and serve total populations nearly as large as that served by the
heuristically best (heuristically optimal) solution discovered.

approaches are almost certainly more effective in combination than isolation; by concentrating on geographic placement of grocery stores, we do not mean to imply that this is the only solution, or the only use for the Philadelphioid, in better understanding food deserts. We hope to address one facet of food deserts as a social ill, but our discussion should not be viewed as a single antidote for combating food-related social injustices.

4.2   Heuristic Optimization

To begin, we frame the problem as a *location-allocation* problem, a constrained optimization problem with the objective of maximizing the number of people served, by the placement of the n outlets (full-line supermarkets). In this example $n = 5$. There is no larger reason $n = 5$ is the selected number, as any number would outline the usability of the Philadelphioid to solve problems just as well. However, even this simple formulation presents a challenging combinatorial optimization problem. We shall now briefly describe our computational approach to solving for $n = 5$ additional supermarkets, which yielded 1024 high-quality solutions. In the next sections, we describe how the Philadelphioid helps us make use of these solutions.

The data is based on the 2010 US census data plus geo-coded locations for the 97 full-service grocery stores in Philadelphia. For each of the 18,874 census blocks, we compute the taxicab distance to the closest supermarket from its centroid. Population and income data are available, as are further demographic data such as population counts for Caucasian American, African American, and other ethnic groups, as well as counts of population above 65 years of age and population under 15 years of age. The current disposition of the existing grocery stores is far from optimal with regard to maximally serving population with supermarkets. Figure 1 shows the current situation of Philadelphia. Figure 2 shows areas that are in/not in a food desert (using taxicab distance, a census block more than 0.5 miles away from a supermarket is counted as located in a food desert).

Fig. 2 Black dots represent supermarkets; dark gray areas surrounding them represent areas that are reasonably covered by the supermarket. The remaining light gray area represents the Philadelphia food desert

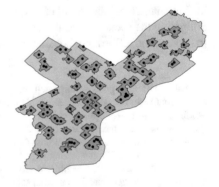

Our heuristic algorithm for placing the n ($= 5$ here) new grocery outlets works as follows. It is a variant of a standard greedy algorithm for location allocation (Kimbrough and Lau 2016). Given census blocks (polygons in GIS) and supermarkets (points in GIS), the goal of the described point-to-polygon location allocation problem is placing five new supermarkets so that a maximum number of people are added to the count of people that do not live in a food desert. This is achieved using a greedy heuristic that places one supermarket after another, meaning placing the first supermarket, updating the situation in the data and then placing the best supermarket given the new updated situation, and so on. At each step, the choice is greedy optimal because we simply enumerate the choices. Overall, however, when placing more than one outlet, this is not optimal (Kimbrough and Lau 2016). The heuristic does reduce the computation from 18874^5 options to about 18874×5 options. (Our algorithm, see below, worked with all 18,874 census blocks in Philadelphia.)

In our greedy algorithm, selection of locations for new supermarkets is purely based on population, i.e., on minimizing population in a food desert. We introduce solution pluralism into our algorithm as a way of circumventing this limitation. When the heuristic places a supermarket, it saves the top four locations for that supermarket. Upon completion of a run, the heuristic algorithm will return 20 different locations, 4 options for each of the 5 new locations. The combinations provide $4^5 = 1024$ options for placing 5 new supermarkets. Of course, 1024 cannot be said to be the best number of options generated, but it is adjustable via the algorithm should experience indicate that other values should be used. We find that 1024 is large enough that it contains a variety of distinct and interesting solutions. As described next, the 1024 options for the position of best solution are further evaluated using utility functions.

4.3   Designing MAD Models

Based on the previous description on how we produced 1024 good solutions for the Philadelphia food desert problem, we now need to discuss how this plurality of solutions can be assessed and deliberated upon in a principled and accessible way. We discuss in this section a very general approach meeting these requirements: multiattribute decision (MAD) models, built with the SMARTER technique. In the following section, we describe the particulars of its application to our food desert data.

It is often the case that we need to assess multiple outcomes or entities on several dimensions or attributes. To generalize the scenario, consider comparing restaurants. We consider price, quality, distance from home, service, as well as other attributes. Rarely, if ever, do we find a single outcome (e.g., restaurant) that is as good as or better than the alternatives on every single attribute of interest. Consider how we might represent the familiar problem of choosing a restaurant on a particular occasion. It is often the case that we need to assess multiple outcomes

Table 1 Restaurants with attributes

Restaurant name	Food	Decor	Service	Cost
Abbey Grill	14	16	16	$26.00
Academy Café	15	16	15	$23.00
Adobe Café	16	12	15	$18.00
Alaina's Fine Food	21	15	20	$19.00
Alberto's Newtown Squire	19	20	19	$31.00
Al Dar Bistro	16	14	14	$20.00
Alexandar's Table at Chaucer's	17	14	16	$19.00
Alexander's Café	17	17	16	$26.00

or entities on several dimensions or attributes. Table 1 presents a generic example of multiattribute data (having nothing to do with food deserts). It shows comparative scores for a number of Philadelphia restaurants on each of the four dimensions, viz., the attributes food quality, decor quality, service quality, and cost.

It often happens that we need to make trade-offs among the attributes in order to arrive at an accurate, as opposed to emotionally driven, overall score (the utility or more generally an *index*) for a possible choice. Multiattribute decision (MAD) modeling has as its purpose the construction of mathematical models for making these trade-offs (Kimbrough and Lau 2016, Yoon and Hwang 1995).

Returning to Philadelphia's recognized problem of food deserts (Cannuscio et al. 2014, Johann et al. 2014, Mayer et al. 2014), we modeled census data at the block level, other data at the census block group level, and the locations of the 97 supermarkets in Philadelphia. Recall that we then asked the question: Supposing resources were available to add five new supermarkets, where should they be added? We implemented a heuristic optimization procedure for location analysis (see **Heuristic Optimization**) to find candidate decisions, based upon maximizing the population served within 0.5 mile of a supermarket. Recall again that employing a philosophy of solution pluralism (finding and using multiple solutions or decisions for a problem; see below), we used the heuristic optimization procedure to find 1024 good decisions for locating these 5 stores. Table 2 displays scores on 6 attributes for the best 12 decisions discovered. Rows correspond to candidate decisions and columns to their served populations on the indicated attributes.

For many purposes, it will be useful to construct a simple additive MAD model, in which the utility or index of each alternative is a weighted sum of the utilities of the alternative's attribute scores. This is readily expressed clearly in mathematical notation. Our additive model is

$$U(x_i) = \sum_{j=1}^{n} w_j u_j(x_{i,j}) \tag{1}$$

where $i \in$ objects or choices, $j \in$ the n attributes, x_i is choice i, w_j is the weight on attribute j, u_j is the utility function on attribute j, and $x_{i,j}$ is the score

Table 2 Attributes of the top 12 discovered decisions for adding five grocery stores in Philadelphia. A: total population served. B: Caucasian American population served. C: African American population served. D: Other ethnic population served. E: Population over 65 served. F: Population under 15 served

Rank	A	B	C	D	E	F
1	649,965	263,256	277,075	109,634	97,419	143,685
2	649,743	263,295	276,784	109,664	97,438	143,680
3	647,220	263,383	274,298	109,539	97,129	142,958
4	649,536	261,676	278,377	109,483	97,333	143,959
5	649,491	262,288	277,321	109,882	97,196	143,571
6	649,269	262,327	277,030	109,912	97,215	143,566
7	646,973	262,673	274,532	109,768	96,954	142,901
8	649,062	260,708	278,623	109,731	97,110	143,845
9	649,054	262,536	277,048	109,470	97,234	143,537
10	648,832	262,575	276,757	109,500	97,253	143,532
11	646,973	263,177	274,291	109,505	97,074	142,922
12	648,625	260,956	278,350	109,319	97,148	143,811

of object/choice i on attribute j. (The scores in Tables 1 and 2 are $x_{i,j}$ values.) We follow the method of Edwards and Barron (1994), called SMARTER. It is maximally simple and has good theoretical backing and empirical success (Dawes 1979, Kimbrough and Lau 2016). Of course, it is possible to develop more complex, and one might hope more accurate, models. There is a good theory for this (Edwards and Barron 1994, Keeney and Raiffa 1993, von Winterfeldt and Edwards 1986), but the burden on the users is much increased. SMARTER models are excellent points of entry to MAD modeling. We shall now unpack the model and discuss how all of its elements may be obtained with minimal user input (if that is what the user wants).

Let X be a table or array of outcomes and their scores. In terms of Table 1, X is the interior twelve rows and four columns. $x_{i,j}$ is the element of X in the ith row and jth column. For example, $x_{3,2} = 12$ and is the score for the Adobe Café on decor. We need to convert all of the scores to a common range so that they may be compared. We choose the $[0,100]$ range and transform each of the scores in X as follows:

$$u_j(x_{i,j}) = 100 \times \frac{x_{i,j} - x_j^-}{x_j^+ - x_j^-} \qquad (2)$$

where:

- $x_{i,j}$ is the score of object/choice i on attribute j.
- x_j^+ (x_j^-) is the best (worst) score on attribute j.

  For example, from Table 1, if the attribute is food (j = food), then $x_j^+=24$ and $x_j^-=14$.

- $u_j(x_{i,j})$ is the utility (desirability, index value) on attribute j of the score on attribute j of object/choice i.

  For example, from Table 1, if the object is Al Dar Bistro ($i =$ Al Dar Bistro) and the attribute is cost ($j =$ cost), then the object is x_{ij} and its utility u_j on i is score

$$u_j(x_{i,j}) = 100 \times \frac{\$20 - \$31}{\$18 - \$31} = 84.6 \tag{3}$$

We also need to find weights, w_j, for each attribute. To do so we use the method of rank weights. We simply ask the user to rank in order the attributes by importance or value, and then we calculate weights based on the rankings only. (This has to be done properly. We pass over the details because they are known and readily available.) Here is the formula for doing this:

$$w_k = \frac{1}{n} \sum_{j=k}^{n} \frac{1}{j} \tag{4}$$

where w_k is the weight on the kth attribute by rank (so w_1 is the weight on the first-ranked attribute), n is the number of attributes, and the highest ranking attribute has a k value of 1 (i.e., the best to worst rank order is 1, 2, 3, ..., n).

With four attributes as in our restaurant example, if the attributes food, decor, service, and cost are ranked in that order, then the (rank, weight) pairs are (1, 0.5208), (2, 0.2708), (3, 0.1458), and (4, 0.0625).

4.4   Using the MAD Models

MAD models of the SMARTER variety potentially apply to any situation in which there is a table of scores, X, in which rows correspond to distinct entities, columns to attributes of the entities, and the $x_{i,j}$ are scores for the entity attributes. In our context, this range of applicability is indeed very large. Synchronically, the entities to be compared co-exist at a given time. These might be different plans for adding grocery stores, different redistricting proposals, geographic entities such as wards, and much else. Attributes of interest might include total population, income distribution, demographics (income, ethnicity, age distribution), voting behavior, access to public transportation, presence of services such as police and fire stations, etc.

Under either perspective, we advocate the philosophy of solution pluralism: use the data and the models to generate multiple possible decisions, and then evaluate this plurality of options, taking into account information not present in the data and models (see Chou et al. 2014, Hall et al. 2013, Kimbrough and Lau 2016). MAD models are entirely apt tools for this purpose.

MAD models, then, plausibly have a wide scope of applicability for socialoids and DMA-GIS. The basic work flow in getting them built is remarkably simple:

1. The user: Based on a system presentation, identifies the collection of entities to be compared.
2. The user: Based on a system presentation, identifies the entity attributes to be included in the model and for each attribute identifies its preference sense (Is more better or is less better?).
3. The user: Based on a system presentation (and using theory about how to do this), rank orders the attributes.
4. The system: Assembles the model and presents a ranking of the selected entities.
5. The user: Explores the results and comes to a judgment.

At this point, it is possible to provide a variety of general services for MAD models that support post-solution analysis (Kimbrough and Lau 2016). The user in this scenario is a human, preferably a user with considerable insight on the models to be chosen and a good understanding of the domain. To note some main examples and the questions they raise:

1. Sensitivity analysis:
   Are there small changes in parameter values that will result in large changes in outcomes according to the model? If so, what are they, and which parameters have the largest sensitivities, i.e., which parameters if changed by small amounts result in large changes in model outcomes? Which parameters have small sensitivities?
2. Missing data and implausible data services:
   Where are the missing data? How should any missing data be handled? What about apparent outliers?
3. Outcome reach analysis:
   Given an outcome predicted or prescribed by the model, and a specific desired (or feared) alternative outcome, how do the assumptions of the model need to be changed in order to reach the outcome(s) in question? If so, what is the cheapest or most effective way to do this? Outcome reach questions arise on the degradation side as well. By opting to accept a degraded outcome, we may free up resources that can be used elsewhere.
4. Robustness analysis:
   Which decisions or policy options of the model perform comparatively well across the full range of ambient uncertainty for the model?

It is evident that a SMARTER MAD model affords much scope for automation of post-solution analysis (including automation to check with the user).

Focusing again on our data and results, Table 2—fundamentally similar in structure to Table 1—presents multiattribute data for the food desert problem. Results show that when adding five supermarkets to Philadelphia minimizing a 0.5-mile taxicab distance as the indicator on living in a food desert, the number of people not living in a food desert can be raised from 557,925 to 640,065. The 1024 discovered solutions raise the number of people not living in a food desert to an average of 639,675, which is an insignificant difference to the solutions discovered by the heuristic.

The perspective of solution pluralism has much to add here. While the 1024 discovered solutions do not differ greatly in the number of people in a food desert, they do differ significantly in other aspects. Considering only the best 12 options, as shown in Table 2, all other columns differ by more than the best population value in column A and the average unserved population (639,675). Thus, the quality of the solutions with regard to the other criteria is more diverse. Solution diversity allows us to differentiate between the solutions considering all criteria—the goal of solution pluralism combined with MAD models. Following up on this observation, we use these differences to evaluate all 1024 solutions, by applying a MAD model to score and rank all of the solutions on an expanded set of criteria.

Table 3 presents the weighted single attributes (columns A–F) and overall utility scores (column G) for a SMARTER MAD model we developed and applied to the 1024 solutions from the greedy heuristic, using additional data, as indicated in the table. As described above, given the data, we need just two additional sources of information in order to build the model, whose results we see, in part, in the table. The first information item we need is the sense for each of the six attributes (A–F). In our model, we stipulated that for attributes A–E, more is uniformly better, but for attribute F (average income), less is better. Thus, we sought to favor lower-income individuals. The second information item we need is the rank order of the attributes

Table 3 Weighted utility values for the top 20 solutions. ID: Solution rank on population served. A: Population served. B: African American population served. C: Other ethnic population served. D: Population over 65 served. E: Population under 15 served. F: Income per year (in $1000). G: Net utility

ID	A	B	C	D	E	F	G
131	2.70	6.04	5.95	22.62	35.81	10.24	83.36
67	2.72	5.93	5.96	23.26	35.80	9.51	83.19
643	2.69	2.81	9.96	12.80	39.40	15.31	82.96
579	2.71	2.70	9.97	13.44	39.39	14.59	82.80
899	2.69	5.88	6.02	22.11	35.08	10.20	81.97
128	2.76	5.67	6.06	23.36	34.67	9.42	81.93
195	2.69	5.88	5.94	23.13	36.08	8.17	81.90
691	2.69	2.80	9.98	12.57	38.75	15.03	81.81
129	2.73	5.58	6.08	23.52	34.65	9.25	81.81
835	2.71	5.77	6.03	22.75	35.07	9.47	81.80
3	2.73	5.84	5.96	22.85	35.84	8.58	81.80
64	2.78	5.56	6.07	24.00	34.66	8.69	81.76
135	2.65	6.11	6.12	20.70	35.34	10.75	81.66
627	2.71	2.69	9.99	13.21	38.74	14.30	81.64
65	2.75	5.47	6.09	24.17	34.64	8.51	81.63
640	2.74	2.43	10.06	13.54	38.26	14.50	81.54
707	2.68	2.65	9.94	13.31	39.67	13.25	81.51
179	2.67	6.02	5.88	22.29	34.84	9.81	81.50
71	2.67	6.00	6.13	21.34	35.33	10.02	81.49
641	2.71	2.35	10.08	13.70	38.24	14.32	81.41

in importance. This we stipulated as A = 6, B = 5, C = 4, D = 2, E = 1, and F = 3. Thus, E = *population under 15 served* is the most important attribute in the model, and A = *total population served* is the least important. Of course, A is what the heuristic optimization procedure sought to maximize. With this ranking, the weights are A = 0.02777778, B = 0.06111111, C = 0.10277778, D = 0.24166667, E = 0.40833333, and F = 0.15833333. Points arising:

1. Comparing Tables 2 (raw data) and 3 (MAD model processed data), we can see that the MAD model has done real work for us in discriminating among the plurality of options. Looking at the raw data in Table 2, it is really not possible to discern a better row from a worse row, yet the MAD model data, excerpted in Table 3, does this comprehensively for all 1024 options.
2. Only one—ID 3, or rank 4—of the top 60 solutions from the heuristic optimization appears in the top 20 solutions identified by the MAD model.
3. Several of the top 20 utility model solutions have rank scores worse than (greater than) 500 in the heuristic (population served only) optimization solutions.
4. Figure 3 shows a portion of Philadelphia. Existing grocery stores are indicated as black dots. The five green dots represent the locations of the five grocery stores in the best heuristic optimization solution.
5. When we examine the top heuristic optimization solutions, they closely resemble what we see in Fig. 3.
6. Remarkably, of the top 10 solutions from the utility model, eight also closely resemble the solution in Fig. 3. However, two are somewhat different, ranks 4 and 8 (rows 4 and 8 of Table 3).
7. Figure 4 adds, as yellow stars, the five locations from the rank 4 solution from the utility model. We see that four of the five locations are quite close to those of the heuristic optimization, yet the fifth location is quite different from its counterpart in the heuristic optimization. The rank 8 solution in the utility model is similar.

Fig. 3 Green dots represent top solution from the heuristic optimization, placing five grocery outlets; black dots indicate existing grocery stores in Philadelphia

Fig. 4 Green dots represent top solution from the heuristic optimization, placing five grocery outlets; black dots indicate existing grocery stores in Philadelphia. Yellow stars represent the rank 4 solution from the utility model

Table 4 (a) (ID 1 to 5) presents information on green dots of Figs. 3 and 4, and (b) (ID 6 to 10) presents information on yellow stars of Fig. 4

ID	Street	Number	Longitude	Latitude
(a)				
1	S 17th Street	1820	−75.175	39.928
2	Ritner Street	1014	−75.165	39.921
3	Potter Street	3150	−75.116	39.996
4	S 18th Street	368	−75.172	39.947
5	S 54th Street	324	−75.231	39.955
(b)				
6	Sigel Street	1750	−75.176	39.928
7	Ritner Street	1014	−75.165	39.921
8	Potter Street	3150	−75.116	39.996
9	Waverly Street	1750	−75.171	39.946
10	N Water Street	3150	−75.129	39.997

Table 4 shows further information pertaining to Fig. 4. As Fig. 4 suggests, the green dots and yellow stars twice coincide at the same supermarket location; these are supermarkets with IDs 2 and 7 as well as supermarkets with IDs 3 and 8. Supermarkets with IDs 5 and 10 are those that are very far away from each other. The last four supermarkets (IDs 1 and 6 (the supermarket couple further south in Fig. 4) and 4 and 9 (the supermarket pair further north in Fig. 4)) are close and so would serve a similar part of Philadelphia. To give an idea about distances: 1 and 6 are 130 meters apart and 4 and 9 are 120 meters apart.

5   Discussion and Future Work

Urban environments are complex and messy arrangements of people, institutions, and infrastructure. Making decisions about how to address a city or neighborhood problem—such as access to healthy food–is not solely a matter of access to data; it is also about being able to model data in such a way as to be usable. More specifically, information systems must be designed in a way that allows for interpretation and can inform difficult decisions through the presentation of distinct possibilities for addressing identified problems. We have described the Philadelphioid as an information system designed to aid in research and deliberation surrounding local socioeconomic concerns. Using real data to model solutions for a known problem, our modeling design leverages solution pluralism to provide a robust set of possibilities for tackling resource allocation in a discrete geographic setting.

In evaluating the efficacy of the Philadelphioid, it is safe to draw two conclusions from the heuristic optimization and MAD exercise discussed above. First, the solution from the optimization, green dots in Fig. 3, is quite robust within the consideration set we explore. Each of the 1024 solutions is distinct, and even adding the MAD model, incorporating information from other attributes does little to change this conclusion. The optimization solution appears to be a good one, but so are very many other solutions nearby geographically. Thus, if we accept it as an anchor point, there is ample room for adjusting locations slightly (by a few census blocks) in response to further information (availability of land, public transit, etc.). We see this proposed solution as a guide rather than a fixed, unyielding demand, i.e., the Philadelphioid is meant to inform rather than dictate decisions. The second point is that there are a few credible, distinctly different alternatives to the heuristic optimization solution, viz., as seen in Fig. 4. In terms of public deliberation, we might think of this solution as in the consideration set, but as having a burden of proof to overcome when compared to any solution very similar to the optimization solution.

The larger point here is that we can see that the Philadelphioid has produced substantial material for affording public discussion presented in a way that aids comprehension of the proposed solutions. It does this in large part by producing a consideration set—a plurality of solutions—of high value. It then evaluates a feasible number that are appropriate for deliberation and presents them in easy-to-digest ways.

This last point serves as a segue to discussion of future work. As a tool with both academic and activist capacities, the Philadelphioid's design and potential use cases are open-ended. We have laid out with considerable specificity important basic elements of a socialoid. The challenge now is to articulate and implement generalizations of what is on display here. These include at a minimum more data, especially diachronic data, richer modeling, further algorithms for generating multiple solutions, more nuanced forms of MAD modeling, and much more in the way of interactive, visualized post-solution analysis. Diachronically, the entities can be conditioned by time frames (e.g., by decade) and the attributes just about anything of interest, particularly where they touch on issues of broad social and cultural import (such as historical patterns of police brutality, indicators of neighborhood change, and so on). For example, the entities might be geographic regions of the city conditioned by a time frame and the attributes quality of life scores for the region-times across multiple dimensions (income, crime, health, etc.). Building chronological accounts of urban environments would provide researchers as well as policymakers with tools for understanding in a more precise and grounded way how city landscapes and neighborhoods are being affected by dynamics of gentrification and fluctuations in population and wealth. We are, in particular, keen to explore this with diachronic data on grocery store locations and population data. Has the Philadelphia food desert problem been getting better or worse since 1960? Addressing this and many related questions is within reach by adding existing data to the present system.

The ability to support diachronic data would allow us to model *time series*; that is, we could observe change in time which, in turn, would allow different models of the factors influencing social and cultural patterns to be tested. For example, if we have a theory that the distribution of grocery stores in the city is influenced by some set of demographic factors distributed over space and time, we could use the time series in the model to test this theory. Analysis of these time series would allow a researcher to model and test a variety of theories against actual spatiotemporal series with different degrees of granularity. We could, for example, look at the impact of demographic changes on both property values and food deserts. Alternatively (or in addition), we could analyze the impact of the introduction of casinos on property values, crime rates, and bankruptcy rates in the surrounding neighborhoods. From a policy perspective, we could also model the impact of potential governmental actions and ordinances on the community, as well as model how past policies have influenced the well-being of various populations in the city.

Other areas of interest for future work could shift from decision support theory in urban data contexts to interpersonal and institutional settings. For example, one could envision evaluating solution quality from the socialoid compared to focus group discussions or expert opinions. Measuring stakeholders' cognitive load in the deliberation and decision process could also be significant. We note that for a richer set of design decisions, this kind of modeling and data gathering should be informed by research on interpersonal and organizational communication, as well as decision theory. Another area of interest is applying the concept of solution pluralism on political redistricting, i.e., the creation of voting districts based on smaller precincts. As a highly politicized issue with many, and often unclear, objectives, initial work shows that a variety of solutions with different properties can be created and evaluated based on several dimensions (Haas et al. 2020, Miller et al. 2018). Finally, we hope that very many socialoids can be built. This will afford comparative analysis between cities and neighborhoods, which can yield insights and is required to undergird provisional findings with any single socialoid. Indeed, as scientists, we are "stronger together" by creating a plurality of solutions with a plurality of socialoids.

References

Bankes S (1993) Exploratory Modeling for Policy Analysis. Operations Research 41(3):435–449
Bernstein J, Shierholz H (2014) The minimum wage: A crucial labor standard that is well targeted to low- and moderate-income households. Journal of Policy Analysis and Management 33(4):1036–1043

Cannuscio CC, Hillier A, Karpyn A, Glanz K (2014) The social dynamics of healthy food shopping and store choice in an urban environment. Social Science and Medicine 122:13–20

Chou C, Kimbrough SO, Murphy FH, Sullivan-Fedock J, Woodard CJ (2014) On empirical validation of compactness measures for electoral redistricting and its significance for application of models in the social sciences. Social Science Computer Review 32(4):534–542

Choudhury MD, Sharma S, Kiciman E (2016) Characterizing dietary choices, nutrition, and language in food deserts via social media. In: Proceedings of the 19th ACM Conference on Computer-Supported Cooperative Work & Social Computing (CSCW '16), ACM, New York, NY, USA, pp 1157–1170

Claes S, Moere AV (2013) Street infographics: raising awareness of local issues through a situated urban visualization. In: Proceedings of the 2nd ACM International Symposium on Pervasive Displays (PerDis '13), ACM, pp 133–138

Cranshaw J, Raz S, Hong J, Sadeh N (2012) The livehoods project: Utilizing social media to understand the dynamics of a city. In: International AAAI Conference on Weblogs and Social Media, pp 58–65

Davies HT, Nutley SM (2000) What works?: Evidence-based policy and practice in public services. Policy Press

Dawes RM (1979) The robust beauty of improper linear models in decision making. American Psychologist 34(7):571–582

De Melo Borges J, Budde M, Peters O, Riedel T, Schankin A, Beigl M (2016) Estavis: A real-world interactive platform for crowdsourced visual urban analytics. In: Proceedings of the Second International Conference on IoT in Urban Space (Urb-IoT '16), ACM, pp 65–70

Di Mascio D, Clarke R, Akama Y, Salim F (2016) Urban HCI: (re)adapting the city together. In: Proceedings of the 2016 ACM Conference Companion Publication on Designing Interactive Systems, pp 89–92

Edwards W, Barron FH (1994) SMARTS and SMARTER: Improved simple methods for multiattribute utility measurement. Organizational Behavior and Human Decision Processes 60(3):306–325

Gallacher S, Golsteijn C, Kalnikaite V, Houben S, Johnson R, Harrison D, Marquardt N (2015) SenCity 2: visualizing the hidden pulse of a city. In: Adjunct Proceedings of the 2015 ACM International Joint Conference on Pervasive and Ubiquitous Computing and Proceedings of the 2015 ACM International Symposium on Wearable Computers (UbiComp/ISWC'15 Adjunct), ACM, pp 1391–1394

Georges V, Courtemanche F, Senecal S, Baccino T, Fredette M, Leger PM (2016) Ux heatmaps: Mapping user experience on visual interfaces. Proceedings of the 2016 CHI Conference on Human Factors in Computing Systems pp 4850–4860

Haas C, Hachadoorian L, Kimbrough SO, Miller P, Murphy F (2020) Seed-fill-shift-repair: A redistricting heuristic for civic deliberation. PloS one 15(9):e0237935

Hafford WB (2014) Linked open data and the Ur of the Chaldees project. Web post: http://dlib.nyu.edu/awdl/isaw/isaw-papers/7/hafford/#p1, iSAW Papers 7.7 (2014). Accessed: 2020-11-01

Hall M, Kimbrough SO, Michalk W, Schneider J, Weindardt C (2013) Making solution pluralism in policy making accessible: Optimization of design and services for constituent well-being. In: Extended abstracts of the 2013 ACM Conference on Human Factors in Computing Systems (CHI). (Workshop on Engaging the Human-Computer Interaction Community With Public Policymaking Internationally)

Halpern O, LeCavalier J, Calvillo N, Pietsch W (2013) Test-bed urbanism. Public Culture 25(2):272–306

Johann H, Hall M, Kimbrough SO, Quintus N, Weinhardt C (2014) Service district optimization: Usage of facility location methods and geographic information systems to analyze and optimize urban food retail distribution. Working paper, SSRN

Keeney RL, Raiffa H (1993) Decisions with multiple objectives: preferences and value tradeoffs. Cambridge University Press, Cambridge, UK

Kimbrough SO, Lau HC (2016) Business Analytics for Decision Making. CRC Press, Boca Ratan, FL

Kitchin R (2013) The real-time city? big data and smart urbanism. GeoJournal

Klauers F, Paasche T, Söderström O (2014) Michel Foucault and the smart city: power dynamics inhering in contemporary governing through code. Environment and Planning 32:869–885

Laurel B, Oren T, Don A (1990) Issues in multimedia interface design: media integration and interface agents. Proceedings of the SIGCHI conference on Human factors in computing systems Empowering people - CHI '90 pp 133–139

Mayer VL, Hillier MA Aand Bachhuber, Long JA (2014) Food insecurity, neighborhood food access, and food assistance in Philadelphia. Journal of Urban Health 91(6):1087–1097

Messeter J, Johansson M (2008) Place-specific computing: conceptual design cases from urban contexts in four countries. In: Proceedings of the 7th ACM conference on Designing interactive systems (DIS '08), ACM, New York, NY, pp 99–108

Miller P, Kimbrough S, Schacht J (2018) Simulating redistricting in the classroom: A binding arbitration decision game using Louisiana census data. PS: Political Science & Politics 51(3):664–668

Odom W (2010) 'mate, we don't need a chip to tell us the soil's dry': opportunities for designing interactive systems to support urban food production. In: Proceedings of the 8th ACM Conference on Designing Interactive Systems (DIS '10), ACM, ACM, New York, NY, pp 232–235

Ploeg MV, Breneman V, Farrigan T, Hamrick K, Hopkins D, Kaufman P, Lin B, Nord M, Smith T, Williams R, Kinnison K, Olander C, Singh A, Tuckermanty E, Krantz-kent R, Polen C, Mcgowan H, Kim S (2009) Access to Affordable and Nutritious Food: Measuring and Understanding Food Deserts and Their Consequences Report to Congress

Schwartz R, Naaman M, Matni Z (2013) Making sense of cities using social media: Requirements for hyper-local data aggregation tools. In: Proceedings of the International AAAI Conference on Weblogs and Social Media, AAAI, pp 15–22

Smyth M, Helgason I (2010) Informing the design of the future urban landscape. In: Proceedings of the 8th ACM Conference on Designing Interactive Systems (DIS '10), ACM, ACM, New York, NY, pp 438–439

Söderström O, Paasche T, Klauser F (2014) Smart cities as corporate storytelling. City 18(3):307–320

Sweller J (1994) Cognitive load theory, learning difficulty, and instructional design. Learning and instruction 4(4):295–312

Todd P, Benbasat I (1994) The Influence of Decision Aids on Choice Strategies - An Experimental-Analysis of the Role of Cognitive Effort. Organizational Behavior and Human Decision Processes 60(1):36–74

Vanolo A (2014) Smart mentality: The smart city as disciplinary strategy. Urban Studies 51(5):883–898

von Winterfeldt D, Edwards W (1986) Decision Analysis and Behavioral Research. Cambridge University Press, Cambridge, UK

Xia C, Schwartz R, Xie K, Krebs A, Langdon A, Ting J, Naaman M (2014) Citybeat: real-time social media visualization of hyper-local city data. In: Proceedings of the 23rd International Conference on World Wide Web, pp 167–170

Yoon KP, Hwang CL (1995) Multiple Attribute Decision Making: An Introduction, Quantitative Applications in the Social Sciences, vol 104. Sage, CA

Yu A, Nahapetian A (2013) Participatory sensing for fighting food deserts. In: Proceedings of the 8th International Conference on Body Area Networks (BodyNets '13), ICST (Institute for Computer Sciences, Social-Informatics and Telecommunications Engineering),, ICST, Brussels, Belgium, pp 221–224

Zheng Y, Capra L, Wolfson O, Yang H (2014) Urban computing: Concepts, methodologies, and applications. ACM Trans Intell Syst Technol 5(3):Article 38

Data Analytics for Smart Decision-Making and Resilient Systems

Benjamin Blau, Clemens van Dinther, Christoph M. Flath, Rico Knapper, and Daniel Rolli

Abstract In a networked world, companies depend on fast and smart decisions, especially when it comes to reacting to external change. With the wealth of data available today, smart decisions can increasingly be based on data analysis and be supported by IT systems that leverage AI. A global pandemic brings external change to an unprecedented level of unpredictability and severity of impact. Resilience therefore becomes an essential factor in most decisions when aiming at making and keeping them smart. In this chapter, we study the characteristics of resilient systems and test them with four use cases in a wide-ranging set of application areas. In all use cases, we highlight how AI can be used for data analysis to make smart decisions and contribute to the resilience of systems.

1 Introduction

Our global economy today is a highly interconnected system. According to Ricardo (1817), open markets lead to comparative cost advantages. Companies specialize and exploit local advantages (e.g., skilled workers or cost advantages due to cheap

B. Blau
SAP SE, Walldorf, Germany
e-mail: benjam.blau@sap.com

C. van Dinther (✉)
ESB Business School at Reutlingen University, Reutlingen, Germany
e-mail: clemens.van_dinther@reutlingen-university.de

C. M. Flath
Universität Würzburg, Würzburg, Germany
e-mail: christoph.flath@uni-wuerzburg.de

R. Knapper
anacision GmbH, Karlsruhe, Germany
e-mail: rico.knapper@anacision.de

D. Rolli
Conemis AG, Karlsruhe, Germany
e-mail: daniel.rolli@conemis.com

© The Author(s) 2021
H. Gimpel et al. (eds.), *Market Engineering*,
https://doi.org/10.1007/978-3-030-66661-3_13

raw materials or low wages). At the same time, companies are under high price and innovation pressure in global competition, which is difficult to counter without a strong partner network. For this reason and due to specialization, there is a dependency of the companies among each other in a value-added network. Close cooperation between companies is also possible due to the global communication infrastructure, as information can be passed on and shared quickly. At the same time, this presents companies with the challenge of being able to process information quickly and effectively, since the dynamics of the markets also require companies to be able to make decisions quickly. First of all, this includes the ability to perceive a change in the market situation on the basis of existing or observable information or, in the best case, to foresee it early on. In addition to the ability to observe and process information, companies use information not only to recognize changes but also to prepare decisions or even to make automated decisions. This means that those companies have a competitive advantage, if they have mastered fast and effective data/information processing and are able to benefit from it, and if they have the organizational capability to react quickly, appropriately, and agilely to changes.

The world economic crisis caused by the COVID-19 pandemic in 2020 highlights both the global economic interdependencies and the importance of rapid response. Resilience is an adaptive capacity, i.e., the ability of a system to stabilize itself after external shocks (Holling 2001, p. 394). Resilient systems are adaptable, i.e., companies are able to react to external events. In order to make the right decisions in a crisis situation, a good information base is required. Modern methods of information processing can help to create this information base. Thus, self-learning algorithms can help to process and deal with the changed situation. However, adaptive systems usually require a certain amount of adaptation time, because on the other hand, too much sensitivity of the system would lead to permanent change—resistance to adaptation is certainly desirable to a certain degree. This shows the dilemma of adaptive systems. Based on this, the research question for the development of information systems is how and where data analytics can be used for smart decisions and thus make systems more resilient. Our chapter is therefore structured as follows. First, in Sect. 2, we look at the state of the art with respect to data science and smart decision-making and discuss in Sect. 3 how data analysis can contribute to the design of resilient systems. Sections 4, 5, 6, and 7 deal with use cases in which data analytics contributes to improved information processing. Section 8 summarizes our results in a conclusion and provides an outlook.

2   Data Analysis for Decision-Making

Decisions are fundamental tasks of management and determine the success and failure of an organization (Edwards et al. 2000). Decisions are based on current, relevant, and accurate information that must be collected or newly created. Organizations have a large amount of structured and unstructured data that is still far too often unused. It should be noted that decisions are not always easy to make, especially in complex situations, where alternatives are difficult to compare, or where there is uncertainty about the available information (e.g., because it relates to the future). Therefore, it is important to prepare and support decisions with appropriate information and information systems.

Data analysis can help to extract new information from the available data. The technical development of the last decades enables a powerful data analysis. Due to the growing computing power and the advanced algorithms of artificial intelligence, it is possible to process and analyze large amounts of data and thus generate new information. In this context, we understand the term *smart decision-making* as the ability to prepare or automatically make decisions with the help of intelligent algorithms for data analysis. In the literature, there are numerous synonymous uses of the term smart decision-making, e.g., intelligent decision-making (Phillips-Wren 2012), algorithmic decision-making (Bader and Kaiser 2019), automated decision-making (Araujo et al. 2020), autonomous decision-making (Kusiak et al. 2000), augmented decision-making (Burton et al. 2020), AI-based decision-making (Shrestha et al. 2019), and computational intelligence-based decision-making (Lakhmi C. Jain 2009). Already in 2006, Phillips-Wren and Jain (2006) pointed out the revolution in decision-making with the help of AI, which is capable of coordinating the provision of data, analyzing data trends, making forecasts, or quantifying uncertainty. Thus, decision-making in complex situations can be improved (Akerkar 2019, p. 6).

However, Stubbs (2014, p. 5) points out that data analysis alone does not create added value but that a benefit only comes from the action, i.e., the decision and the resulting action. Companies typically show different stages of development with regard to the ability to process information. Analytics maturity models can be useful in determining the level of development and skills. IBM has already presented such a model in 2013. Maturity refers both to the ability to use data and to how companies can use this information to their own advantage. Figure 1 shows the IBM information and analytics maturity model with the five maturity levels.

In principle, we can distinguish between decision support and automation. At the level of "differentiating," the IBM model shows the use of predictions, i.e., the use of historical data to identify trends or for pattern recognition as well as the use of forecast models. This is also known as predictive analytics. At the "breakaway" level, it is referred to as the use of prescriptive analytics with real-time pattern-based strategies. Here, prescriptive analytics means "going beyond the forecast to actually determine the optimal decision to make" (Frank Stein and Arnold Greenland 2014, p. 35). For this purpose, for example, simulation models can be developed. Such simulation models can be based on intelligent agents (van Dinther 2007; 2008). AI technologies are used for both predictive and prescriptive analytics. For example, fuzzy logic, expert systems, case-based reasoning, evolutionary algorithms, intelligent agents, random forests, artificial neural networks, or other machine learning algorithms are used. Lepenioti et al. (2020) provide a good overview of different AI methods for analytics. We illustrate in several use cases how such techniques can assist smart and resilient decision-making.

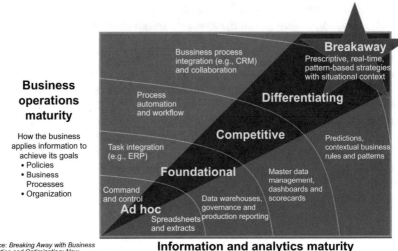

Fig. 1 IBM analytics maturity model

3 Resilient Systems and the Supporting Role of Data Analytics

Resilient systems are known to us from nature. Therefore, the terms "resilience" and "system" first appear in the context of ecosystems (Gunderson and Holling 2002). Folke et al. (2002, p.438) describe resilience in socioecological systems in relation to *(i) the magnitude of shock that the system can absorb and remain within a given state, (ii) the degree to which the system is capable of self-organization,* and *(iii) the degree to which the system can build capacity for learning and adaptation.* The term resilience was later on picked up in systems engineering by Jackson and Ferris (2013). The definition mainly builds upon the three criteria as shown in Table 1 which differ in aspect 2 and 3 from the aspects provided by Folke et al. (2002).

While these criteria are derived from engineering systems, it is feasible and meaningful to abstract them to complex systems in general (e.g., social systems, large companies as described in Cheema-Fox et al. 2020, service value networks as described in Blau et al. 2009). With the recent example of the COVID-19 crisis,

Table 1 Criteria of a resilient system based on Jackson and Ferris (2013)

Criteria	Description
Flexibility	The ability of the system to adapt to a threat
Tolerance	The ability of the system to degrade gracefully in the face of a threat
Cohesion	The ability of the system to act as a unified whole in the face of a threat

Table 2 Strategy map along resilience criteria and target audiences

	Customer experience	Employee experience	Stakeholder experience
Flexibility	Meet customers where they are	Prepare for "unknown unknowns"	Move quickly to preserve trust
Tolerance	Listen, care, and support	"Show the beach, not the trip"	Build up predictable revenue streams
Cohesion	Make customer success the ultimate metric	End-to-end processes beyond functions	Build sustainable business

the relevance and importance of resiliency of complex systems to be able to deal with external shocks has been proven in an unplanned and unprecedented macroeconomic "experiment."

While the criteria of resilient systems have proven to be essential for companies to persist and perform in the face of external shocks, it is important to create and implement a strategy map outlining measures that turn the criteria into action tailored for each major stakeholder. Table 2 shows such a strategy map of SAP.

The pandemic caused by COVID-19 shows the vulnerability of global supply chains (Golan et al. 2020, Pierre Haren and David Simchi-Levi 2020, Sharma et al. 2020) and the need for resilient systems and analytics. Simulations of the supply chain help to better understand this vulnerability (Ivanov 2020) and to design resilient systems.

Focusing on customer experience, "meeting customers where they are" is essential to quickly adapt to changing needs in B2B (Hartmann and Lussier 2020). Accelerated roadmaps for digital touch points, digital supply chains, and a seamless digital front-to-back-office experiences are essential to cater for a changed buying behavior. This requires thorough data analysis of customer behavior along the full life cycle. This allows for early prediction of altering patterns and adaptation of the roadmap accordingly. Customer data analytics is applied to forecast sales (cp. Fan et al. 2017, Foxall 2017, Loureiro et al. 2018). Increased system tolerance and "acting as a whole" can be achieved by implementing team incentives for customer success across all roles of the value chain. The design of such incentive schemes requires modeling of historic data and simulation of worst-, mid-, and best-case scenarios. To drive change, especially in sales, requires a proactive winner-loser analysis. This helps to eliminate uncertainty related to fear of loss of control in the affected group.

Catering for employee experience in a resilient manner is another important pillar to assure safety and retain productivity. When it comes to flexibility, i.e., the ability of the system to adapt to the threat, agile employee-related processes are important to deal with the unknown unknowns. There is a large portion of events and external shocks that are beyond predictability/the horizon of possibly anticipated threats. Only agile processes can adapt quickly in case of non-anticipated unknown influences. Event-based and data-driven systems can help to detect unknown unknowns quickly and automatically adapt agile processes to the new circumstances. Tolerance according to the definition of Jackson and Ferris (2013) in the context of employee experience can be achieved by a clear target state that demonstrates the benefits for the employees beyond times of crisis. The design of such a target state requires data-intense analysis and simulations based on historic and external data sources. The "beach" is an analogy for such a target state. It is of utmost importance from a change management perspective to mainly communicate that "beach" instead of the process to get there, i.e., the related "trip." In addition to flexibility and tolerance, cohesion is an important aspect especially among the employee population to achieve resiliency. To foster collaboration and a team identity, end-to-end processes beyond functional silos are a key ingredient. For example, if companies manage to establish streamlined marketing to sales handover processes supported by event- and data-based routing systems and respective team incentives such as revenue contribution, cohesion will be a logical end result.

The third important experience customers need to cater for is the shareholder experience. Flexibility needs to be demonstrated by quickly adapting to the new normal, that is, radically rethinking existing structures and processes (e.g., changing service delivery model from on-site to almost purely remote within less than a month which can only be achieved by eliciting customer expectations based on vast data lakes). The ability to keep a stable and believable market guidance while quickly adapting to safeguard the top and bottom lines is crucial for resilient companies. Tolerance, i.e., the ability of the system to degrade gracefully in the face of a threat—in other words, endurance, can be achieved by building and sustaining predictable revenue streams radically shifting to subscription- or consumption-based commercial models. Demonstrating cohesion to shareholders requires fundamentally relevant and long-term objectives such as sustainability measures and ambitions. Profitable sustainability and sustainable profitability as a common goal rallies the troops moving as a single unit.

The following use cases illustrate the main aspects of resilient systems, flexibility, tolerance, and cohesion and how they can be achieved with data-driven decision-making based on real-world scenarios.

4   Use Case 1: Improving Employee Experience Through the Listen-Learn-Act Approach and Reasoning on Semi-structured Data

For many employees, their personal well-being and a good work-life balance are now more important than the basic employment contract conditions such as salary, company car, etc. Not least because of this development, there has been a shift from a job market to an applicant market for some time. Companies must therefore address these points and ensure satisfaction not only during the application phase but also during the course of their employees' work—at the same time, of course, increase work output as much as possible. The listen-learn-act approach is a possible instrument for controlling this issue. Regular "listening" is possible at an almost exclusively software-supported global, country, or location level via (semi-)structured surveys. This is already established in practice, in particular in large companies such as SAP (as mentioned in Sect. 3). Such surveys, if they are carried out regularly, can be used to implement the "listen" part of the approach presented. However, the question arises as to the evaluation of the answers obtained in the survey, especially if there are a large number of free-text answers. For the implementation of the "learn" and "act" parts, this must be done in an automated and resilient manner. We use a multistage approach for the evaluation concerning the resilience criteria for employer experience as displayed in Table 1:

- Analysis of the survey results and response texts with the help of data analysis methods, especially with regard to the topics and sentiments contained therein. Algorithms from the area of topic modeling (including latent Dirichlet allocation, Blei et al. 2003; Yin and Wang 2014; and sentiment analysis, Gilbert and Hutto 2014) are used.
- Technical and business-driven (but also partly automated) derivation of hypotheses with regard to the areas of interest (e.g., employee satisfaction, relationship between the manager and the employee, problems in everyday work of the employees).
- Verifying or falsifying the hypotheses with the help of targeted data analysis (which, e.g., are also based on the hierarchy structure).
- Combination of the data analysis results with operational data for further verification or falsification.

The last step is the most challenging but also the most important one. For example, can the challenges often mentioned by employees also be recognized in the performance of agile development teams (e.g., burndown rate)? Can correlations between financial indicators and the problems mentioned (or positive effects) be identified? If this step is carried out successfully, the organization can learn from it and act accordingly. The basic requirements for such a system to be resilient are, in addition to the criteria listed in Table 1, regular surveys and a standardized process to carry out the abovementioned four steps.

5 Use Case 2: Manufacturing

The manufacturing sector has undergone a tremendous digital transformation. Ubiquitous computing, connectivity combined, and integration of diverse sensors have created a next-generation industrial infrastructure (Feng and Shanthikumar 2018). These investments help manufacturing companies to further increase efficiency of production processes (Wuest et al. 2016). However, these efforts are often focused on equipment monitoring and automation solutions. Typical examples include predictive maintenance for key productive assets (McKone and Weiss 2002) or automated quality control of outputs (Flath and Stein 2017, Wuest et al. 2014). However, oftentimes, humans still play an important role in manufacturing processes, in particular when complex or highly variant operations are necessary (assembly, customized products). Still, analytics can pave the way to resilient manufacturing processes by supporting workers to improve along the dimensions of flexibility, tolerance, and cohesion. Empowered by artificial intelligence innovations, IoT solutions stand at the forefront of digital transformation. Augmented intelligence solutions which enhance human performance in complex tasks are of particular interest. However, there are no turnkey solutions for developing and implementing such systems. One possible avenue is to complement multipurpose hardware with flexible AI solutions which are adapted to a given task.

Stein et al. (2018) describe how advanced analytics can assist human workers in a high-tech production process, namely, vacuum resin infusion. During this process, molds are placed in vacuum bags. Any leakages will impair quality. Therefore, leak detection is of highest priority. This is a manual activity (e.g., using ultrasonic microphones or thermal cameras), and therefore, the production of large components (e.g., aircraft wings) becomes extremely expensive. The research augments the standard search process by means of generic, multiuse vibration sensors collecting data during the infusion process. Subsequently, predictive models based on machine learning algorithms provide high-accuracy predictions for leak locations. Using prescriptive analytics, these predictions can be directly transformed into better search paths which can substantially reduce the work required for leak detection. This increases organizational flexibility as workers are relieved of nonproductive tasks.

Krenzer et al. (2019) illustrate the bottom-up development of a machine learning backend for an augmented intelligence system for assembly environments. A wearable sensing device is paired with a deep neural network to monitor connector systems assembly in real time. This system can monitor the correctness of assembled plugs based on structure-borne noise signals. The initial study yields promising results and establishes the feasibility of the suggested approach. Furthermore, it serves as a blueprint for similar IoT applications which facilitate improved process tolerance through high transparency.

Oberdorf et al. (2020) elaborate on the design, evaluation, and roll out of an escalation management system with integrated data-driven decision support. The decision support functionalities leverage state-of-the-art machine learning algorithms for disruption-type classification as well as prediction of the escalation handling duration. These predictions are then embedded in an integrated planning procedure leveraging diverse organizational data sources (e.g., personnel availability, production plans) to instantiate a prescriptive analytics solution. The proposed escalation management system generates significant business value by reducing escalation duration. This improvement is due to automation as well as improved decision support. In the long term, the informational and transformational business value enabled by the decision support system may even exceed the automational business value. This highlights the special importance of tight integration of Industry 4.0 applications within business processes. In particular, such a solution ensures the flexibility of troubleshooting processes and introduces a tolerant process control through transparency. Ultimately, analytics support improves organizational cohesion as workers complement themselves in an optimized fashion.

6   Use Case 3: Purchasing and Logistics

Purchasing and logistics processes are subject to fluctuations in demand. Therefore, knowledge of demand is advantageous for optimizing internal processes (warehousing, supplier management, etc.). The challenge is that demand varies over time and is different for each product. In this respect, the creation of a forecast model depends on industry- or product-specific factors. AI can help to build such forecasting models (van Dinther and Mauch 2019).

Economic advantages through forecasts in purchasing can be achieved in particular by optimizing processes. For example, storage costs can be lowered, or transports can be reduced by bundling orders or the number of short-term transports (e.g., due to subsequent orders). In addition, targeted supplier management can improve the negotiating position with suppliers and thereby achieve price advantages. An optimization of sales management is also possible.

In this case, we consider a dealer of rubber products in the B2B sector with over 20,000 customers. The ERP system records 250,000 product numbers, which can be grouped into classes so that similar products are easier to identify. The dealer purchases these products from over 2000 suppliers worldwide. The products range from simple standard articles to special products with specific properties depending on the intended use. Special products require knowledge of the properties of the materials, require intensive consultation, and are often part of a project business. For such products, forecasting is difficult and, with regard to logistics processes, also superfluous, since the lead times in projects are long enough to effectively manage internal processes. For example, customers for the construction of special machines order hoses of certain sizes and lengths for hydraulic applications, i.e., the hoses are filled with oil and must withstand certain pressures. Advice is needed here as to which types of rubber are suitable, and internal knowledge is required from which supplier they can be obtained. These special hoses are not standard goods and are therefore only ordered from the supplier after the customer has placed his order. Therefore, it is not necessary to develop a forecast for these products.

In contrast to such products, the forecast for the demand of standard goods is much more interesting, both from a business point of view and from a scientific point of view. Standard products must be in stock in sufficient quantities to be able to process customer orders reliably. However, the demand for standard goods varies greatly and ranges from continuous demand to products that are in regular but not continuous demand. This makes the forecast problem challenging.

The distribution of product order quantities is a typical long-tail distribution, i.e., few products are ordered in large quantities and continuously, while many products are ordered in varying quantities and infrequently. The latter are called lumpy time series. Especially for such lumpy time series, forecasting is difficult because both the time interval between orders and the order quantity vary. For the medium-term forecast, the aim is to forecast sales at the industry and divisional level for the top 1200 customers and top 2000 articles for up to 6 months into the future. This is done using data from the past 12 months with information on the order date and the industry and division, general data such as public holidays and external data such as the ifo Business Climate Index, or industry data from the Federal Statistical Office and Google Trends. Various algorithms were implemented and compared, including naive periodic approaches, linear regression, SARIMAX, Holt-Winters triple exponential smoothing, Support Vector Regression, Random Forests and Gradient Boosted Trees, multilayer perceptron artificial neural networks, or LSTM-RNN.

The procedures were compared using R2 and RMSE. It is not surprising that the naive approaches were not well suited. Similarly, bad results were obtained with SARIMAX, but good results were obtained with the other approaches. Classical forecasting methods such as Croston (1972) or Peter R. Winters (1960) perform well compared to AI-based methods. Compared to classical approaches, long short-term memory (LSTM) neural networks show similarly good results for lumpy time series forecasting (Kiefer and van Dinther 2020). This revealed considerable savings potential. For example, the medium-term forecast of the RMSE was reduced by up to 80% compared to the previously used forecast.

High-quality forecasts are particularly valuable in the retail sector, as errors affect stock levels and delivery times. In this respect, resilient forecast models represent an important economic value. However, with regard to the three characteristics of resilient systems, there is a trade-off with forecast models. In the present case study, forecasts are mainly based on historical data, i.e., on order patterns in the past. It is assumed in the model that there are repeated time cycles. Without external sources that provide a reliable indication of a trend change or shock, it is almost impossible to anticipate abrupt events like the COVID-19 crisis. Therefore, the question on the adaptability (flexibility) of the model after an external shock is much more important, i.e., the question of how quickly the system takes up and adapts to a permanent change. The weighting of historical data in the forecast plays a role in this respect in that more recent data receive a stronger weighting than events further in the past. On the other hand, there is a risk of underweighting long-term trends or seasonal events. The aim in the forecast models is therefore to correctly determine the tolerance in the model's adjustment speed. It is necessary to take up permanent changes without at the same time distorting the forecast results by short-term deviations. With regard to the third property of resilient systems, cohesion, it should be noted on the basis of the present case study that the interaction between employees and forecast models is important. Especially in the application case with lumpy time series, this trade-off between short-term adjustment and long-term trends is difficult. In this respect, we do not yet see any possibility of fully automating orders on the basis of the forecast model results. This is where employees are called upon to check plausibility, who may come to different decisions based on context information or information that is not taken into account in the model.

7 Use Case 4: Software Transition

Hyper-distribution of teams makes the management of projects even harder than it has already been. Complex transformation projects to new standard software are always a state of exception, and a pandemic potentiates this.

According to Friedman (2009), a majority of 83% of data migrations fail or significantly exceed time and budget. And this is only one part of a software transition that can go wrong. It not only hurts user adoption and the value of the new system but can cause the respective transition and transformation project to fail overall, which in turn means losing tens or hundreds of millions of euros in large transformations. It also means a traumatizing experience for project participants. Many of them typically take care of the already challenging but well-practiced job of maintaining and managing a familiar application and are in a state of exception during a transition.

Transition issues are hardly ever technical in nature. The challenges lie in translating evolving business needs into change that remains consumable for the customer organization and in the complexity of coordinating many thousands of operational activities in a compact timeframe. In addition, many organizations lack a complete understanding of circumstances to successfully undertake the complex changes required in their legacy systems to attain advantages of migration (Gholami et al. 2017, Strobl et al. 2020). Distributed teams do not make this easier. Following the megatrend of the recent past, namely, outsourcing IT services, teams are oftentimes not only distributed across different customer locations but include one or several offshore locations as well. Even before the COVID-19 pandemic, most transition projects were fragile and far from resilient with respect to timing and risk. As shown in multiple studies, delay risk prediction is one of the main concerns in the migration projects (Manekar and Gera 2017).

7.1 *Key Challenges in Transition Projects*

Inherent key challenges in such transition projects—with and without a pandemic—are:

- Understanding legacy software applications and what remains relevant thereof
- Understanding how functionality and data translate from the old applications to new ones
- Reliably planning the efforts and duration of a transition endeavor
- Coordination of a multitude of tasks in configuring new software, migrating data, and taking decisions for issue resolution
- Monitoring overall progress and remaining risks
- Susceptibility to errors in the many manual activities executed by on- and off-shore teams

- Managing change and ensuring that customer organization can consume that
  change

Until the pandemic affected IT projects, it remained best practice to have off-shore teams co-located and on-site teams at customer facilities either co-located or at least meeting physically on a regular basis. This has become impossible during full lockdowns and remains extraordinarily challenging in a hyper-distributed environment where people work primarily from home and even off-shore teams are scattered. However, all of the above challenges become even harder in a hyper-distributed world. Each of them relies on a number of decisions that are traditionally taken by humans and based on information that is compiled by humans.

7.2   AI-Automated Platform with Consistent Digitalization

The vision is to fundamentally change transitions for the better and address its challenges with a consistent digitalized solution. Instead of mere human experience, and individual handling of tasks and tools, a cohesive platform not only enables inherent guidance through processes, a foundation for automation in each and every task, and all the information for automatically tracking progress but is also the necessary enabler for AI to encompass the entirety of activities in transition projects. It can learn the processes, patterns, and pitfalls of projects. With enough projects captured over time, it can derive recommendations for the project participants and eventually control the automation of certain sequences of steps directly.

Building a solution begins with a consistent digital coverage of all operational processes in transition projects. This may start with the assessment of existing applications to be replaced. It continues with capturing scope and requirements, configuration of the destination applications, data profiling, data cleansing, and data migration. And it doesn't end there. The goal is to take every manual task and scattered tool, which may often be run on a local machine, and move it to a central cloud platform that guides and follows experts through a project from beginning to end. With such a foundation arise two major possibilities that were impossible before, seamless automation support of all the individual activities in a project and immediate digital insight into each and every activity, no matter if it is triggered manually or executed in a fully automated fashion. This in turn means that the latter can feed an AI with sufficiently comprehensive data, and the AI can guide more and more of the steps in the former.

Such a platform for consistent digitalization captures a unique digital fingerprint consisting of up to hundreds of thousands of data points for each project. It enables seamless collaboration and data-driven communication with real-time insight. This gives the project members a better overview and lets them see the patterns in the project across members and, hence, take smarter decisions on how to proceed. The platform also preserves the knowledge of how projects are executed in detail beyond the limited memory of the people who executed them. It retains a wealth of information on which projects are fast, which projects are slow, what leads to success, what leads to failure, what healthy patterns to adhere to, what unhealthy patterns to avoid, and much more. And all of this is represented in an AI-accessible format. So, the AI can draw on a wealth of information and present suggestions to the project participants that help them to take even smarter decisions faster. Having all data accessible for AI models is one of the goals we strive to tackle. As studies show in recent years, the use of AI models will only be as good as the data they are fed with. As seen in a critical case like a pandemic, not having enough meaningful data will hinder any AI technology. Collecting big enough data for transitions and transforming it into a knowledge base, which an AI model can be trained on, are the biggest challenges for every AI. Only when this is achieved, AI will reach its full potential in learning and finding insights for predictions on new projects and for smarter decisions.[1]

7.3 Resilience with the Platform

Consistent digitalization, a central home for project knowledge, and AI greatly add to the resilience of transition projects.

Flexibility is provided for a team working on such a platform both in terms of space and time. When formerly co-located teams are forced to physically isolate every individual, they can rely on a central live dashboard and status information to stay coordinated and base their decisions on facts. Team members are truly enabled to work from anywhere. Tasks and partial results can be handed over within the platform to be flexible with time zones. If certain regions are severely impaired over a longer period of time—due to issues in public infrastructure, government regulation, etc.—all of the work can temporarily be shifted from one region to another, given that enough expert resources are available. Moreover, it is common that projects within a larger transformation initiative have dependencies on other projects for reasons like technical interfaces or expert availability. The comprehensive storage of the project work including its status also helps a team to be more flexible in adapting timelines to such external dependencies.

Tolerance is enabled, as not only all project-specific knowledge like mapping of functionality and data conversion rules is stored in a safe central place but also the most recent state of progress including every prior activity leading to the current state. Progress of the configuration of the destination applications including all fields, picklist values, workflows, and more is kept in the platform—even the latest state of source application setup: the exact state of how many records of which object have been extracted when from the source applications, converted to what extent, and imported into the destination applications at what time; how many

---

[1]More details and a commercial platform striving to fulfill this vision can be found at http://www. conemis.com.

necessary activities for running all of that work have already been executed; and how many are left according to the plan. With all that knowledge in the platform, even a sudden interruption of the project by a pandemic incident can be tolerated. After such an interruption, humans participating in the project may require some time for finding orientation again and familiarizing themselves with the latest status of the project. But all of the information for that is in the system and does not depend on any distributed information on local devices. As shown in several studies, legacy data challenges and their storage during migration are key concerns that project stakeholders have in their planning and designing phase of migration (Gholami et al. 2017, Manekar and Gera 2017). In the most dire of circumstances, even a different team familiar with how the platform works in general could pick up work and continue it after some time of orientation. AI could continue with its suggestions and assistance in coordination regardless of the interruption. We nevertheless hope this will remain a merely hypothetical scenario.

Cohesion is achieved by having complete digitalization as the ultimate goal. End-to-end processes beyond functions are covered by the platform. Formerly distributed information and information solely in the heads of people is externalized and stored by the software. Interruptions of the project do not disturb cohesion in retaining the knowledge of the project. All information necessary for AI to consume remain available in a consistent form.

Cohesion is provided across projects. When leveraging a proven platform for several projects—past and present—processes and recorded experience can easily be leveraged across projects to benefit all. Experience silos, typically in the heads of a few experienced experts, are opened up for an overall increased level of quality and success in projects supported by the platform. An added benefit that is not to be neglected is that the platform automatically documents every step in every project. So even in the most exceptional and hectic of times, detailed documentation continues.

In general, existing AI approaches mainly target delay risks prediction and estimation of efforts that are unforeseen for the management team. Yet in addition, AI solutions can be the key for data protection and security of critical data that an organization has, as shown in a recent study (Diener et al. 2016). Collecting and storing big data before starting any migration is a hot topic, where the integration of AI approaches can help in handling data challenges, extractions from different resources, and designing data lakes in a migration project (Manekar and Gera 2017).

Understanding the market dynamics and evolving business needs of an organization, their translation into enabling technology, and the response to unforeseen impacts like a pandemic will require clever human minds for as far as we can see into the future. They need to take smart decisions both based on data available to them and sometimes under uncertainty. But our vision implies that all the operational tasks, including assessment, planning, configuration, data migration, and more, will sometime in the future be fully executed by an AI that builds on a vast amount of recorded knowledge to automatically orchestrate workflows with full automation in all individual tasks. This will become better with every bit of recorded project experience that can be fed into AI algorithms. Major decisions and the response to exceptions like a pandemic will still remain the responsibility of humans. But, although an AI-automated platform will take human direction, even in complex transformation projects, the operational execution of the transition may one day be fully autonomous.

8 Conclusion

The current global economic system is vulnerable to external shocks at various levels. Companies work together in value networks and are thus interdependent. Disruptions in such networks can have far-reaching consequences. Companies use IT systems to control and automate their own processes and to communicate and exchange information in value networks. As a result, the amount of digital data is constantly growing, and the demands on IT and data analysis are increasing. Technological advances in hardware and software as well as networking and sensor technology have brought major advances in the field of artificial intelligence over the last decade. Thus, AI becomes applicable in many areas and helps to advance decision-making toward smart decisions. The development of resilient systems places high demands on information systems. Thus, AI can make an important contribution in the field of smart decision-making for resilient systems.

Global-acting firms and global value networks require management attention and fast reaction on major changes such as external shocks. Therefore, more attention is to be paid to data analysis and application of AI. Such settings require firms to go the next step and embrace digitization beyond their machinery. This necessitates a paradigm shift where AI complements humans instead of replacing them (Bansal et al. 2019, Kamar et al. 2012). Such smart decision-making has been discussed in many different domains including chess-playing (Kasparov 2017), medical decision-making (Paul et al. 2018), as well as data science projects (Wang et al. 2019). Oftentimes, these human-AI teams have demonstrated higher resilience (avoiding pitfalls such as biased training data or implausible decisions) or even better performance in their respective tasks.

In our contribution, we study four use cases from very different application domains. All use cases apply AI to specific decision-making context. The interesting point to note is that the application of AI is very diverse. In the first use case, AI is applied to employee management and team development. AI analyzes text information from employee surveys in order to identify necessary actions in team development. In manufacturing, AI is applied to improve quality processes by using visual defect detection. AI is trained to identify defects (such as cracks or holes) in packaging. In sales, the focus is on improving customer order forecasts in order to optimize logistics and purchasing. The challenge here is to forecast orders for products with irregular and fluctuating demand (lumpy time series). Especially here, an optimization of resilient systems is advantageous. Inventory processes can be automated based on improved forecasting processes. AI can also be successfully used in IT projects to analyze and optimize data migration processes. Data migration and transformation is a critical process within IT projects due to the complexity caused by data volume and data properties. Analysis of project data can help to better manage or automate transformation processes and to identify and eliminate errors. Furthermore, AI can support the data transformation process itself.

However, the use cases also show that full automation is not yet available. However, the development advances permanently, so that an increase in the resilience of the systems becomes possible. So far technology is already advanced; it must nevertheless be stated that still further research and development remain necessary. Nevertheless, we can state that we can already use data analysis for smart decisions in resilient systems.

References

Akerkar, R. 2019. *Artificial Intelligence for Business: Springer Briefs in Business.* Springer.

Araujo, Theo, et al. 2020. "In AI we trust? Perceptions about automated decision-making by artificial intelligence". *AI & SOCIETY* ISSN: 1435-5655. https://doi.org/10.1007/s00146-019-00931-w.

Bader, Verena, and Stephan Kaiser. 2019. "Algorithmic decision-making? The user interface and its role for human involvement in decisions supported by artificial intelligence". *Organization* 26 (5): 655–672. ISSN: 1350-5084. https://doi.org/10.1177/1350508419855714.

Bansal, Gagan, et al. 2019. "Updates in human-AI teams: Understanding and addressing the performance/compatibility tradeoff". In *Proceedings of the AAAI Conference on Artificial Intelligence*, 33:2429–2437.

Blau, B., et al. 2009. "Service Value Networks". In *2009 IEEE Conference on Commerce and Enterprise Computing*, 194–201.

Blei, David M, Andrew Y Ng, and Michael I Jordan. 2003. "Latent Dirichlet allocation". *Journal of machine Learning research* 3 (Jan): 993–1022.

Burton, Jason W., Mari-Klara Stein, and Tina Blegind Jensen. 2020. "A systematic review of algorithm aversion in augmented decision making". *Journal of Behavioral Decision Making* 33 (2): 220–239. ISSN: 0894-3257. https://doi.org/10.1002/bdm.2155.

Cheema-Fox, Alexander, et al. 2020. "Corporate Resilience and Response During COVID-19". *Harvard Business School Accounting and Management Unit Working Paper No. 20-108.*

Croston, J. D. 1972. "Forecasting and Stock Control for Intermittent Demands". *Operational Research Quarterly (1970-1977)* 23 (3): 289. ISSN: 00303623. https://doi.org/10.2307/3007885.

Diener, Michael, Leopold Blessing, and Rappel Nina. 2016. "Tackling the Cloud Adoption Dilemma - A User Centric Concept to Control Cloud Migration Processes by Using Machine Learning Technologies". In *International Conference on Availability, Reliability and Security (ARES)*.

Edwards, J. S., Y. Duan, and P.C. Robins. 2000. "An analysis of expert systems for business decision making at different levels and in different roles". *European Journal of Information Systems* 9 (1): 36–46.

Fan, Zhi-Ping, Yu-Jie Che, and Zhen-Yu Chen. 2017. "Product sales forecasting using online reviews and historical sales data: A method combining the Bass model and sentiment analysis". *Journal of Business Research* 74:90–100. ISSN: 0148-2963. https://doi.org/10.1016/j.jbusres.2017.01.010. http://www.sciencedirect.com/science/article/pii/S0148296317300231.

Feng, Qi, and J George Shanthikumar. 2018. "How research in production and operations management may evolve in the era of big data". *Production and Operations Management* 27 (9): 1670–1684.

Flath, Christoph M., and Nikolai Stein. 2017. "Towards a Data Science Toolbox for Industrial Analytics Applications". *Computers in Industry* 94:16–25.

Folke, Carl, et al. 2002. "Resilience and Sustainable Development: Building Adaptive Capacity in a World of Transformations". *AMBIO: A Journal of the Human Environment* 31 (5): 437–440. https://doi.org/10.1579/0044-7447-31.5.437.

Foxall, Gordon R. 2017. *Advanced introduction to consumer behavior analysis.* Elgar advanced introductions. Cheltenham, UK: Edward Elgar. ISBN: 1784716928.

Frank Stein and Arnold Greenland. 2014. "Producing Insights from Information through Analytics". In *Business Analytics*, ed. by Jay Liebowitz, 29–54. CRC Press Taylor and Francis Group.

Friedman, Ted. 2009. "Risks and Challenges in Data Migrations and Conversions". *Retrieved from Gartner Research Portal.*

Gholami, Mahdi Fahmideh, et al. 2017. "Challenges in migrating legacy software systems to the cloud — an empirical study". *Information Systems* 67:100–113. ISSN: 0306-4379. https://doi.org/10.1016/j.is.2017.03.008. http://www.sciencedirect.com/science/article/pii/S0306437917301564.

Gilbert, CHE, and Erric Hutto. 2014. "Vader: A parsimonious rule-based model for sentiment analysis of social media text". In *Eighth International Conference on Weblogs and Social Media (ICWSM-14). Available at (20/04/16) http://comp.social.gatech.edu/papers/icwsm14.vader.hutto.pdf*, 81:82.

Golan, Maureen S., Laura H. Jernegan, and Igor Linkov. 2020. "Trends and applications of resilience analytics in supply chain modeling: systematic literature review in the context of the COVID-19 pandemic". *Environment systems & decisions*: 1–22. https://doi.org/10.1007/s10669-020-09777-w.

Gunderson, Lance H., and C. S. Holling. 2002. *Panarchy: Understanding transformations in human and natural systems.* Washington, DC: Island Press. ISBN: 9781559638579.

Hartmann, Nathaniel N., and Bruno Lussier. 2020. "Managing the sales force through the unexpected exogenous COVID-19 crisis". *Industrial Marketing Management* 88:101–111. ISSN: 0019-8501. https://doi.org/10.1016/j.indmarman.2020.05.005 http://www.sciencedirect.com/science/article/pii/S0019850120302972.

Holling, C. S. 2001. "Understanding the complexity of economic, ecological, and social systems". *Ecosystems* 4:390–405. https://doi.org/10.1007/s10021-00-0101-5.

Ivanov, Dmitry. 2020. "Predicting the impacts of epidemic outbreaks on global supply chains: A simulation-based analysis on the coronavirus outbreak (COVID-19/SARS-CoV-2) case". *Transportation research. Part E, Logistics and transportation review* 136:101922. https://doi.org/10.1016/j.tre.2020.101922.

Jackson, Scott, and Timothy L. J. Ferris. 2013. "Resilience principles for engineered systems". *Systems Engineering*16 (2): 152–164. doi: 10.1002/sys21228. eprint: https://onlinelibrary.wiley.com/doi/pdf/10.1002/sys.21228

Kamar, Ece, Severin Hacker, and Eric Horvitz. 2012. "Combining human and machine intelligence in large-scale crowdsourcing." In *AAMAS.* 12:467–474.

Kasparov, Garry. 2017. *Deep thinking: where machine intelligence ends and human creativity begins.* Hachette UK.

Kiefer, Daniel, and Clemens van Dinther. 2020. "Demand Forecasting Intermittent and Lumpy Time Series: Deep Learning a magic bullet?"

Krenzer, Adrian, et al. 2019. "Augmented Intelligence for Quality Control of Manual Assembly Processes using Industrial Wearable Systems". In *Proceedings of the 40th International Conference on Information Systems (ICIS).*

Kusiak, A., et al. 2000. "Autonomous decision-making: a data mining approach". *IEEE transactions on information technology in biomedicine: a publication of the IEEE Engineering in Medicine and Biology Society* 4 (4): 274–284. ISSN: 1089-7771. https://doi.org/10.1109/4233.897059.

Lakhmi C. Jain. 2009. "Advances in Decision Making". In *Recent Advances in Decision Making*, ed. by Janusz Kacprzyk et al., 1–6. Berlin, Heidelberg: Springer Berlin Heidelberg. ISBN: 978-3-642-02186-2.

Lepenioti, Katerina, et al. 2020. "Prescriptive analytics: Literature review and research challenges". *International Journal of Information Management* 50:57–70. ISSN: 02684012. https://doi.org/10.1016/j.ijinfomgt.2019.04.003.

Loureiro, A.L.D., V. L. Miguéis, and Lucas F.M. da Silva. 2018. "Exploring the use of deep neural networks for sales forecasting in fashion retail". *Decision Support Systems* 114:81–93. ISSN: 01679236. https://doi.org/10.1016/j.dss.2018.08.010

Manekar, S, and Pradeepini Gera. 2017. "Opportunity and Challenges for Migrating Big Data Analytics in Cloud". *IOP Conference Series: Materials Science and Engineering* 225 (): 012148. https://doi.org/10.1088/1757-899X/225/1/012148.

McKone, Kathleen E, and Elliott N Weiss. 2002. "Guidelines for implementing predictive maintenance". *Production and Operations Management* 11 (2): 109–124.

Oberdorf, Felix, et al. 2020. "ADR for Big-Data IT Artifact Development: An Escalation Management Example". In *Proceedings of the 41st International Conference on Information Systems (ICIS)*.

Paul, H Yi, Ferdinand K Hui, and Daniel SW Ting. 2018. "Artificial intelligence and radiology: collaboration is key". *Journal of the American College of Radiology* 15 (5): 781–783.

Peter R. Winters. 1960. "Forecasting Sales by Exponentially Weighted Moving Averages". *Management Science* 6 (3): 324–342.

Phillips-Wren, G., and L. Jain. 2006. "Knowledge-based intelligent Information and Engineering Systems". Chap. Artificial Intelligence for Decision Making, ed. by Bogdan Gabrys, Robert J. Howlett, and Lakhmi Jain, 531–536. Springer.

Phillips-Wren, G. (2012).Phillips-Wren, Gloria. 2012. "AI tools in Decision Making Support Systems: a review". *International Journal on Artificial Intelligence Tools* 21 (02): 1240005. ISSN: 0218-2130. https://doi.org/10.1142/S0218213012400052.

Pierre Haren and David Simchi-Levi. 2020. "How Coronavirus Could Impact the Global Supply Chain by Mid-March". *Harvard Business Review* 2020 (03).

Ricardo, David. 1817. *The Principles of Political Economy and Taxation*. Reprint from 1926. London and Toronto: J.M. Dent/Sons.

Sharma, Amalesh, Anirban Adhikary, and Sourav Bikash Borah. 2020. "Covid-19/s impact on supply chain decisions: Strategic insights from NASDAQ 100 firms using Twitter data". *Journal of Business Research* 117:443–449. ISSN: 0148-2963. https://doi.org/10.1016/j.jbusres.2020.05.035. http://www.sciencedirect.com/science/article/pii/S0148296320303210.

Shrestha, Yash Raj, Shiko M. Ben-Menahem, and Georg von Krogh. 2019. "Organizational Decision-Making Structures in the Age of Artificial Intelligence". *California Management Review* 61 (4): 66–83. ISSN: 0008-1256. https://doi.org/10.1177/0008125619862257.

Stein, Nikolai, Jan Meller, and Christoph M Flath. 2018. "Big data on the shop-floor: sensor-based decision-support for manual processes". *Journal of Business Economics* 88 (5): 593–616.

Strobl, Stefan, Mario Bernhart, and Thomas Grechenig. 2020. "Towards a Topology for Legacy System Migration". In *Proceedings of the IEEE/ACM 42nd International Conference on Software Engineering Workshops*, 586–594. IC-SEW'20. Seoul, Republic of Korea: Association for Computing Machinery. ISBN: 9781450379632. https://doi.org/10.1145/3387940.3391476.

Stubbs, Evan. 2014. "Business Analytics: An Introduction". Chap. The Value of Business Analytics, ed. by Jay Liebowitz, 1–28. CRC Press, Taylor / Francis Group.

Wang, Dakuo, et al. 2019. "Human-AI Collaboration in Data Science: Exploring Data Scientists' Perceptions of Automated AI". *Proceedings of the ACM on Human-Computer Interaction* 3 (CSCW): 1–24.

Wuest, Thorsten, Christopher Irgens, and Klaus-Dieter Thoben. 2014. "An approach to monitoring quality in manufacturing using supervised machine learning on product state data". *Journal of Intelligent Manufacturing* 25 (5): 1167–1180.

Wuest, Thorsten, et al. 2016. "Machine learning in manufacturing: advantages, challenges, and applications". *Production & Manufacturing Research* 4 (1): 23–45.

Yin, Jianhua, and Jianyong Wang. 2014. "A Dirichlet multinomial mixture model-based approach for short text clustering". In *Proceedings of the 20th ACM SIGKDD international conference on Knowledge discovery and data mining*, 233–242.

van Dinther, Clemens. 2007. *Adaptive Bidding in Single-Sided Auctions Under Uncertainty: An Agent-based Approach in Market Engineering*. Whitestein Series in Software Agent Technologies and Autonomic Computing. Basel: Birkhaäuser Verlag. ISBN: 978-3764380946.
– 2008. "Agent-based Simulation for Research in Economics". In *Handbook on Information Technology in Finance*, ed. by Detlef Seese, Christof Weinhardt, and Frank Schlottmann, 421–442. Berlin, Heidelberg: Springer Berlin Heidelberg. ISBN: 978-3-540-49487-4. https://doi.org/10.1007/978-3-540-49487-4_18.
van Dinther, Clemens, and Svenja Mauch. 2019. "Chancen der künstlichen Intelligenz zur Prognose im Mittelstand". *Decision Growth*, no. 3: 21–27. https://decision-growth.de/Magazin//catalogs/Growth_Magazin_III/growth-Magazin-Ausgabe-3/pdf/complete.pdf.

Academic Poem for Christof

Kurt Kammerer, Ulrike Smetsers, and Anna Maier

For reasons of academic ambition, this poem was not compiled in Hohenloher-Fränkisch, Alemannisch, Badisch-Karlsruherisch, Westerwälder Platt or scientific English, but in High-German. This poem is contributed by Christof's first academic family of the early 1980s. This work would not have been possible without the inspiring spices and brain calories of Jule's delicious quiche that turned a long poetic session into a memorable scientific breakthrough event.

> Vier Erstsemester aus Baden und Franken,
>   kamen nach Karlsruhe, um Wissen zu tanken.

> Zum Wohnen wählten sie sich aus,
>   vier Zimmer, Küche, Bad im selben Haus.

> Sie machten sich tiefe akademische Gedanken,
>   zuvorderst der Christof aus Unterfranken.

> Der Wirtschaftsingenieur oder kurz WI,
>   braucht viel Praxis neben der Theorie.

> An der Uni gab es zwar reichlich Theorie,
>   doch Bezug zur Praxis, den gab es nie.

> In unserer WG dafür um so mehr,
>   Household-Engineering kreuz und quer.

K. Kammerer (✉)
Regify GmbH, Hüfingen, Germany
e-mail: kurt.kammerer@regify.com

U. Smetsers
Königsbach-Stein, Germany
e-mail: ulrike@smetsers.de

A. Maier
Karlsruhe, Germany
e-mail: maieraa@web.de

© The Author(s) 2021
H. Gimpel et al. (eds.), *Market Engineering*,
https://doi.org/10.1007/978-3-030-66661-3_14

241

Christof, damals schon Experte für gutes Essen,
  war zuständig für kulinarische Delikatessen.

Besuchte er seine Familie, eine Feinkost-Dynastie,
  dann ging der WG-Kühlschrank tief in die Knie.

Boxbeutel, Kristallweizen und fränkische Wurst,
  stillten Tag und Nacht unseren Hunger und Durst.

Nicht zuletzt Christof's Feinkost-Mekka aus Franken,
  hatten wir unseren akademischen Drive zu verdanken.

Sogar abends haben wir Wirtschaft studiert,
  eifrig Kippe, Bacchus und Zwiebel frequentiert.

Selbst nachts um zwei war's uns nicht zuviel,
  für eine Extra-Lerneinheit im Krokodil.

Derlei Überstunden standen uns gut zu Gesicht,
  es lebe das volkswirtschaftliche Gleichgewicht!

Solchen Stress wussten wir klaglos zu ertragen,
  unter der Woche und erst recht an Sonn- und Feiertagen.

War sie auch manchmal kurz die Nacht,
  die Vorlesung startete immer um Acht.

Schnelles Frühstück, Müsli und Tee,
  Beginn war für uns pünktlich c.t.

So ergatterten wir ohne viel Hetze,
  die besten, die hinteren Hörsaalplätze.

Dort hat man den Überblick und mit Glück und Zeit
  ist der Durchblick auch nicht weit.

Merke: Hohe akademische Weihen
  können auch fern von der Tafel gedeihen.

Programmieren lernen ging nicht lang,
  Miele, Vor- und Hauptwaschgang.

Und noch vor Erfindung des Parallel-Prozessor
  hatten wir mit Christof den ersten Parallel-Professor.

Als Pionier im Multi-Tasking kann er telefonieren
  sowie gleichzeitig duschen, lesen und delegieren.

Wenn es zeitlich eng wird, ein anderer schon rennt,
  dann ist Christof erst in seinem Element.

Er erreicht mühelos den ICE um 8:00
  selbst wenn er um 8:10 noch Frühstück macht.

Lamentiert der Durchschnittsakademiker über solche Pleiten
  rechnet Christof mit „Verspätungswahrscheinlichkeiten".

Nach Kaffee und Mathe-Übungen immer fleißig,
  erwischt er so den verspäteten ICE um exakt 8:30.

Zuvor noch die Küche geputzt und flott abgewaschen,
  inklusive Entsorgung der Boxbeutelflaschen.

Der Standard-Ingenieur ist zwar hocheffizient,
riskiert aber, dass er sein Leben spaßfrei verpennt.

Christof hingegen fand, fürwahr,
den Weg zum diplomierten Ausnahmeexemplar.

Er kann akademisches Wissen sogar in fränkisch vorsingen
und auch der trockensten Materie ein Lächeln abringen.

Multi-lingual parliert er in Sprachen aus fernen Landen,
selbst in „Badisch for Academics" wird er weltweit verstanden.

Derart üppig munitioniert für sein späteres Leben,
konnten wir Christof der akademischen Community übergeben.

Durch die WG-Ausbildung gestählt für das weitere Leben,
wird es für Ihn keine unlösbaren Probleme mehr geben.

Dres Gaudimonium, Dipl.- Amicitia Ulrike Smetsers, Anna Maier, Kurt Kammerer

Printed in the United States
by Baker & Taylor Publisher Services